KYOTO

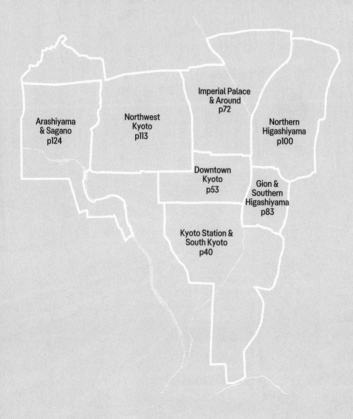

Arashiyama
& Sagano
p124

Northwest
Kyoto
p113

Imperial Palace
& Around
p72

Northern
Higashiyama
p100

Downtown
Kyoto
p53

Gion &
Southern
Higashiyama
p83

Kyoto Station &
South Kyoto
p40

Tom Fay, Rob Goss, Thomas O'Malley

Arashiyama Bamboo Grove (p127)

CONTENTS

Plan Your Trip

COWARDLION/SHUTTERSTOCK ©

Tea garden, Kinkaku-ji (p120)

The Guide

Toolkit

Storybook

Sannen-zaka (p89)

KYOTO
THE JOURNEY BEGINS HERE

Japan's capital city for more than a thousand years, Kyoto was not only the centre for politics and the imperial court, but also art, religion, cuisine, philosophy and culture. Packed with over 2000 temples and shrines, the city feels like one great big World Heritage Site, and there is so much to see and do that you would need a lifetime to experience all that is on offer.

But despite the history seeping from its pores, Kyoto somehow never feels like a relic. On the contrary, there is a spirit of fresh thinking and vibrant creativity that runs through Kyoto's very core, evident in all of the tiny boutique art galleries, artisan workshops and stylish cafes to be found down almost every street – the mishmash of modernity and old-school tradition only adds to the never-ending allure of Japan's cultural capital.

Tom Fay

@tomfay.jp / ✕ @T_in_Japan

Tom is a British travel and outdoors writer who has been living in Japan since 2007 and is based in rural Kyoto.

My favourite experience
is wandering along Ninen-zaka and Sannen-zaka and exploring the backstreets leading towards **Kiyomizu-dera** (p98); there are few places that are more brilliantly atmospheric or evocative of 'old Japan'.

WHO GOES WHERE

Our writers and experts choose the places that, for them, define Kyoto

Picking just one favourite place in Kyoto is close to impossible, but revisiting **Myōshin-ji** (p122) for this book was one of the standouts. With its peaceful collection of sub-temples and walled pathways, it always feels like entering another world. Yet, like Kyoto's other traditions, it's not entirely removed from the present day: you might see people taking their dogs on walks through the grounds or even groups of nursery kids running about on playtime.

Rob Goss

@robgosswriter

Rob is a Tokyo-based writer and author focusing on travel and culture in Japan for media around the world.

Ōkōchi Sansō (p127) breaks the mould of Kyoto's gardens because it's not attached to a temple or an imperial villa. This hillside nirvana was created by a movie star, Ōkōchi Denjirō, who played a sword-swinging samurai in over 200 films between the 1920s and 1960s. The Arashiyama crowds tend to bypass his creation, leaving it wonderfully free of visitors. A stepped path winds through the garden revealing new vistas at every turn, and you can finish at a teahouse for a cuppa. Wonderful.

Thomas O'Malley

tomfreelance.com

Thomas is an East Asia specialist and the author of over a dozen Lonely Planet guidebooks.

ICONS OF THE CITY

Nestled in a compact basin with steep mountains hemming it in on three sides, Kyoto is a richly storied city packed to the brim with interesting sights and famous spots. This is the Japan of wood-block prints and old samurai movies, where geisha float down lantern-lit streets, but there are striking modern landmarks too – it is this juxtaposition that helps to make Kyoto such a fascinating destination.

Plan Your Trip

Unless you are staying in Kyoto for a long time, choose the sights carefully and savour your visits there, rather than rushing to cram everything in.

Time It Right

Many of the most scenic spots are almost deserted early in the morning or late at night, and tend to be wonderfully atmospheric at these times too.

National Holidays

Kyoto can be packed at any time, but try to avoid Golden Week and national holidays when half of Japan seems to decamp to the city.

Maiko (apprentice geisha)

MOST ICONIC EXPERIENCES

Traipse through the corridors of stately **Nijō-jō** ❶ (p56) and be transported back to feudal-era Kyoto.

Go for an evening stroll and do some geisha-spotting in **Gion** ❷ (p84), Kyoto's lovingly preserved traditional entertainment district.

Marvel at the towering red *torii* gate and colourful buildings of **Heian-jingū** ❸ (p103), Kyoto's most striking Shintō shrine.

Cross the iconic 'moon-viewing' bridge and wander up to the otherworldly **Arashiyama Bamboo Grove** ❹ (p127).

Get a bird's-eye view of the city from **Kyoto Tower** ❺ (p46) from where you can study the controversial contemporary pizzazz of nearby Kyoto Station.

CITY OF GARDENS

The stunning temples and shrines of Kyoto, while undoubtedly impressive feats of architecture in their own right, often owe much of their visual impact and beauty to the carefully landscaped gardens that frame them so perfectly. These masterpieces of moss, rocks and flora are not only carefully designed for their visual appeal, but are also imbued with deeper layers of meaning, giving visitors something to contemplate beyond the obvious nature-inspired forms. There are thousands of them in the city.

Entry Fees

Even if the temple grounds are free, most gardens require a small extra fee to enter, usually around ¥500 or so.

Autumn Colours

In around late November when the maples are burning red, yellow and gold, expect crowds at the most popular gardens such as Ginkaku-ji (pictured; p104).

Garden Types

Kyoto is home to gardens of all kinds: *karesansui* are dry rock (Zen Buddhist) gardens, *cha-niwa* are tea gardens and there are *tsubo-niwa* (indoor gardens).

Rock garden, Ryōan-ji (p115)

PLAN YOUR TRIP

OUR PICKS

BEST GARDEN EXPERIENCES

Kyoto's most famous rock garden, **Ryōan-ji ❶** (p115) is a place for contemplation as you ponder the meaning of its 15 mystical rocks.

The beautiful temple grounds of **Tōfuku-ji ❷** (p43) are home to an abstract expressionist garden that is unlike any other in the city.

Nicknamed Koke-dera (the Moss Garden), **Saihō-ji ❸** (p132) is a verdantly green oasis and one of the city's best gardens.

The gardens of **Ginkaku-ji ❹** (p104) offer a little of everything, including a bamboo grove, pond, waterfall and luxuriant carpets of moss.

Kyoto Botanical Gardens ❺ (p77) are a place to escape the crowds and find some-thing in bloom no matter the season.

9

FOODIE HEAVEN

Kyoto has a rich foodie heritage. Called *kyō-ryōri*, the principles of Kyoto cooking focus on seasonality and fresh local produce, and this dates back to the imperial courts of the Heian period, where only the finest ingredients and presentation would do. The vegetarian Zen Buddhist diet also influenced things, but today you can find far heartier fare and a plethora of restaurants ranging from cheap eats to Michelin-starred establishments at the cutting edge of Japanese cuisine.

Haute Cuisine

Kaiseki is Kyoto's celebrated form of culinary art; these multi-course banquets focus heavily on seasonal ingredients, with the presentation and setting as important as the food.

Local Specialities

Shōjin-ryōri is the traditional vegetarian fare of Buddhist monks; *obanzai-ryōri* incorporates simple ingredients in a home-cooked style; and specialist tofu restaurants are a Kyoto mainstay.

Where to Eat

Downtown Kyoto is the place to head for the widest selection of restaurants, although almost every neighbourhood is home to genuinely excellent establishments.

BEST FOOD EXPERIENCES

Indulge in an exquisite *kaiseki* multi-dish banquet at **Kikunoi Honten ❶** (p94), where every bite is a sensory experience to savour.

Try a tofu-themed lunch set and admire the stunning Zen garden at **Yudōfu Sagano ❷** (p129) in Arashiyama.

Slurp down thick udon noodles served in hot or cold broth at **Omen ❸** (p106), a short hop from Ginkaku-ji.

Head for lunch at **Yoshi-kawa ❹** (p71), a rustic ryokan restaurant serving the best tempura in all of Kyoto.

Queue up for some of Kyoto's best ramen served in a rich pork-based broth at **Ippūdo ❺** (p66).

Kimono demonstration, Nishijin Textile Centre (p81)

MARVELLOUS MUSEUMS

Kyoto isn't all about temples, shrines, tea ceremonies and fancy food. You can also find some excellent museums and art galleries, showcasing cultural and historic treasures from Kyoto's storied past, plus more quirky exhibitions that are sure to delight young and old alike.

Discount Pass

If you plan on visiting numerous museums consider the Gurrutto Pass Kansai, which grants entry to many museums in the region for ¥1200.

Opening Times

Most museums are open from around 10am to 4pm, and many are closed on Mondays (or the following day if Monday is a national holiday).

BEST MUSEUM EXPERIENCES

Browse the extensive collections and stunning wonders of Japan's artistic heritage at the **Kyoto National Museum ❶** (p95).

Delve into the world of Japanese comics at the **Kyoto International Manga Museum ❷** (p59), with its special exhibitions and resident artists.

Admire the world-class collections of hanging scrolls, decorative folding screens and other art work at the architecturally-stunning **Fukuda Art Museum ❸** (p133).

Learn all about kimonos and fabrics at **Nishijin Textile Centre ❹** (p81), where you can get hands-on and watch a kimono fashion show.

Sneak into a world of ninja and samurai in Downtown Kyoto, and learn to throw shuriken at **Samurai Ninja Museum Kyoto ❺** (p62).

KYOTO WITH KIDS

Japan is safe and welcoming to kids, and Kyoto is no different, with plenty of things to keep them occupied. While the finer charms of the city's temples and shrines may be lost on little ones, their grounds and gardens can be fun to explore, and child-friendly attractions are not in short supply either.

Eating Out

Kaiseki and some local fare may not be to all tastes, but 'family restaurants' such as Saizeriya offer Western-style dishes and some places have kids menus.

Getting Around

Some temples and shrines can be tricky with strollers. Children under six ride trains for free, while those up to 12 pay half the adult fare.

Outdoor Fun

Kids who like running around will enjoy Kyoto's parks and outdoorsy shrines such as Fushimi Inari-Taisha. The Kamo-gawa is a popular river for summertime splashing.

BEST KID-FRIENDLY EXPERIENCES

Train-crazy kids (and like-minded adults) will love the vintage locomotives and recently retired engines at the multi-floored and interactive **Kyoto Railway Museum** ❶ (p48).

Be entranced by all manner of mesmerising shapes and colours at the mini-treasure trove that is the **Kaleidoscope Museum of Kyoto** ❷ (p62).

Explore the mocked-up streets and movie sets of **TŌEI Kyoto Studio Park** ❸ (p118), a small Edo-inspired theme park packed with plenty of family-friendly attractions

Hike up to **Arashiyama Monkey Park** ❹ (p133), the hilltop nature reserve where monkeys and humans roam freely, with only the latter caged in for feeding.

While away a few happy hours around **Okazaki Park** ❺ (p103), a popular park in Northern Higashi-yama with a playground, zoo, playing fields and a couple of museums.

CULTURAL PLAYGROUND

Few other cities in the world pack in as much culture heritage as Kyoto; Japan's former capital city is the cultural heart of the country, and its imperial courts and temple districts were a breeding ground for the development of everything from tea ceremony to ikebana flower arranging. For 1000 years new and old art forms were refined, as artisans perfected their crafts, and this rich cultural legacy is still very much alive to this day.

Book Online

Many experiences are best booked in advance, and, today, this is often easily done online; if not, ask your accommodation for help.

Try Something New

Even if kabuki theatre or formal tea ceremonies don't initially float your boat, such unique Kyoto experiences rarely disappoint and can be a surprising highlight.

Meditative Vibes

A number of temples offer reasonably priced or even free meditation sessions; combine with a temple stay for a truly Zen experience.

Garden, Enkō-ji (p108)

BEST CULTURAL EXPERIENCES

Get a short introduction to the varied facets of Japanese culture by heading to an evening show at **Gion Corner** ❶ (p87).

Delve into the world of tea ceremony at **Camellia** ❷ (p92), where you can learn the intricacies of this thirst-quenching art form.

Join in the revelry of Japan's most famous summer festival during the month-long **Gion Matsuri** ❸ (p70).

Catch a kabuki performance at **Minamiza** ❹ (p97) and enjoy trying to make sense of the story at Gion's iconic old theatre.

Meditate and become at one with the universe under the instruction of a Zen Buddhist monk at **Enkō-ji** ❺ (p108).

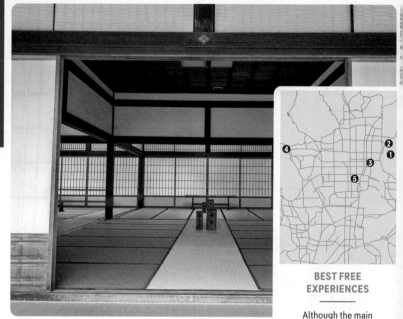

Tenryū-ji (p134)

FOR FREE

Japan is not the eye-wateringly expensive destination it once was, and despite catering to big tourist crowds, Kyoto has plenty of things you can do completely for free – it can be worth seeking out low-cost thrills, so that you can splurge on more expensive treats such as a high-end dinners or ryokan stays.

Spiritual Savings

The grounds of many of Kyoto's best temples and shrines can be entered for free, so you can see famous landmarks without it costing at all.

Take a Walk

Some of the best experiences can be had simply by walking from place to place, taking the backstreets and noticing the little details of daily Kyoto life.

BEST FREE EXPERIENCES

Although the main hall requires an entry fee, you can tour the extensive grounds of **Nanzen-ji ①** (p110) with-out spending a penny.

Make a small detour from the Philosopher's Path and discover **Hōnen-in ②** (p107), a must-see temple that sometimes has free art exhibits.

Time your visit to watch the giant floats and enjoy the revelry of **Gion Matsuri ③** (p70), a summer festival spectacle like no other.

Find your inner self and join in a free *zazen* morning meditation session at **Tenryū-ji ④** (p134), held on the second Sunday of the month.

Make a beeline from Kyoto Station to see the spectacular structures of the monumental temple complex of **Higashi Hongan-ji ⑤** (p47).

UNDER THE RADAR

Kyoto is frequently cited as a case study in over-tourism; bus routes are packed with travellers and their suitcases, popular sights are overrun with tourist crowds, and some fear the city may lose the characteristics that set it apart. But there are still quiet neighbourhoods and corners where the understated local essence of Kyoto can be found.

Two Wheels

Kyoto is relatively flat and pleasant to cycle around, so grab a bicycle from one of the many rental shops and get around like a local.

Get Off-Road

Don't just stick to strict itineraries or follow the crowds; wandering down side streets often leads to memorable discoveries such as hidden shrines and other interesting sights.

Mix Like a Local

Festivals, especially smaller neighbourhood ones, are great for mingling with the locals; likewise *hanami* (cherry-blossom viewing) picnics in the park or eating at an *izakaya*.

BEST UNDER-THE-RADAR EXPERIENCES

Escape the crowds at Ginkaku-ji (the Silver Pavilion) and enjoy the peace and solace of neighbouring **Hōnen-in ❶** (p107).

Pick up an end-of-day bargain *bentō* box just before closing time at the gourmet basement food floor in **Takashimaya ❷** (p59).

Join in-the-know locals admiring the pretty gardens of **Enkō-ji ❸** (p108), while avoiding the crowds of nearby Shisen-dō.

Explore the sprawling temple grounds of **Ninna-ji ❹** (p119), a favourite with locals during cherry-blossom season.

Stroll or sit along the banks of the **Kamo-gawa ❺** (p65), and take in the view of the fires lit on Daimonji-yama on 16 August.

Perfect Days

Many travellers visit Kyoto as part of a wider Japan itinerary. To really do the city justice, try to give yourself at least four days, and tackle the city's dispersed sights in chunks.

Philosopher's Path (p107)

COWARDLION/SHUTTERSTOCK ©

DAY 1

Southern Higashiyama

☀ Beat the crowds by starting out first thing at **Kiyomizu-dera** (p98). Take in the dreamy views from the temple's raised terrace, purify yourself at the sacred springs, then exit the temple for a stroll along charming (if busy) **Sannen-zaka** (p89). At **Maruyama-kōen** (p92) you can get a breather under the trees, before a quick detour to **Yasaka-jinja** (p89) on route to monumental **Chion-in** (p90), the grandest of Kyoto temples.

Lunch Refuel with a signature bowl of *oyakodon* (chicken and egg over rice) at **Hisago** (p89).

Kyoto Station & South Kyoto

☀ Ride the rails south to **Fushimi Inari-Taisha** (p44), Kyoto's most famous shrine. Climb up through mesmerising Senbon Torii, a passage formed by hundreds of flame-red shrine gates, then hike your way along paths to the summit of Inariyama in time for sunset.

Dinner Head to **Giro Giro Hitoshina** (p58) in Downtown Kyoto for a laid-back take on refined *kaiseki* cuisine.

Downtown Kyoto

☾ Stroll under twinkling lanterns along **Ponto-chō** (p58), a charming paved alley with drinking spots for all budgets, from craft beer dives to more exclusive establishments.

DAY 2

Arashiyama & Sagano

☀️ Hit up **Tenryū-ji** (p134) to marvel at the Zen temple's 700-year-old pond garden with its mountain backdrop. Stroll through Arashiyama's ethereal **Bamboo Grove** (p127), then escape the crowds at **Ōkōchi Sansō** (p127), a serene hillside garden. Head down to the river to admire the famous **Togetsu-kyō** (Moon-Crossing Bridge; p127), and if you've got the energy, hire a row boat.

Lunch Discover the multifarious joys of tofu at **Yudōfu Sagano** (p129).

Northwest Kyoto

☀️ Ride Kyoto's last remaining tram line, the Keifuku Randen, to **Ryōan-ji** (p115), a Zen temple home to perhaps the world's most pondered patch of raked-gravel. After you've contemplated its cryptic secrets, hail a taxi for the short hop to **Kinkaku-ji** (p120), a temple complex that draws huge crowds for its iconic pavilion clad in gleaming gold leaf.

Dinner Savour an (early-ish) sushi and sashimi feast at **Tai Sushi** (p66) in Downtown Kyoto.

Gion & Southern Higashiyama

🌙 Catch the hour-long evening show at **Gion Corner** (p95), a touristy whirl of geisha dances, traditional music recitals, tea ceremony and ikebana flower arrangement, then go for classy cocktails at **Gion Finlandia Bar** (p84).

DAY 3

Downtown Kyoto

☀️ Head out early and explore **Nijō-jō** (p56), mighty castle of the Tokugawa shoguns. Listen for the telltale squeak of the 'nightingale' floors, then head to **Nishiki Market** (p68), dubbed 'Kyoto's kitchen' for its specialist retailers selling *tsukemono* (pickles), sticky rice cakes, local heirloom veggies and samurai-sharp Japanese knives.

Lunch Take your pick from the many tempting restaurants at **Nishiki Market** (p68).

Northern Higashiyama

☀️ Catch the bus to **Ginkaku-ji** (p104), Kyoto's most aesthetically sublime temple. Flit between moss gardens, bamboo groves, wooden halls and austere raked sand, then depart for a stroll along the **Philosopher's Path** (p107), a canal-side promenade famous for cherry blossoms. Finish up in the hallowed precincts of **Nanzen-ji** (p110), a hillside haven of Zen temple halls and exquisite gardens set amid a forest.

Dinner Pair perfectly crisp tempura with premium sake at **Gion Tempura Koromo** (p95).

Downtown Kyoto

🌙 Cross the Kamo-gawa and have a wander along bar-and-nightlife-filled **Kiyamachi-dōri** (p60), stopping in for innovative cocktails at **Bee's Knees** (p65), an intimate speakeasy. If you've anything left in the tank, hit up one of Downtown's clubs, like friendly, multi-floored **World Kyoto** (p67).

WHEN **TO GO**

Especially lovely in spring and autumn, Kyoto is a year-round destination where every season holds its own appeal.

Few places cherish the seasons as intensely as Kyoto – a *maiko* (apprentice geisha) has a different hair ornament for every month of the year. The city's Zen-inspired concept of beauty embraces transience, and nothing is more prized than the fleeting loveliness of spring's pale-pink *sakura* (cherry blossoms), a media-tracked event that starts as early as late March and lasts around two weeks. Arguably even more spectacular, though, is *kōyō* (autumn-foliage season), an eruption of fire-red *momiji* (Japanese maples) and honey-yellow gingko trees from mid-November to early December. Both periods draw the crowds, which thin a little in May and October when the weather is at its finest. Sticky-hot summer is the season for festivals, while winter brings the faint chance of snow, and uncrowded temples afford rare moments of quiet.

Book Accommodation Early

Kyoto is busy most of the year, but all the more so in cherry blossom season and peak autumn-foliage season, so organise your stay well in advance.

Kiyomizu-dera (p98)

⊛ I LIVE HERE

SEASON CHANGES

Ayako Takemoto is Deputy Director of Fukuda Art Museum in Arashiyama

In Kyoto there's always great excitement and anticipation for each new season. As winter comes to an end, you start to see Kyoto ladies wearing spring-themed kimonos, and sweet shops displaying the coming season's *wagashi*. One of my favourite seasonal sweets is *sakura mochi*, sticky rice cakes made with *sakura* (cherry blossom petals) preserved in salt. When the *sakura* arrives in Arashiyama, I love the visual contrast of its pink blossoms against the fresh green of the spring mountains.

SAKE AND SAKURA IN SPRING

In early April, cherry-blossom-viewing parties called *hanami* bring together friends, family, and colleagues for boozy picnics on blankets spread out under the *sakura* trees. **Maruyama-kōen** (p92) is Kyoto's most famous *hanami* spot.

Weather Through the Year

JANUARY	FEBRUARY	MARCH	APRIL	MAY	JUNE
Ave. daytime max: **8°C**	Ave. daytime max: **9°C**	Ave. daytime max: **13°C**	Ave. daytime max: **19°C**	Ave. daytime max: **24°C**	Ave. daytime max: **27°C**
Days of rainfall: **8**	Days of rainfall: **9**	Days of rainfall: **11**	Days of rainfall: **11**	Days of rainfall: **11**	Days of rainfall: **13**

RIVER DINING ALFRESCO

To beat the summer heat, restaurants along the Kamo-gawa set up elevated riverside platforms called *kawayuka*. In Kibune (p148), restaurants offer *kawadoko,* where diners sit on platforms just centimetres above the rushing waters of the Kibune-gawa.

Kyoto's Grandest Festivals

Gion Matsuri (p70) Kyoto's biggest festival peaks with a parade on 17 July, during which enormous floats and portable shrines, some up to 25m tall, are hauled through Downtown Kyoto. ☀ **July**

Aoi Matsuri On 15 May, 600 people in Heian-era period dress parade from Kyoto Gosho to **Shimogamo-jinja** (p77). Named after the *aoi* (hollyhock) plant, the festival dates back to the 6th century. ☀ **May**

Jidai Matsuri (p103) Commemorating the founding of Kyoto as capital in 794 CE, the comparatively recent 'Festival of the Ages' features a procession of revellers in period dress marching from Kyoto Gosho to Heian-jingū. ☁ **October**

Daimon-ji On 16 August, huge fires in the shape of Chinese characters are set ablaze on the Kyoto hillsides. This magical 'Sending-Off Festival' is watched by onlookers lining the banks of the Kamo-gawa. ☀ **August**

Quirky Kyoto Gatherings

Nagoshi no Harae On the last day of June, shrines in Kyoto erect enormous grass wreaths called *chinowa*, which visitors walk through to be cleansed of their misdeeds from the first half of the year. ☀ **June**

Kurama no Hi Matsuri This popular fire festival takes place in the mountain village of Kurama, where hundreds of young men in loincloths bear giant flaming torches. The festival peaks on the evening of 22 October at Yuki-jinja. ☁ **October**

Tōshiya At **Sanjūsangen-dō** (p88) on the Sunday closest to 15 January, hundreds of kimono-clad participants shoot arrows in a competition of accuracy and strength. ☀ **January**

Yabusame Shinji On 3 May, this archery contest adds galloping horses into the mix for a truly thrilling spectacle. An event associated with Aoi Matsuri, it takes place on Tadasu-no-mori, the tree-lined approach to **Shimogamo-jinja** (p77). ☀ **May**

SAKURA GAZING

Jay Crystall is a musician based in central Kyoto
Spring in Kyoto brings on a freshness and vitality that seems to permeate everywhere the moment the pink and white blossoms burst forth. *Sakura* (cherry blossoms) decorate the surrounding hills and cluster in ancient temples and shrines, along rivers and in parks. Under their shade we gather to celebrate spring with a picnic, always a time of warmth and laughter. For those of us fortunate enough to be in Kyoto at this time, a serene stroll among the *sakura* feels timeless, almost sacred.

Geisha, Gion Matsuri (p70)

BLOSSOMS AND CLIMATE CHANGE

In 2021, the cherry blossoms in Kyoto peaked on 26 March, the earliest date since records began over 1200 years ago. Studies have also shown that a temperature rise of 2°C to 3°C could mean trees only partly blossom or not at all.

JULY	AUGUST	SEPTEMBER	OCTOBER	NOVEMBER	DECEMBER
Ave. daytime max: **31°C**	Ave. daytime max: **33°C**	Ave. daytime max: **28°C**	Ave. daytime max: **22°C**	Ave. daytime max: **17°C**	Ave. daytime max: **11°C**
Days of rainfall: **13**	Days of rainfall: **9**	Days of rainfall: **11**	Days of rainfall: **9**	Days of rainfall: **7**	Days of rainfall: **8**

FROM LEFT: MATTEO COLOMBO/GETTY IMAGES ©, BUN-BUKU/NETFLIX/ALBUM/ALAMY STOCK PHOTO ©

Arashiyama Bamboo Grove (p127)

GET PREPARED FOR KYOTO

Useful things to load in your bag, your ears and your brain.

Clothes

Slip-on shoes You'll be removing footwear constantly to enter temples, shrines, ryokan, restaurants and people's homes – avoid fiddly shoelaces or awkward boots for your own sanity.

Nice socks See above! That toe poking out is not a conversation starter.

Neat, casual clothes Fine for almost all situations – some swanky restaurants have a 'no shorts, sleeveless shirts or sandals' rule for men. There's no special dress code for religious sites.

Wallet/Money container Cash is still king in Kyoto, particularly for small purchases like temple tickets, casual dining and vending machines.

Packable waterproofs Kyoto is an open-air destination – even at temples and shrines you'll mostly be admiring the buildings from the outside.

Manners

Follow shoe etiquette. Think 'shoes on stone, socks on wood', and don't forget to remove toilet slippers after going to the loo.

Don't eat and walk. Scoff that delicious snack where you bought it.

Maintain a quiet demeanour in public spaces, especially on trains and buses.

Take your trash with you. Rubbish bins are almost non-existent.

Don't tip. It can lead to awkwardness and might be refused.

Sun protection See above. Kyoto gets particularly hot and sunny in August.

Light jacket/Sweater Handy for cool evenings, especially during the shoulder seasons. Between December and February you'll need something warmer.

📖 READ

Another Kyoto
(Alex Kerr; 2016) Delve deeper into Kyoto's cultural history with a true expert – it's like having a brilliant, if slightly stoned, travel guide.

Geisha of Gion: The True Story of Japan's Foremost Geisha
(Mineko Iwasaki; 2002) A top-tier geisha lifts the lid on Kyoto's esoteric 'flower and willow world'.

The Old Capital
(Yasunari Kawabata; 1962) Novel set in Kyoto by a Nobel Prize–winning author. A young woman's past is disturbed by the discovery of a twin sister.

Kyoto: A Cultural History (John Dougill; 2006) A sprawling study that touches on everything from Zen Buddhism to geisha and modern film.

Words

Kon-nichi wa (こんにちは) Hello, good day. Used any time of day but especially late morning to late afternoon.

Ohayō gozaimasu (おはようございます) Good morning.

Konban wa (こんばんは) Good evening.

Mata ne/Bye bye (またね/バイバイ) Informal goodbye, 'see you soon'.

Oyasumi nasai (おやすみなさい) Good night. Use only just before bedtime.

Sumimasen (すみません) Excuse me. Said to get someone's attention or when you have committed a minor offence (eg bumped into someone). Use to call waiting staff (or they'll probably keep their distance).

Sayōnara (さようなら) Goodbye. Rarely used – very formal and implies finality.

Onegai shimasu (お願いします) Please.

____ o kudasai (____を下さい) Please give/bring me _____, when asking for a specific thing, such as when ordering food. If you can't pronounce a food name, point to it on the menu and say *kore o kudasai* (translation: This, please).

Dōzo (どうぞ) Please. Used when offering something.

Arigatō gozaimasu (ありがとうございます) Thank you. Can be shortened to *arigatō*.

Arigatō gozaimashita (ありがとうございました) Past tense of thank you. Used for a completed action.

Dō itashimashite (どういたしまして) You're welcome. Used surprisingly rarely.

Kekkō desu (けっこうです) No thank you.

🎬 WATCH

The Makanai: Cooking for the Maiko House (pictured; Netflix; 2023) Whimsical, food-oriented Japanese drama series set in a Kyoto geisha house.

The Last Samurai (Edward Zwick; 2003) Tom Cruise plays a 19th-century US military officer hired by the Japanese emperor, with scenes shot at Kyoto's Nijō-jō.

Rashomon (Kurosawa Akira; 1950) Kurosawa's classic uses Kyoto's former south gate as the setting for a 12th-century crime story told from several perspectives.

Sisters of the Gion (Mizoguchi Kenji; 1936) Riveting black-and-white portrayal of two very different sisters working in Kyoto's geisha district.

🎧 LISTEN

Otoboke Beaver
Explosive, feminist-tinged, impeccably crafted songs by Kyoto's all-woman punk quartet.

Michiru Aoyama
Prolific, Kyoto-based ambient music producer known for releasing new albums daily!

JapanesePod101
One of the most established Japanese language-learning tools, with thousands of audio lessons and both free and paid tiers.

Sakamoto Ryūichi
From Tokyo, a genre-defying composer, pianist and producer who collaborated with musicians, film directors and DJs.

KZO/SHUTTERSTOCK ©

Saba-zushi

DINING OUT

A city of culinary perfectionists, Kyoto is an edible wonderland finely tuned to nature and the seasons.

The capital of Japan for over a thousand years, Kyoto has evolved into a city of kitchen obsessives where only perfection is good enough. Restaurants guard recipes passed down through generations, farmers nurture heirloom vegetables unique to the Kyoto countryside, and Michelin-starred chefs muse like artists over plates of food to ensure they are as pleasing on the eye as they are on the taste buds.

That Kyoto, a medium-sized Japanese city, punches so far above its weight in matters culinary is partly down to history. Chefs were obliged to tantalize the palates of emperors, discerning courtiers and the leaders of powerful monasteries and temples. Kyoto's sophisticated Imperial kitchens, married to the health-focused vegetarianism of Zen, gave rise to *kaiseki*,

the multicourse pinnacle of Japanese haute cuisine. But Kyoto isn't all highbrow dining and food as art – the city is a great place to taste the full spread of Japanese cuisine, from steaming bowls of ramen to sushi and *matcha* (green-tea powder) desserts, all done with Kyoto's trademark finesse.

Kyoto Cuisine

You can sample the traditional cuisine of Kyoto, known as *kyō-ryōri,* all over the city. As a food philosophy, *kyō-ryōri* is intensely seasonal. Ingredients (mostly vegetables) are selected at the absolute peak of freshness and presented in the context of the season – on a fresh, green *sakura* leaf in spring, for example. Flavourings are subtle in order to tease

Best Kyoto Dishes	YUDŌFU	NISHIN SOBA	TSUKEMONO	YUBA
	Fresh cubes of tofu in a *kombu* broth, simmered in a clay pot.	Buckwheat noodles topped with dried herring simmered in a sweet sauce.	Assorted Kyoto pickles, often served as a side dish.	Paper-thin sheets of tofu 'skin', often used in *kyō-ryōri* dishes.

out the natural taste of the ingredients, and great care is taken to ensure that the setting and atmosphere in which *kyō-ryōri* is enjoyed aligns with the seasonal mood and hues.

Offshoots of *kyō-ryōri* include *kaiseki-ryōri* (Japanese haute cuisine) and *shōjin-ryōri* (Buddhist vegetarian cuisine), both typically reserved for special occasions. For everyday eating, there's *obanzai-ryōri* – traditional home-style cooking that's straightforward, nourishing and tasty, while still adhering to *kyō-ryōri's* principles of seasonality and freshness. A set meal of *obanzai-ryōri* features multiple small dishes prepared simply. As well as vegetables from the Kyoto area *(kyō-yasai),* you can expect dishes such as miso soup, pickles, tofu, fish and stews.

For a satisfying introduction to *obanzai-ryōri,* try Menami (p58) in Downtown Kyoto, a neighbourhood favourite.

Kaiseki

Top of the list of culinary experiences for many visitors to Kyoto, *kaiseki* is a special-occasion banquet where food is only part of the experience. Historically associated with the art of tea ceremony, *kaiseki* was conceived as a way to provide nourishment to tea-ceremony guests, but in later centuries evolved independently. As in the tea ceremony, great importance is placed on the tools and setting – precious lacquerware and ceramics are carefully chosen to match each course, while the space itself, usually the private room of a *ryōtei* (traditional, high-class Japanese restaurant) or ryokan, might feature calligraphy, flowers and other subtle touches chosen to reflect that particular season.

MEALS OF A LIFETIME

Kikunoi Honten (pictured; p94) One of the finest restaurants in Kyoto, foodies flock to this secluded spot close to Maruyama-kōen for Michelin-starred *kaiseki* banquets and exemplary service.

Yoshikawa (p71) Take a counter seat to watch chefs cook up the city's best tempura at this intimate restaurant in a traditional building that surrounds a Japanese garden.

Izusen (p79) Savour the sublime, meat-free fare of Buddhist monasteries at this stunning restaurant inside the temple complex of Daitoku-ji.

Kitcho Arashiyama (p132) *Kaiseki* meals resemble works of art at this legendary riverside restaurant in Arashiyama, considered by many to be the pinnacle of Kyoto dining.

Matcha ice cream

MATCHA DESSERTS	AYU	MITARASHI DANGO	SABA-ZUSHI
Sweet treats made with powdered green tea, from *mochi* to ice cream.	A trout-like fish caught in Lake Biwa during spring and summer. Usually served grilled.	Skewers of rice-flour dumplings bathed in a soy sauce-based syrup.	Pickled mackerel sushi pressed together using a box-shaped mould.

Kaiseki meals unfold over multiple courses, starting with appetisers, sashimi, then something boiled, grilled, deep-fried, steamed, and vinegared, before ending with rice, pickles, miso soup, and dessert or fruit. A *kaiseki* dinner generally costs upwards of ¥10,000 per person (sometimes considerably more). A cheaper way to sample *kaiseki* is to visit a restaurant for lunch. If you stay in an upscale Kyoto ryokan and select the dinner option, you'll usually have elegant *kaiseki* served inside your room.

Vegetarian and Vegan
Vegetables are frequently the star component of a meal in Kyoto, a city surrounded by green mountains and historically far from fresh sources of seafood. Kyoto is also known for its pure groundwater and fertile soil, which helped give rise to distinct subspecies of heirloom veggies known as *kyō-yasai* (Kyoto vegetables), some of which are afforded official protection similar to France's Appellation d'Origine Contrôlée. Unique Kyoto varieties of spring onion, chillies, carrots, eggplant, bamboo, daikon radish and leafy greens are each prized for their special taste, texture and appearance.

Kyoto's high-quality water is also a key ingredient in the region's famous tofu, which together with *kyō-yasai* and *fu* (wheat gluten) make up the traditional, meat-free banquet cuisine served at Buddhist temples and monasteries. Called *shōjin-ryōri*, it's like a simpler, meat-free version of *kaiseki*, though still very much obsessed with seasonality, subtlety and presentation. Some Kyoto temples even have their own on-site restaurants serving *shōjin-ryōri*, like Tenryū-ji (p134) in Arashiyama.

Japanese Favourites
The number, quality and variety of Kyoto's restaurants make it a great place to sample the full smorgasbord of Japanese gastronomy. While you can find classic *nigiri-zushi* (vinegared rice topped with raw fish) all over town, Kyoto also has its own take on sushi, using cooked or cured fish rather than raw, reflecting the city's historically landlocked location.

Kyoto is also a fantastic place to eat ramen (wheat noodles in meat broth). Kyoto-style ramen typically features a clear, light-tasting *shōyu* (soy sauce) broth, or a version involving chunks of pork fat in the soup for extra richness. Japan's answer to Chinese-style ramen are *soba* (thin, brown buckwheat noodles) and *udon* (thick, white wheat noodles).

A favourite of Kyoto's speciality noodle dishes is *cha soba*, made by mixing buckwheat flour with *matcha* (green-tea powder). It's the dish to eat when visiting Uji (p51).

You can find literally hundreds of other restaurants that specialise in dishes like *tempura* (vegetables and seafood deep-fried a light batter), *yakitori* (skewers

THE YEAR IN FOOD

SPRING	SUMMER	AUTUMN	WINTER
Spring brings the *sakura* as people gather under confetti-pink cherry blossoms for *hanami* picnics. A seasonal favourite is *sakura mochi* – sweet rice cakes wrapped in pickled cherry-blossom leaves (pictured).	Various ways to beat the stifling heat include *kakigōri* (shaved ice with sweet toppings), and the teahouse treats of *warabi mochi* (pictured; bracken jelly) and *kuzu-kiri* (arrowroot noodles).	Autumn is the season for earthy foods like mushrooms, particularly the highly-prized (and priced) *matsutake* (pictured), along with chestnuts, pumpkins and bright orange persimmons.	Warming dishes like *nabe* (hot pot) take centre stage as the winter chill descends. *Yudōfu* (pictured) is traditionally eaten, and you can warm up with piping hot *yaki-imo* (roasted sweet potatoes) at food stalls.

Cha soba

of chicken and other meats grilled over charcoal), *unagi* (grilled eel), *tonkatsu* (pork cutlet), as well as countless *izakaya* (Japanese pubs) and *shokudō* (common everyday restaurants) that cook up a little bit of everything. Downtown Kyoto is the centre of the city's dining scene, but you can find pretty much whatever you fancy in most Kyoto neighbourhoods.

Dine Like a Local

Nowadays Kyoto restaurants make a decent effort explaining to non-Japanese what the various dishes are in a meal and in what order they should be eaten. Plenty of places also have an English menu. Some restaurants give you a printed QR code after you've taken your seat, which you scan with your phone to read the menu and order dishes.

If you're not sure no what to order, try these phrases: *o-susume wa nan desu ka* (What do you recommend?) and: *o-makase shimasu* (Please decide for me). Before digging in, it's customary in Japan to say *itadakimasu* ('I gratefully receive'). At the end of the meal you can thank the host or chef with the phrase *gochisō-sama deshita*, which means 'It was a real feast'.

Something Sweet

Time for dessert? Kyoto is famous for its sugary *wagashi* (confectionary), a tradition rooted in the tea ceremony, where a little morsel of something sweet takes the edge off the bitter-tasting green tea. As you might expect, *kyo-gashi* (Kyoto sweets) are closely tied to the seasons and festivals throughout the year, with *wagashi* makers coming up with different styles like *sakura mochi* in spring, made with preserved cherry blossoms. Various types of *wagashi* available year-round include *dango* (soft rice-flour balls), *daifuku* (sticky rice cakes filled with red bean paste) and *mochi* (pounded rice made into cakes).

Places to try tea and kyō-gashi include Kagizen Yoshifusa (p97) in Gion and Toraya Karyō Kyoto Ichijō, Kazariya and Kamo Mitarashi Chaya (p81) near Imperial Palace Park.

OSAKA SNACKS

Tako-yaki Golf-ball shaped octopus dumplings topped with sauce and bonito flakes.

Okonomiyaki Savoury pancake of grated yam, cabbage, pork belly, shrimp, squid, green onions, sauce and mayo.

Kushikatsu Skewers of meat, seafood and veggies which are crumbed, deep-fried, and served with a tangy dipping sauce.

Kitsune udon Thick udon noodles served in a dashi broth and topped with strips of *age* (deep-fried tofu).

CEZARY WOJTKOWSKI/SHUTTERSTOCK ©

Ponto-chō (p58)

BAR OPEN

Underneath its cultured and refined veil, Kyoto is a
city that welcomes all with its varied drinking options.

After a full day of traipsing around
temples, galleries and cultural sites,
the primal desire for a thirst-quenching
beverage can be hard to ignore, and Kyoto
caters to everyone, no matter your tipple of
choice. Not always immediately apparent,
Kyoto has a well-established drinking
scene, although you may need to do some
digging as many bars and drinking holes
are tucked away down alleyways and not
easy to spot when wandering the main
streets. There are chic, high-end bars
where you can sip on seasonally themed
cocktails, rowdy *izakaya* (Japanese pub-
eateries) for glugging cheap draught beers
with locals while wolfing down hearty
dishes, sophisticated sake and whisky
bars, and an ever-increasing number of

cool craft-beer spots to sample local brews.
Non-drinkers are amply catered for too,
with cosy, traditional tearooms serving
bowls of rich *matcha* (powdered green
tea), and hip coffee houses offering single-
origin blends and relaxed spaces in which
to unwind and relax.

Where to Drink

Kyoto has a couple of main drinking districts,
but Downtown Kyoto is undoubtedly the
best place to start and can't be beaten for
sheer breadth of choice. The wonderfully
atmospheric Ponto-chō alleyway (p58) is
home to countless bars and restaurants,
with a good mix ranging from low-
key and casual joints to high-end and
exclusive. Nearby Kiyamachi-dōri (p60)

Lonely Planet's Top Drinking Spots	KYOTO BREWING CO.	FUSHIMI SAKE VILLAGE	NOKISHITA 711
	Possibly Kyoto's finest beer, with an on-site brewpub (open Friday to Sunday only).	Sample a lifetime's worth of sake varieties with piping-hot ramen at this *izakaya* hot spot.	One-of-a-kind gin and cocktail bar with crazily creative food and drink pairings.
	p51	**p51**	**p65**

is another prime drinking strip, with a similar mix of cheap and cheerful to intimidatingly upmarket establishments. Across the river, Gion is Kyoto's traditional entertainment and drinking quarter, and while an evening of drinking, song and dance in the company of a geisha may be beyond the means of most travellers (high-end establishments usually require an invitation), there are a number of excellent restaurants and bars open to everyone.

Don't miss the opportunity to visit an *izakaya* too – they can be found all over the city, usually welcome locals and visitors alike, and often have a cosy yet lively 'only in Japan' vibe. They serve a wide variety of beer, sake and other (including non-alcoholic) drinks, which are ordered along with platefuls of heart-warming Japanese dishes.

Boozy Tipples

Beer remains the favourite drink for most, and thanks to an ever-growing craft-beer scene, there are now far more choices than the old classic draught choices of Kirin, Asahi and Sapporo. Sake *(nihonshu)* is another firm favourite; it goes especially well with sushi or *kaiseki* (Japanese haute cuisine) and is popular at *izakaya*. The good stuff is generally drunk cold, but it is a nice winter-warmer when served hot too. *Shōchū* (a potato- or barley-based spirit) is popular as well, although it packs a punch at 30% – it's usually served diluted with hot water *(oyu-wari)* or mixed with soft drinks to form a cocktail-like *chūhai* (a popular convenience-store beverage). For aficionados, Japanese whisky is some of the best in the world, and there are dedicated bars tucked away here and there.

Sake

NEED TO KNOW

Opening Hours

Bars are usually open from around 6pm (*izakaya* an hour earlier) until late. Cafes are open all day; traditional ones close by 4pm or 5pm, though more contemporary establishments may stay open until around 9pm.

Drinking Etiquette

It's considered bad form to fill your own glass; instead, fill the glass of your drinking partners, and they'll reciprocate. In group situations, drinking begins with raised glasses and a chorus of *kampai* (cheers!).

On the Door

Most bars don't have strict entry policies, although beware of brazenly walking into small, exclusive-looking establishments, as some places (in Kyoto more than other cities) prefer guests to be introduced by an established patron.

Cover Charge

Many bars in Japan include a 'seating charge' of around ¥500 per person, although this is rare in foreigner-friendly places in Kyoto.

BAR KOHAKU	JITTOKU	GION FINLANDIA BAR	BEER KOMACHI	13F COFFEE
Sophisticated cocktail bar with amazing views across the city.	Atmospheric bar in an old sake brewery, with frequent live music.	Stylish bar for Kyotoites in-the-know, located inside an old Gion townhouse.	Pint-sized casual bar with seven Japanese craft beers on tap.	Renovated and arty townhouse cafe with a friendly vibe.
p84	**p77**	**p84**	**p92**	**p80**

Miyako Odori (p92)

SHOWTIME

Kyoto is the best city in Japan to see traditional performing arts, thanks to its rich history as a centre for artistic expression and development. But culture vultures can also find exciting contemporary theatre, a thriving cinema scene and plenty of live-music venues catering to all tastes.

Geisha Performances

Kyoto is the geisha capital of the world, and every year the city's *geiko* (the Kyoto word for geisha) and *maiko* (apprentice geisha) come together and take to the stage to perform at various *odori* (dance) events, typically with a seasonal theme.

Three of the geisha districts perform their dances in April to coincide with the cherry-blossom season; these are the Kyō Odori (held between the first and third Sunday in April) Miyako Odori (held throughout April), and the Kitano Odori (held between 15 and 25 April). The Kamogawa Odori is held a little later (throughout most of May), and towards the end of the year is the Gion Odori (held between 1 and 10 November), which coincides with the autumn foliage.

These dazzling dance performances are highly recommended if you happen to be in town when they are on.

If the timing doesn't work out, there are other ways to witness geisha in full-performing flow – daily evening shows at Gion Corner (p95) include a segment of geisha dancing, along with other cultural performances, for a bite-sized (and slightly more touristy) taste of Kyoto's entertainment heritage.

Traditional Drama

Visitors to Gion will likely walk past Minamiza (p97), the beautifully facaded theatre on Shijō-dōri. This is said to be the birthplace of kabuki, Japan's most exciting and colourful form of performance art, where acrobatic actors leap about the stage in flamboyant costumes and retell dramatic stories from Japan's feudal past.

While much of the plot may be lost to non-Japanese speakers (although even natives often struggle to keep up!), there is a lot to enjoy among the visual drama and over-the-top theatre of it all.

If it sounds like your bag and you have a couple of hours to spare, then taking in a show could be a memorable foray into a cultural rabbit hole where few foreigners venture – tickets can be bought at the box office or online.

Downtown Entertainment

Music lovers should hit Downtown Kyoto for its venues and clubs; small dedicated live-music venues are known as 'live houses' and tend to feature local artists and occasional touring international acts.

NEED TO KNOW

Listings & Events

Most popular theatres have their own English-language websites where you can find out about the latest shows and schedules and make bookings. Otherwise check out *Kyoto Visitor's Guide* (kvg-kyoto.com) for news and info on a range of topics and events, from festivals to geisha performances. Tourist information centres are also usually a good bet for upcoming listings.

Buying Tickets

If an online search doesn't yield any results, pay a visit to the Kansai Tourist Information Center Kyoto (p46) for help with booking tickets, plus any other travel, restaurant or accommodation queries you may have. Higher-end hotels or ryokan may be able to assist guests with show bookings too.

ENTERTAINMENT BY NEIGHBOURHOOD

Kyoto Station & South Kyoto	There are cinemas here, plus a number of theatres within walking distance of the station. Kyoto Theatre is probably the best of the bunch and always has a varied roster of shows; it is conveniently located inside the station building.
Downtown Kyoto	Head here for the best entertainment and nightlife options in the city, ranging from live-music halls to traditional arts and modern theatre, plus a number of art-house-style cinemas.
Imperial Palace & Around	A generally quiet area with limited entertainment options, though it has some nice venues for lovers of classical music.
Gion & Southern Higashiyama	Kyoto's traditional entertainment quarter is arguably less bustling at night than it was in its heyday, but is still the place to go for geisha performances and kabuki.
Northern Higashiyama	If you're interested in seeing a *nō* performance then head to the beautiful Kyoto Kanze Kaikan (*nō* theatre).
Northwest Kyoto	A very quiet area of the city after dark, but it can be a good place to see geisha dances in Kamishichiken, Kyoto's oldest geisha district.
Arashiyama & Sagano	Mostly very quiet at night, with not much in the way of entertainment – perhaps go for a leisurely stroll instead.

Nishiki Market (p68)

TREASURE HUNT

Kyoto is one of Japan's greatest cities when it comes to shopping – while Tokyo has the glitz, choice and world-famous brands that come with being the capital city, and Osaka combines modern commercialism with deep merchant-city roots, Kyoto has a long history as Japan's cultural and artistic workshop.

Many of Kyoto's districts are dedicated to a particular craft, be it textiles, ceramics or antiques, making Kyoto undoubtedly the best place to find traditional arts and crafts in the whole of Japan. The city has countless craft shops and artisan workshops dotted throughout. But it's not just all old-fashioned wares: Downtown Kyoto has luxury department stores to rival anything in Tokyo or Osaka, and around Kyoto Station you can find cutting-edge electronics and variety stores for all of your needs.

The city also hosts some of Japan's best monthly flea markets, where you might be able to pick up a rare bargain.

Shopping Central

Downtown Kyoto should be your first stop when you've got yen burning a hole in your pocket. The bustling area around Shijō-dōri and where it intersects Kawaramachi-dōri is Kyoto's main shopping hub; here you'll find extravagant department stores such as Takashimaya and Daimaru, plus many high-end brand stores interspersed with smaller shops selling souvenirs and traditional goods.

This part of town also has a number of *shōtengai* (covered shopping streets), such as Teramachi (p70) and Shinkyōgoku (p71), which have an eclectic range of shops and are great for a rainy day; nearby Nishiki Market (p68) is Kyoto's premier food market and a must-visit.

A little south of downtown, Kyoto Station has shopping malls within the building itself and around its vicinity, and the famous electronics shop Yodobashi Camera (p49) just a block or so away.

Traditional Arts & Crafts

Kyoto is home to a multitude of expert craftmakers, specialising in everything from kimono fabrics to handmade *washi* (traditional paper) and wooden dolls – if you have an interest in a particular traditional craft, then the chances are that Kyoto has a shop, or sometimes a whole district, dedicated to it. Some of the most important craft neighbourhoods are Nishijin for textiles and fabrics, Gojō-zaka (near Kiyomizu-dera) for pottery and Shinmonzen-dōri (near Gion) for antiques.

Flea Markets

If your Kyoto visit coincides with one of its monthly flea markets, then it's well worth taking the time to swing by, as they're among Japan's best flea markets.

The Kōbō-san Market is held on the 21st of the month under the towering five-storey pagoda at Tōji-ji; it's a great place to hunt for bargains, and there are also usually food stalls for munching on castella cakes or *tako-yaki* (grilled octopus dumplings).

Alternatively, head to the Tenjin-san Market at Kitano Tenman-gū on the 25th of each month – here you can haggle for goods such as kimonos, pottery, tools and antiques, and there are numerous food stalls here too, helping to create a mini-festival atmosphere. Don't miss either if you're in town!

COURTESY OF IPPODŌ TEA ©

Ippodō Tea

LONELY PLANET'S TOP... INDEPENDENT SHOPS

Aritsugu (p71) Legendary knife-makers in Nishiki Market, serving chefs, locals and tourists.

Zōhiko (p71) Kyoto's best lacquerware shop.

Ippodō Tea (p71) One of Kyoto's finest traditional tea shops; great for a souvenir.

Wagami no Mise (p67) Staggering selection of *washi*-related goods.

Kyūkyodō (p71) Old shop in Teramachi selling a wide range of traditional crafts.

Tsujikura (p71) Shop specialising in exquisite and colourful *wagasa* (waxed-paper umbrellas).

Kungyoku-dō (p49) Pick up a Kyoto-inspired scent at the city's oldest incense shop.

Asahi-dō (p95) Kyoto-style pottery specialist since 1870, not far from Kiyomizu-dera.

SHOPPING BY NEIGHBOURHOOD

Kyoto Station & South Kyoto	There are big electronics and camera shops close to Kyoto Station, and a few interesting craft shops away from the main streets.
Downtown Kyoto	This whole neighbourhood seems to be built around shopping, so it should be your first stop for burning some cash.
Imperial Palace & Around	It's not packed with shops, although the historic Nishijin district is the best place in Kyoto for handcrafted textiles.
Gion & Southern Higashiyama	Come here for traditional souvenirs, ceramics and other crafts.
Northern Higashiyama	The area has many small and traditional craft shops.
Northwest Kyoto	Visit for one of the city's best monthly flea markets.
Arashiyama & Sagano	Here you can find bamboo-related products and edible souvenirs.

Sanmon gate, Chion-in (p90)

TRIP PLANNER

TEMPLES & SHRINES

Kyoto's astonishing assortment of temples and shrines is one of the city's big draws, as these symbolic structures feature some of the most magnificent religious architecture on Earth. With over 1600 Buddhist temples and 400 Shintō shrines packed into a relatively compact area, there are enough to fill a lifetime of visits.

TEMPLE OR SHRINE?

Japanese temples and shrines have quite different origins and purposes. Shrines belong to the indigenous Shintō religion, a belief system that holds that all beings, objects and things are inhabited by *kami* (deities), and shrines are where they reside. Temples, on the other hand, are Buddhist in origin (introduced to Japan from the continent via China), and are places where the devout come to learn and practise their beliefs, and where sacred Buddhist artefacts (usually statues) are kept and displayed. In shrines the sacred objects are usually hidden away.

Over the years, Buddhism and Shintō became intertwined, with many people adopting and practising a mix of traditions from each religion, and temples and shrines often being built at the same sites, which can make it hard to discern one from the other. Perhaps the easiest indicator is that shrines always have a *torii* (entrance gate), usually in the form of two upright pillars joined at the top by two horizontal bars, often painted a bright vermilion colour. Temples are usually entered via a more robust-looking *mon* (gate), topped by a multi-tiered roof, with the structure housing intricately carved guardian figures called *niō*.

SHRINE ETIQUETTE

Visitors to shrines traditionally follow a basic procedure, although it is not a requirement. First, at the stone *chōzuya* (basin), rinse both hands and use the *hishaku* (bamboo ladle) to pour water into

With so many to choose from and only limited time, here are a selection of Kyoto's very best and most famous temples and shrines to visit.

Temples

Kinkaku-ji (p120) Possibly Kyoto's most famous and iconic temple, the Golden Pavilion is a stunning sight in any season.

Kiyomizu-dera (p98) Known for its enormous wooden veranda, this hillside temple has many interesting sights spread across its grounds.

Nanzen-ji (p110) A temple with a little bit of everything, from breathtaking architecture to intimate landscaped gardens.

Tenryū-ji (p134) Lovely temple in Arashiyama; its 14th-century Zen garden is one of the best in Kyoto.

Sanjūsangen-dō (p88) Japan's longest wooden building houses a breathtaking collection of 1001 life-size Kannon statues.

Ginkaku-ji (p104) The 'Silver Pavilion' is well known for its wonderful gardens and picturesque views.

Chion-in (p90) Secluded mountainside temple with magnificent architecture and always brimming with religious activity.

Daitoku-ji (p78) A self-contained temple town within the city, Daitoku-ji is particularly notable for its many excellent Zen gardens.

Shrines

Fushimi Inari-Taisha (p44) Kyoto's most famous shrine, where you can stroll mountain paths lined with thousands of bright red *torii*.

Heian-jingū (p103) A red shrine dedicated to the imperial family, with one of the biggest *torii* in Japan.

Shimogamo-jinja (p77) An ancient shrine steeped in history at the north end of the city, with a lovely tree-lined approach.

---

a cupped hand to rinse your mouth; spit it out onto the gravel (and not in the basin!). Next head to the *haiden* (worshippers' hall) in front of the main hall where you can toss a coin into the offering box, and then shake the rope that hangs below a bell to 'wake the gods'. Bow twice, loudly clap twice and bow twice more (once deeply, then lightly) before stepping back and to the side.

VISITING A TEMPLE

Unless you're taking part in meditation or some other instruction, there are no particular rules for visiting a Buddhist temple, other than taking your shoes off when climbing the stairs to the main hall. Note that indoor photography is generally prohibited.

Kinkaku-ji (p120)

ESSENTIAL INFORMATION

Opening Hours

Most shrines are open 24 hours a day and temples from around 9am to 5pm daily. But for some temples this does vary by season, with slightly shorter hours in winter and longer hours in summer; some also have evening light-ups and other seasonal events.

Admission

Most shrines and many temple grounds are free to enter, although entry to shrine treasure houses usually requires a small fee, and most temples charge between ¥400 and ¥600 for entry to the buildings and/or gardens.

Dress Code

There are no particular rules, but use common sense. Visitors are usually required to take off their shoes when entering any building.

KYOTO

THE GUIDE

Chapters in this section are organised by hubs and their surrounding areas. We see the hub as your base in the destination, where you'll find unique experiences, local insights, insider tips and expert recommendations. It's also your gateway to the surrounding area, where you'll see what and how much you can do from there.

Jizō statue, Enkō-ji (p108)
PONGSAKORN TEERAPARPWONG/SHUTTERSTOCK ©

NEIGHBOURHOODS AT A GLANCE

Find the neighbourhoods that tick all your boxes.

Kinkaku-ji

Ryōan-ji

Shuzan-kaidō

Nishiōji-dōri

Kita Tenma

Tenryū-ji

Arashiyama Bamboo Forest

Sanjō-dōri

Kameyama-kōen

Iwatayama Monkey Park

Nishiōji-dōri

Sanjō-dōri

Arashiyama & Sagano (p124)

Explore temples and bamboo groves in popular, scenic neighbourhoods surrounded by nature.

Northwest Kyoto (p113)

A peaceful retreat that's home to two of Kyoto's most popular temples: Kinkaku-ji and Ryōan-ji.

Downtown Kyoto (p53)

Kyoto's main shopping and dining district also boasts big-hitting attractions.

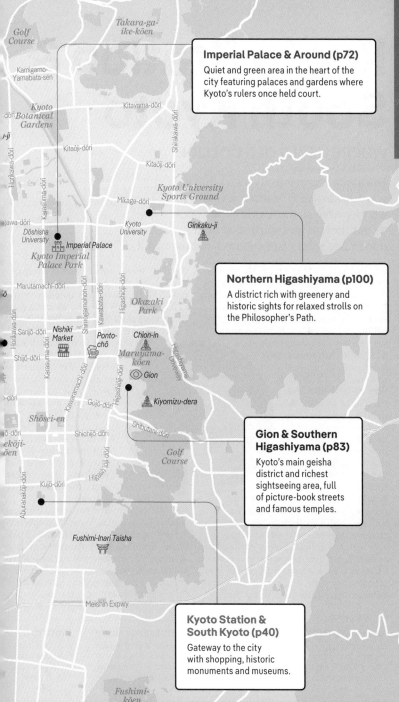

Imperial Palace & Around (p72)
Quiet and green area in the heart of the city featuring palaces and gardens where Kyoto's rulers once held court.

Northern Higashiyama (p100)
A district rich with greenery and historic sights for relaxed strolls on the Philosopher's Path.

Gion & Southern Higashiyama (p83)
Kyoto's main geisha district and richest sightseeing area, full of picture-book streets and famous temples.

Kyoto Station & South Kyoto (p40)
Gateway to the city with shopping, historic monuments and museums.

Golf Course

Takara-ga-ike-kōen

Kamigamo-Yamabata-sen

Kyoto Botanical Gardens

-dōri

-ji

Kitayama-dōri

Shirakawa-dōri

Kitaōji-dōri

Horikawa-dōri

Karasuma-dōri

Kitaōji-dōri

-gawa-dōri

Kitaōji-dōri

Dōshisha University

Kyoto University Sports Ground

Mikage-dōri

Kyoto University

Ginkaku-ji

Imperial Palace

Kyoto Imperial Palace Park

Marutamachi-dōri

Higashiōji-dōri

Kawabata-dōri

Shinmonzen-dōri

Okazaki Park

ō

Horikawa-dōri

Sanjō-dōri

Nishiki Market

Ponto-chō

Chion-in

Maruyama-kōen

Shijō-dōri

Kawaramachi-dōri

Karasuma-dōri

Gion

Higashiyama Driveway

Gojō-dōri

Higashiōji-dōri

Kiyomizu-dera

-dōri

Shōsei-en

Shichijō-dōri

Shibutani-dōri

ō-dōri

ekōji-ōen

Higashi kōji-dōri

Golf Course

Kujō-dōri

Aburanakōji-dōri

Fushimi-Inari Taisha

Meishin Expwy

Fushimi-kōen

Kyoto Station & South Kyoto

WHERE NEW & OLD COLLIDE

The stock Japanese cityscape that greets you outside Kyoto Station can make you wonder what all the fuss is about. Look closer, though, and you'll soon spot Kyoto's trademark history and culture, if not the beauty.

Whether you glide in on the shinkansen or arrive squeezed among suitcases on the Kansai Airport express, Kyoto Station (京都駅) will probably be your first encounter with Japan's fabled city of culture. A colossal beast of glass and steel, it's perhaps not the vibe you were anticipating. But fear not! Kyoto has many faces, and here is a reminder that the city that gave the world geisha, *nō* theatre and *kaiseki* cuisine is also the tech-savvy birthplace of two pixelated plumbers, messrs Mario and Luigi. But before you race off to Kyoto's hillside temples and beauty spots, don't overlook the neighbourhood's own gems, starting with a scramble up the retro Kyoto Tower, a great way to orient yourself as you gaze out over the city's uniform blocks, enclosed by a horseshoe of temple-studded mountains.

Unlike the narrow, hilly lanes you probably associate with the city, in Kyoto Ekimae (literally 'in front of the station')

the flat, broad streets form a compass-aligned grid, divided into square divisions called *chō*. Karasuma-dōri, the city's central thoroughfare, cuts a swathe due north from Kyoto Station all the way to the Imperial Palace, while the main east–west streets are arranged in numerical order from north to south. This is no modern-day Manhattan though, but the vestiges of Kyoto's original design, modelled on ancient Chang'an (Xi'an), the capital of China when Kyoto was founded. Appropriately, Kyoto Station is positioned just a few blocks from where Rashōmon, the original city gate, once stood.

Although most of the action happens north of Kyoto Station, in the other direction are two unmissable sights in Fushimi Inari-Taisha, Kyoto's most popular shrine, and the wondrous Zen monastery of Tōfuku-ji. if you have time on your hands, the sake breweries of Fushimi and the *matcha* merchants of Uji make for rewarding side trips.

DON'T MISS...

FUSHIMI INARI-TAISHA	TŌFUKU-JI	KYOTO RAILWAY MUSEUM	KYOTO TOWER
Hike through a hypnotic tunnel of red *torii* at Kyoto's most mesmerising shrine. **p44**	Ponder the modern Zen gardens at this marvellous temple complex in a sublime natural setting. **p43**	Clamber aboard real-life locos and try a train simulator at this engaging, family-friendly attraction. **p48**	Fly up to a 131m-high observation deck for panoramic Kyoto views. **p46**

TOP TIP

The area around Kyoto Station is packed with hotel rooms of all stripes, from executive shoeboxes to stylish midrange digs. More affordable than other parts of Kyoto, and with excellent transport links, Kyoto Station is a decent if unromantic sightseeing base, particularly if you're passing through on a wider Japan rail itinerary.

Left: Kyoto Tower (p46); Above: Fushimi Inari-Taisha (p44)

HIGASHI HONGAN-JI

Pad across a sea of tatami through one of the world's largest wooden buildings at this monumental Buddhist temple.
p47

TŌ-JI

Dig for treasures at a UNESCO-listed temple complex that also hosts a monthly flea market.
p49

FUSHIMI SAKE VILLAGE

Sample a tasting flight of 18 sakes or try a bowl of sake-infused ramen.
p51

KYOTO STATION & SOUTH KYOTO

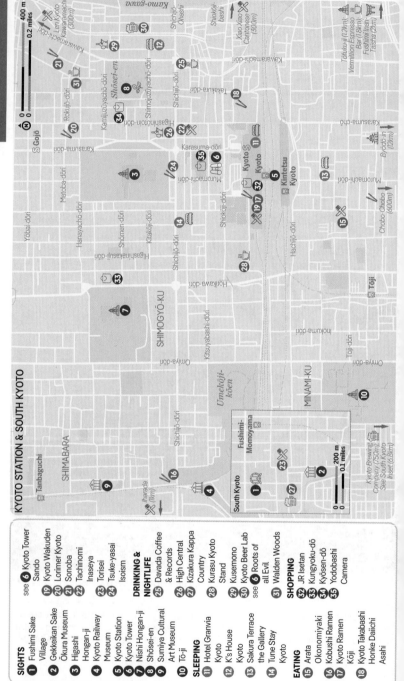

SIGHTS
1. Fushimi Sake Village
2. Gekkeikan Sake Ōkura Museum
3. Higashi Hongan-ji
4. Kyoto Railway Museum
5. Kyoto Station
6. Kyoto Tower
7. Nishi Hongan-ji
8. Shōsei-en
9. Sumiya Cultural Art Museum
10. Tō-ji

SLEEPING
11. Hotel Granvia Kyoto
12. K's House Kyoto
13. Sakura Terrace the Gallery
14. Tune Stay Kyoto

EATING
15. Arata Okonomiyaki
16. Kobushi Ramen
17. Kyoto Ramen Kōji
18. Kyoto Takabashi Honke Daiichi Asahi
see 6 Kyoto Tower Sando
19. Kyoto Wakuden
20. Lorimer Kyoto
21. Sonoba
22. Tachinomi Inaseya
23. Torisei
24. Tsuke-yasai Isoism

DRINKING & NIGHTLIFE
25. Davada Coffee & Records
26. High Central
27. Kizakura Kappa Country
28. Kurasu Kyoto Stand
29. Kusemono
30. Kyoto Beer Lab
see 6 Roots of all Evil
31. Walden Woods

SHOPPING
32. JR Isetan
33. Kungyoku-dō
34. Kyōsen-dō
35. Yodobashi Camera

KYOTO STATION & SOUTH KYOTO

Tōfuku-ji

The Bridge to Heaven
Marvellous Modern Zen Gardens

One of Kyoto's earliest and largest Zen monasteries, **Tōfuku-ji** (東福寺) charms with a three-pronged assault – the sublime architecture of its halls, gates and bridges, intriguing Zen gardens by a modern master, and the manner in which the complex flows across a maple-filled gorge that blazes red and gold in autumn. The covered **Tsūten-kyō** (Bridge to Heaven) is the prime spot for autumn foliage viewing, and joins the main temple precincts to the *hōjō* (abbot's quarters), around which are four dry landscape gardens by Shigemori Mirei, a freethinking artist of the 20th century. Combining myth and modernity, the south-facing garden features clusters of rocks on raked gravel representing the Islands of the Immortals, while the east garden has antique stone pillars arranged like the Big Dipper constellation. Another highlight is the spectacular **San-mon** (main gate), one of the oldest temple gates in Japan. Tōfuku-ji is one stop south of Kyoto Station on the Nara Line.

AUTUMN COLOURS
Tōfuku-ji is one of Kyoto's most famous spots for autumn foliage viewing. Another is out west in **Arashiyama** (p124), where the mountains blaze red and gold between November and December.

BEST PLACES TO STAY AROUND KYOTO STATION

Tune Stay Kyoto ¥¥
Great value, design-forward hotel that feels like a posh hostel with its polished-steel shared kitchen, short film screenings and craft gin sets.

K's House Kyoto ¥
Excellent hostel in a great location close to a leafy canal. Bonus points for clean dorms, bike hire and a substantial rooftop terrace with mountain views.

Hotel Granvia Kyoto ¥¥¥
The ultimate in convenience, this behemoth attached to Kyoto Station has over 500 supersized rooms (by Japanese standards) and a bevy of restaurants.

Sakura Terrace the Gallery ¥¥
More stylish than it should be for the price, Sakura Terrace boasts a striking open-air lounge with fire pit, and modern rooms kitted out with balconies.

Scan for maps, history and a month-by-month guide to festivals and events.

TOP EXPERIENCE

Fushimi Inari-Taisha

Chances are you've seen photos of the flame-hued tunnel of *torii* (Shintō gates) at this shrine to Inari, the god of rice and prosperity. But Fushimi Inari-Taisha (伏見稲荷大社) is more than just a selfie op or a movie location – it's a world unto itself, populated by fox guardians and woven together by wooded trails. There's magic in these hills.

DON'T MISS

Rōmon (tower gate)

Honden (main shrine building)

Senbon Torii

Inariyama summit

Sub-shrines

Shinseki (sites where sub-shrines used to be)

Kitsune guardian statues

Legends and Lore

Fushimi Inari-Taisha is older even than Kyoto. Historical records date the shrine's founding to the early 700s, though it is believed that Inari, a Shintō *kami* (god or spirit) whose name means 'carrying rice', was worshipped in Japan before the arrival of Buddhism in the 6th century. Variations of a founding myth involve a member of the ancient Hata clan shooting an arrow at a rice cake, which promptly transformed into a swan and settled on a hill where rice miraculously started to grow. In the 10th century Fushimi Inari-Taisha was promoted to the highest rank afforded to shrines, receiving imperial patronage. Today it serves as the head shrine for over 30,000 Inari shrines nationwide.

Thousands of Torii

The approach to the shrine is a press of crowds, souvenirs and snacks, and that's before you've reached the palatial **Rōmon** (tower gate), which leads to the **Honden**, the main shrine hall. Most visitors head directly to the **Senbon Torii**, the shrine's spectacular avenue of vermilion gates, planted shoulder to shoulder to form passageways on the slope. *Torii* are said to mark the boundary between the physical and spiritual, symbolising the passing of prayers from people to gods, so walking through hundreds of them in a row is a serious spiritual trip! As sunlight glints fleetingly between *torii* as you climb, the effect is hypnotic.

Investing in Blessings

All of the mountain's 10,000-plus gates have been donated by businesses and individuals as offerings to Inari, with larger *torii* costing well over ¥1 million. You'll see names and prayers inscribed in black ink on each *torii*. The reason businesses seek the blessing of a rice god is because rice and wealth have an ancient connection. Long ago in Japan rice was currency, collected as tax and paid as wages.

Hiking Mount Inari

Around 4km to 5km of pilgrimage trails climb from the main shrine precincts to the summit of **Inariyama**, the southernmost of Higashiyama's 36 peaks. A fun half-day hike takes you past **sub-shrines**, teahouses, **shinseki** (sites where shrines used to be) and panoramic views. Most visitors turn around after Senbon Torii, meaning it's more peaceful up top. Allow two or three hours for a relatively zippy up and down, and come early or late to sidestep the selfie-stick crowd. The shrine is open 24 hours, though the paths are not extensively lit after dark.

Fantastic Foxes

What's with all the fox statues? In Japanese folklore, **kitsune** (foxes) are believed to be intelligent and possess magical abilities. White foxes *(byakkosan)* are considered servants and messengers of Inari – flitting between rice field and woodland, it's thought they can mediate between the earthly and spiritual realms. If you want to make a wish, buy a fox-shaped *ema* (votive tablet) – write whatever you desire on one side and draw a fox face on the other.

SPIRITUAL STAMP COLLECTING

You'll probably visit loads of temples and shrines in Kyoto, so why not gamify the experience and get yourself a *goshuinchō* (book of seals)? Essentially a blank notebook, you can purchase one at Fushimi Inari-Taisha and start collecting. Pay a small donation and temples and shrines will paste in a calligraphic stamp that records your pilgrimage. You'll end up with a beautiful (if unreadable) souvenir.

TOP TIPS

- Visit in the first few days of January for *hatsu-mōde* (first shrine visit of the New Year) when thousands crowd the main courtyard to pray for good fortune.
- The **Sangyō-sai** festival takes place on 8 April, during which offerings are made and dances performed to ensure prosperity for national industry.
- When it's time for a break, head to **Vermillion Espresso Bar** for superior coffee and cake.
- If you have time on your hands, veer off the main paths and explore the side trails; finds include waterfalls and a bamboo grove minus the crowds.

BEDS FOR EELS

It wouldn't be Kyoto without *machiya*, those old-timey wooden townhouses often squeezed between modern constructions.

Narrow but deceptively deep, *machiya* functioned as both home and workplace for Japan's burgeoning bourgeoisie in the Edo period, featuring a slatted shopfront and living quarters deeper within. Their skinny shape came about because homes were once taxed on the width of their street frontage, earning *machiya* the nickname '*unagi no nedoko*' (bed for an eel).

Despite their cultural value, *machiya* are costly to maintain and some are still being demolished.

The Takase-gawa, a tree-lined canal northeast of Kyoto Station, has some lovely *machiya* repurposed as holiday lets, bookable at sites like Airbnb and machiya-inn-japan.com.

Reflection of Kyoto Tower

Eye in the Sky
Climb Kyoto Tower

Too modern for an ancient capital? That's been the criticism of the 131m-tall **Kyoto Tower** since it was built in the boom years of the 1960s. From the observation deck, Kyoto's horseshoe of surrounding mountains reveal temple roofs nestled on green hillsides, and you can see the skyscrapers of Osaka on a clear day. Head to the 3rd floor for the **Kansai Tourist Information Center** and down to the basement for a street-food-style food court.

EATING IN KYOTO STATION & SOUTH KYOTO: RAMEN & SOBA NOODLES

Kobushi Ramen
Broth pepped up with duck and sea bream elevates the ramen at this neighbourhood joint by the Railway Museum. *11.30am-2.30pm & 6-10pm ¥*

Kyoto Ramen Kōji Take your taste buds on a ramen tour of Japan at this themed food 'street' on the 10th floor of Kyoto station. *11am-10pm ¥*

Sonoba Handmade soba is the star at this minimalist hangout. An attached pottery studio provides some of the gorgeous tableware. *11.30am-3pm Fri-Tue ¥¥*

Kyoto Takabashi Honke Daiichi Asahi
A Kyoto fixture since 1947, this no-frills ramen joint is known for its clean-tasting yet umami-rich broth. *6am-1am Fri-Wed ¥*

Next Stop the Future
Explore Kyoto's Divisive Train Station

You might feel compelled to flee the orbit of Hiroshi Hara's jarring spaceport of a station, a gigantic architectural statement that sparked protests in the 1990s and kick-started a wave of new high-rise developments. Or you could surrender to this glass-and-steel vision of Kyoto's future by the same architect as Osaka's Umeda Sky building. Ride the escalators up through the central hall for soaring views, shop for goodies at **Isetan Department Store**, grab noodles at **Kyoto Ramen Kōji** (p46) then walk the **Skyway**, a viewing tunnel suspended 45m above the ground.

The station was built to mark 1200 years since Kyoto's founding. A century earlier, Kyoto marked its anniversary by building the stately Heian Shrine...how times change.

Monumental Masterpiece
True Pure Land Temple

Unlike other Buddhist sects that demanded endless meditation and study, Jōdo Shinshū (True Pure Land) Buddhism, practised at **Higashi Hongan-ji** (東本願寺) just north of Kyoto Station, opened its gates to all who could convey their faith by chanting a simple mantra: *namu amida butsu* – a prayer to the Amida Buddha. Unsurprisingly, this proved highly popular.

Enter the cavernous **Amida-dō** with its sea of tatami mats and gleaming gold altar and you'll see it was built to accommodate massed ranks of worshippers.

Things get even more monumental in the **Goei-dō**, one of the largest wooden buildings in Japan. Such mighty structures exude a sense of muscular permanence, but Higashi Hongan-ji has been rebuilt after fire five times – the present buildings date from 1895. Look for the display between halls that hints at the human toil in their reconstruction.

A python-like coil of rope was made from the donated hair of female worshippers – hemp ropes weren't strong enough to raise the 90 massive timber pillars that hold up the Goei-dō's roof.

A TALE OF TWO TEMPLES

What's the deal with Higashi Hongan-ji's doppelganger?

A few blocks away, **Nishi Hongan-ji** (西本願寺) is almost a mirror image of its neighbour. Both temples belong to Jōdo Shinshū, founded in the 13th century and the most popular branch of Buddhism in Japan today. In 1591, the warlord Toyotomi Hideyoshi granted land in Kyoto for the building of Hongan-ji to serve as the sect's headquarters. But just 11 years later, an internal schism led to the founding of Higashi Hongan-ji a few blocks away (*higashi* means east, *nishi* west). Jōdo Shinshū was becoming so powerful that the new shōgun Tokugawa Ieyasu encouraged a succession dispute as part of a divide-and-conquer tactic to weaken its influence.

EATING IN KYOTO STATION & SOUTH KYOTO: LIVELY & LOCAL

Tachinomi Inaseya
None of your Kyoto airs and graces at this friendly standing bar; just delicious nibbles, cheap drinks and an English menu. Smoking permitted. *11.30am-11pm* ¥

Arata Okonomiyaki
Between Kyoto Station and Tō-ji, this *okonomiyaki* (Japanese savoury pancake) joint is perpetually crammed with lively locals. Book ahead. *5-11pm* ¥

Torisei Gorge on charred *yakitori* (grilled skewers) paired with house-brewed sake at this traditional restaurant in the Fushimi sake district. *11am-10pm* ¥

Kyoto Tower Sando
All bare concrete and buzzing neon, this food court beneath Kyoto Tower mixes Japanese counter dining with burgers, banh mi and cocktails. *10am-11pm* ¥¥

Shōsei-en

Going Loco in Kyoto
All Aboard for Railway Nostalgia

FAMILY FUN IN KANSAI

Kyoto Railway Museum is one of the few dedicated child-oriented attractions in Kyoto. For much more family fun, catch a train to **Osaka** (p140) and take your pick from Osaka Aquarium, Universal Studios Japan, Legoland Discovery Centre and umpteen giant Ferris wheels.

A fitting tribute to Japan's enduring love affair with rail travel, the **Kyoto Railway Museum** (closed Wednesdays) showcases over 50 full-size locos, from vintage steam spewers to the first iteration of the shinkansen, c1964. Kids will love the miniature railway displays, train simulators and the chance to take a 10-minute jaunt on a real steam train. Older trainspotters can take a deep dive into the history of rail travel and learn how, in the early days, Japanese passengers would remove their shoes before boarding.

 DRINKING IN KYOTO STATION & SOUTH KYOTO: COOL COFFEE SPOTS

Kurasu Kyoto Stand
Skip Kyoto Station's chain cafes and seek out Kurasu for perfect espresso drinks and pour-overs. Also sells its own line of coffee homewares. *8am-6pm*

Davada Coffee & Records
Thumb though racks of vinyl records while you wait for your lovingly crafted latte at this hip little hangout behind a retro brick shopfront. *11am-7pm*

Vermillion Espresso Bar Fuel up at this cool cafe before taking on the crowds at Fushimi Inaria-Taisha. The name refers to the colour of Japan's *torii* (shrine gates). *7.30am-2.30pm*

Walden Woods
Pay homage to the stunning all-white interiors and Instagram-worthy coffee at this backstreet cafe space. *9am-6pm*

Secret Walled Garden
Paths, Ponds and Teahouses

A little-visited gem, **Shōsei-en** (渉成園) was created in the 17th century as a retirement villa for the 13th abbot of Higashi Hongan-ji. The traditional strolling garden, winding between reception halls, teahouses and pond, is brought to life by an excellent free guide booklet. Garden views designed to incorporate the hills of Higashiyama as *shakkei* (borrowed garden scenery) have long since been tainted by encroaching buildings and powerlines, but in a modern twist, the Kyoto Tower does a similar job, providing a fine backdrop to photos.

Cultural Treasures of Tō-ji
Pagoda, Halls and Market Stalls

Boasting Japan's tallest pagoda and a tō-do (lecture hall) crammed with muscled Niō statues and enlightened Buddhas, the impressive temple complex of Tō-ji (東寺) is the main reason to explore the streets south of Kyoto Station. On the 21st of each month, Tō-ji hosts **Kōbō-san**, a festival-like flea market that marks the passing of Kōbō Daishi, the founder of Shingon Buddhism to which Tō-ji belongs. Haggle for Japanese crafts, curios and secondhand kimonos, or graze at the many food stalls on offer.

Sake, Sake Everywhere
Sipping and Strolling in Fushimi

Ten minutes from Kyoto by train, the area of Fushimi Ward north of Chūshojima Station is a time warp of tree-lined canals, wooden sake warehouses and multiple invitations to knock back a cup of Japan's famous fermented rice drink. Thanks to its river port location between Kyoto and Osaka and sweet-tasting spring water, Fushimi became a major sake hot spot and still hosts 20 or so sake breweries, including industry giant Gekkeikan, founded here in 1637.

The **Gekkeikan Sake Ōkura Museum** introduces the history of the craft and offers tastings. Canal cruise boats ply the waterways just south of the museum (lovely in cherry-blossom season), while nearby **Kizakura Kappa Country** is a sake and beer brewery with on-site bar-restaurant and shop.

BEST SHOPS AROUND KYOTO STATION

Kungyoku-dō
Shop for incense sticks, hand creams and candles infused with cherry-blossom, *yuzu* (a citrus) and other Kyoto-inspired scents at Japan's oldest incense shop. *9am-5.30pm*

Kyōsen-dō
All handmade on site, the Kyoto-style paper or silk fans at this long-established shop east of Higashi Hongan-ji make lovely gifts. *9am-5pm Mon-Sat, 10am-6pm Sun*

Yodobashi Camera
It's not just cameras at this gigantic emporium; there's also a cycle track, golf-club testing range, every gadget going, fashion on the 5th floor and food up top. *9.30am-10pm*

JR Kyoto Isetan
Attached to Kyoto Station, this department store has 11 floors of retail, restaurants and a delicious basement *depachika* (food market). *10am-8pm*

 EATING IN KYOTO STATION & SOUTH KYOTO: TREAT YOURSELF

Tsuke-yasai Isoism	Kyoto Wakuden	Iharada Savour a *kaiseki*	Lorimer Kyoto
Creative *izakaya*-style fare featuring pickled vegetables sourced from the restaurant's own farm. Call to book. *11.30am-3pm & 5-11pm* ¥¥	Splurge on seasonal set menus with a view at this Kyoto *kaiseki* restaurant on the 11th floor of Kyoto Station. *11am-3.30pm & 5-10pm* ¥¥	set made with ingredients like aged Tajima beef and *matsutake* mushrooms. Reservations via its website (iharada.jp/en). *5-11pm Mon-Sat* ¥¥¥	Breakfast or brunch on beautiful set meals of grilled fish, miso soup and fresh veggies. *8am-3pm Mon-Fri, from 7:30am Sat & Sun* ¥¥

HIGHLIGHTS OF KYOTO STATION AREA ON FOOT

THE GUIDE

KYOTO STATAION & SOUTH KYOTO

Allow around 2½ hours for this looping walk, much of it along residential lanes and backstreets. Take a moment to drink in the scale of futuristic ❶ **Kyoto Station**, then exit through the main entrance and head north to the ❷ **Kyoto Tower** (p46).

When you've taken in the views from its 100m-high observation deck, keep going north to ❸ **Higashi Hongan-ji** (p47), a monumental Buddhist temple complex. Remove your shoes to enter the Founder's Hall (Goei-dō), so enormous that it takes 927 tatami mats to cover the floor. Exit through Goei-dō-mon, one of the grandest temple gates in Kyoto, and continue west to the garden sanctuary of ❹ **Shōsei-en** (p49).

After a stroll along the garden paths, head back around the north wall of Higashi Hongan-ji then south along Shinmachi-dōri, before turning right (west) when you hit Shōmen-dōri. Continue past shops selling accessories for *butsudan* (household altars) until you reach

Higashi Sōmon, an ornate gate. Turn right to find wonderful ❺ **Kungyoku-dō** (p49), Japan's oldest incense shop. Cross the main road and enter ❻ **Nishi Hongan-ji** (p47), almost a facsimile of Higashi Hongan-ji (*nishi* means west and *higashi* east). Though both temples belong to the same branch of Buddhism, they fell out and diverged in the 16th century.

Exit the temple through the north gate and head west around the sturdy outer wall. Keep going along Hanayachō-dōri and you'll reach the gate that marks the boundary of Shimabara, a former pleasure district. Here, you'll find a beautifully preserved wooden *ageya* (pleasure house), now the ❼ **Sumiya Cultural Art Museum**.

Wander south to the ❽ **Kyoto Railway Museum** (p48), packed with retired locos, including the first edition of the shinkansen (bullet train). Finish with a stroll through peaceful Umekōji Park back to Kyoto Station.

50

Byōdō-in

HIDDEN HANGOUTS

Leon Cameron from Kyoto Beer Lab shares some of his favourite spots in the neighbourhood.

Len Kyoto Kawaramachi It's a hostel, cafe and restaurant in a beautiful space. Great morning coffee, and even better beer at night.

Chobo-chobo A unique *teppan* (hot plate) restaurant and a great place to relax with a larger group. Try the house special Chobo yaki.

Xiao Xiao Cantonese An outlier you've got to taste! Funky 1970s decor and some of the best Cantonese food and sake pairings.

Kusemono sake bar A local's favourite, you can try speciality *nihonshu* (Japanese sake) from all over Japan, many of which are shop exclusives. Quality sake at ¥500 a pop.

Find your way to **Fushimi Sake Village**, a sake-themed *izakaya* cluster, for head-spinning tasting flights of 18 sakes (with accompanying English explanations) and steaming bowls of sake-infused ramen.

Meet Your Matcha

Tea and Temples Uji Excursion

The small city of Uji, 20 minutes south of Kyoto on Nara-bound trains, is a pleasant spot to escape the crowds, taste the area's esteemed *matcha* (powdered green tea) and visit a first-rate temple in **Byōdō-in** (平等院), whose shapely Hōō-dō (Phoenix Hall) is depicted on the ¥10 coin. Built over water with corridors fanning outwards like outstretched wings, it's a stunning sight, and it's survived here since 1053. A contemporary museum houses impressive temple treasures including Byōdō-in's original bell. The **Omotesandō** (approach road) to Byōdō-in is lined with *matcha* merchants where you can buy high-grade tea, wooden whisks and *matcha* bowls, or snack on *matcha*-infused ice-cream, *mochi* and doughnuts.

DRINKING IN KYOTO STATION & SOUTH KYOTO: BEERS & COCKTAILS

Kyoto Beer Lab This Australian-Japanese brewpub makes all its beers on site, which lean to the strong and punchy. *3-11pm Mon-Fri, from 1pm Sat-Sun*

Kyoto Brewing Co. Some of Kyoto's best beer is brewed at this meticulous facility adrift in the sprawl of southern Kyoto. The on-site brewpub opens Friday to Sunday only. *5-9pm Fri, noon-6pm Sat & Sun*

Roots of All Evil Try innovative gin-based cocktails and unusual gin infusions at this fun and friendly counter bar in Kyoto Tower Sando's basement. *11am-11pm*

High Central Smartly attired bartenders mix signature and bespoke drinks at this pint-sized hideaway with a civilised, low-key vibe. English spoken. *7.30pm-2am Tue-Sun*

TOP TIP

Kyoto is one of the world's great food cities, but the sheer choice of establishments – particularly downtown – can at times make eating out a bewildering ordeal. For straightforward but reliable options, the restaurant floors of Takashimaya and Daimaru offer a good selection of high-quality eateries in a compact area.

Above: Ponto-chō (p58); Right: Preserved vegetables, Nishiki Market (p68)

WHY I LOVE DOWNTOWN KYOTO

Tom Fay, Lonely Planet writer

Downtown isn't packed with many of Kyoto's classic must-see sights, but unlike the shrine- and temple-filled neighbourhoods at the city's edge that become eerily quiet after dark, the centre of Kyoto always feels like a lively place, and its almost limitless selection of shops, restaurants and bars means there is always somewhere new to discover.

Nishiki Market is not just a tourist trap – locals still come here to pick up ingredients, and so it retains a real sense of authenticity; that's not to mention the Teramachi and Shinkyōgoku neighbourhoods with their old-school charm.

On warm summer evenings it's always a pleasure to stroll through the wonderfully atmospheric Ponto-chō, and perhaps end the day sipping a *chū-hai* on the banks of the Kamo-gawa.

Downtown Kyoto

THE BUSTLING COMMERCIAL HEART OF KYOTO

Hemmed in by Nijō-jō to the west and the Kamo-gawa to the east, Downtown Kyoto is a melting pot of new and old.

Slap bang in the middle of the city, Kyoto's downtown district packs a lot into its relatively compact area. For serial shoppers and well-heeled browsers, there are contemporary brands, boutique shops and famous luxury department stores such as Takashimaya and Daimaru, meaning that Kyoto has high-end shopping to rival anything Tokyo or Osaka have to offer. At the other end of the spectrum, Nishiki Market has been selling traditional wares, local produce and street food under the same roof for generations, and the city is well-known as a melting pot for traditional crafts and art forms that have been honed to perfection over the centuries – around almost every corner you will find skilled artisans, galleries, workshops and specialist shops, and a deep sense of history, creativity and accumulated knowledge runs through Kyoto's core.

Much of Kyoto's commercial activity is centred on the hustle and bustle of Kyoto's busiest streets, Shijō-dōri and Kawaramachi, but it's worth branching off to explore the many shops and restaurants of Downtown Kyoto's four covered shopping streets (known as *shōtengai*): Sanjō is good for restaurants; Teramachi has a mixture of clothing, art and souvenir shops; Shinkyōgoku offers cheap souvenirs; and Nishiki Market is the city's main food shopping district.

If you would prefer to eat than shop, then Downtown Kyoto has countless restaurants covering the whole spectrum of Japanese and foreign cuisines – at times it can seem to offer almost too much choice! On top of that, there are cafes to while away an hour or two on a rainy afternoon, and bars, clubs and cosy drinking holes for an evening on the town. With plenty of accommodation options and cultural heavyweight attractions such as Nijō-jō, plus excellent museums and art galleries and its good subway and bus connections to other parts of the city, Downtown Kyoto makes for a great base during any visit.

DON'T MISS...

NIJŌ-JŌ	NISHIKI MARKET	PONTO-CHŌ	TAKASHIMAYA
Stunning monument of feudal Japan with extensive and attractive grounds and gardens.	Historic gourmet food market selling fresh local produce and unique street food.	Atmospheric alleyway packed with people, bars and eateries, and perhaps even a geisha or two.	Upmarket department store featuring luxury brands and a high-end food floor.
p56	p68	p58	p59

DOWNTOWN KYOTO

Nijō-jō

Nijō-jō-mae Ⓢ

Shinsen'en

Cafe Phalam (400m)

Oike-dōri

Nijō-dōri

Oshikōji-dōri

Karasuma-Oike

Aneyakōji-dōri

Aneyakōji-dōri

Sanjō-dōri

Sanjō-dōri

Rokkaku-dōri

NAKAGYŌ-KU

Takoyakushi-dōri

Nishikikōji-dōri

Nishikikōji-dōri

Ōmiya

Shijō-Ōmiya

Shijō-dōri

Ka

Bukkōji-dōri

Mimure (250m)

Aburanokōji-dōri
Ogawa-dōri
Shinmachi-dōri
Koromonotana-dōri
Muromachi-dōri
Ryōgaemachi-dōri
Horikawa-dōri
Kamaza-dōri
Shinmachi-dōri
Koin-dōri
Horikawa-dōri
Nishinotōin-dōri
Ōmiya-dōri
Kuronon-dōri

35 Tai Sushi
36 Tōsuirō
37 Yasubee
38 Yoshikawa

DRINKING & NIGHTLIFE
39 Atlantis
40 Bar K6
41 Beer Bar Miyama 162
42 Bee's Knees
43 Bungalow
44 Cafe Bibliotic Hello!

45 Jam House Rock Bar
46 Kaboku Tearoom
47 Karafuneya Coffee
   Sanjō Honten
48 Kitsune Kyoto
49 Kyoto Chambers
50 Maikoya Nishiki
51 Motoan
52 Nokishita 711
see 32 Rocking Bar ING
53 Smart Coffee
54 Tribute Coffee

55 World Kyoto
56 Zen Kashoin

ENTERTAINMENT
see 3 Gear Theatre
57 Kaburen-jō Theatre

SHOPPING
58 Aritsugu
59 BAL
60 Erizen
61 Fujii Daimaru
   Department Store

62 Hands Kyoto
63 Harajuku Chicago
see 46 Ippodō Tea
64 Kamiji Kakimoto
65 Kyūkyodō
see 9 Rakushikan
66 Takashimaya
67 Tsujikura
68 Wagami no Mise
69 Zōhiko

Scan this QR code for detailed background information.

TOP EXPERIENCE

Nijō-jō

Just a short distance northwest of the shops and crowds of Downtown Kyoto is a mighty monument that has stood for centuries as a symbol Japan's shogun power. Nijō-jō (二条城) is a fascinating place to visit and one of the historical highlights of the city, with its sublime feudal-era palace architecture and extensive gardens and grounds.

DON'T MISS

Karamon Gate

Ninomaru Palace

Ōhiroma Yon-no-ma

Honmaru Palace

Ninomaru Garden

Seiryū-en Garden

Nijō-jō Castle Painting Gallery

Deep History

Nijō-jō was built in 1603 as the Kyoto residence of the first Edo-period (1603–1867) shōgun, Tokugawa Ieyasu. It was expanded in later years with additional palace buildings and a five-storey castle keep. At the end of the Edo era and the fall of the Tokugawa shogunate in 1867, the castle was briefly used as an imperial palace before being donated to the city and then opened to the public as one of Kyoto's key historical monuments, and a UNESCO World Heritage Site.

Outer Defence

Nijō-jō comprises three main areas and is entered through a large gate to the east; go here to pick up an English-language audio guide. Further in is the magnificent Azuchi Momoyama–era (1568–1600) **Karamon Gate** with its exquisite woodcarvings and metalwork, and beyond here is the Ninomaru, the castle's outer defensive structure.

Here you can find the castle's main draw, **Ninomaru Palace**, the residence and office of the shōgun when he visited. Designated a national treasure, it is the only surviving example of a fortified palace complex. Its numerous connected buildings are full of intriguing features, such as squeaking 'nightingale' floors, said to be designed as an intruder alert, and hidden alcoves from where bodyguards could watch and leap out from. The almost rococo-style interiors are also full of finely decorated ceilings and painted *fusuma* (sliding doors). The *Matsutaka-zu* is the palace's most impressive wall painting, and depicts a hawk perched on an enormous pine tree – it can be found in the **Ōhiroma Yon-no-ma** (Fourth Chamber), where weapons were once kept and displayed. Originally, access to the palace's tatami-mat inner rooms required a high ranking, but they can now be entered simply by paying an extra fee.

The Honmaru

This was the main circle of defence, and used to be the site of a second palace complex and the castle keep, but both burned to the ground in the 18th century and were never rebuilt. The remaining **Honmaru Palace** has served as an imperial residence since the fall of the shogunate, but is only open to the public for special autumn viewings. However, you can wander around the gardens and take in the views from the top of the old keep's stone foundations.

The Grounds

Nijō-jō's grounds form an extensive oasis of green in the heart of the city, and with its various types of cherry blossoms, the *hanami* (blossom-viewing) season stretches from late March and throughout April. The **Ninomaru Garden** should not be missed – it was laid out when the castle was originally built and designed by Kobori Enshū, Japan's most celebrated garden designer, and is arguably one of the finest landscaped gardens in the city. Its centrepiece is a pond with three islets spanned by stone bridges; allow about an hour to explore both the palace and its gardens. In the northwest corner of the castle grounds you can find the **Seiryū-en Garden** (pictured left); this eclectic garden comprises a Western-style area with grass lawn, and a more traditional *chisen-kaiyū* (strolling pond garden) with two teahouses.

ORIGINAL TREASURES

Most of the wall paintings and sliding screen art in the castle are reproductions, so you will have to visit the **Nijō-jō Castle Painting Gallery** in the northwest area of the grounds to see a selection of the original works. Exhibitions change quarterly and are usually arranged by a specific room or theme; entry is an additional ¥100.

TOP TIPS

● The castle is open from 8.45am to 5pm, and it is definitely worth arriving late or early to beat the crowds. However, note that last admission to the castle grounds is at 4pm if you plan on arriving late in the day.

● To add a deeper layer of richness to your visit, an English audio guide can be rented for ¥500.

● One-hour-long guided tours (in English and Japanese) run daily at 10am and noon and cost ¥1000; to book a place, see the website.

● Just west of the castle, Café Phalam (p61) offers great veggie burgers, vegan cakes and single-origin coffee.

GETTING THERE & AROUND

Most visitors to Kyoto arrive at Kyoto Station, some way south of downtown.

To get to Downtown Kyoto from here use the subway; the Karasuma line offers a direct connection, while the Tōzai line runs east–west across the neighbourhood, including a stop next to Nijō-jō.

JR trains don't service the downtown area, but the privately run Hankyū line stops at Karasuma and Kawaramachi stations, and also has direct trains to Osaka Umeda.

Also make use of the buses; many Kyoto City buses have stops in the downtown area, though taxis are a better option if you have heavy luggage, as the buses can be cramped and crowded.

Sukiyaki, **Mishima-tei**

Drinking District

Take in the After-Dark Ambience of Ponto-chō

Possibly the most atmospheric street in the whole of Kyoto, **Ponto-chō** (先斗町) is a long and narrow paved pedestrian alleyway lined by traditional wooden buildings. Here you can find a mixture of enticingly upmarket and exclusive restaurants and bars frequented by Kyoto's fashionable and most well-to-do denizens, but there are also a few much more affordable eateries and drinking holes tucked away too, such as the cosy craft-beer spot Beer Bar Miyama 162 (p59).

The street is fairly quiet and unremarkable during the daytime – it is at night when it really comes alive, with the soft light of lanterns creating a magical ambience, like the

EATING IN DOWNTOWN KYOTO: MIDRANGE MEALS

Giro Giro Hitoshina Delicious *kaiseki* cuisine stripped of formality, making for a more laid-back (and cheaper) dining experience; chat with the energetic chefs as they work. *5.30-11pm ¥¥*

Menami Friendly establishment specialising in *obanzai-ryōri* (home-style cooking using local and seasonal ingredients). Plenty of small fish, vegetable and meat dishes. *3-9.30pm Thu-Tue ¥¥*

Mishima-tei At the intersection of two shopping arcades, this restaurant serves *sukiyaki* – thin slices of beef cooked in a sweet broth, dipped in raw egg. *11am-8pm ¥¥*

Tōsuirō Marvel at the number of supremely varied tofu-based dishes offered at this specialist tofu restaurant. Lovely Japanese setting, with summertime outdoor riverside seating. *11.30am-3pm & 5-9pm ¥¥*

dreamy Kyoto of many people's imaginations. Be advised that on weekends it can get very crowded, but the bustling crowds don't detract from the experience much (unless you're trying to take the perfect photo!). The Shijō-dōri end of the street can also be a good place to spot *geiko* (geisha) or *maiko* (apprentice geisha) as they make their way to appointments in the early evening. A leisurely evening stroll of Ponto-chō only takes 15 minutes or so, but it can be combined with a walk around nearby Gion (just across the river) for a longer tour of Kyoto's most ambient nighttime entertainment districts

Shopping With Kyoto's Well-Heeled Crowd
Treat Yourself at Takashimaya Department Store

Founded in 1831, **Takashimaya** is one of Japan's most famous luxury department stores, and the Kyoto branch is probably the most lavish shopping experience in the city. Located on Shijō-dōri, Takashimaya is the place to go for high-end luxury items, from clothes and electronics to kimonos, jewellery and homeware – if you are so inclined, it would be quite feasible to spend a whole day here. It's not all just fancy goods, however – a new official Nintendo store on the 7th floor has proved incredibly popular too. One of the store's real highlights is the enormous food court in the basement; here you can buy the highest-quality sweets, cakes, *bentō* boxes, fruit and almost anything your heart desires – just don't go there on an empty stomach unless you want to leave with a big dent in your wallet. For a proper sit-down meal, there are numerous excellent restaurants on the 7th floor as well.

School Yourself in Manga
Comic Heaven at Kyoto International Manga Museum

Situated in a wonderfully evocative old primary-school building replete with many of the old fittings, the **Kyoto International Manga Museum** (京都国際マンガミュージアム) houses a comprehensive collection of comic books covering all eras and genres, with a small but ever-growing selection of foreign-language titles too. The museum, in essence, functions as a mind-bogglingly comprehensive manga (Japanese comics) library, but it's more than just that, as there are displays chronicling the historical development of manga, allowing

STATUE STORIES

As you wander around central Kyoto you may notice a number of statues dotted around the neighbourhood.

On Sanjō-dōri, on the west side of the bridge just before it crosses the river, are a pair of bronze statues called *Yaji-san* and *Kita-san;* these characters walked the Tōkaidō (an ancient route between Tokyo and Kyoto) in an early-19th-century book (and later silent film) chronicling their long and amusing trip – here they can be found at the end of their journey.

Just across the river outside Gion-Shijō Station is a statue of Izumo no Okuni, an entertainer and shrine maiden born in 1578; she is said to be the original inventor of kabuki (traditional theatre mixing drama and dance).

DRINKING IN DOWNTOWN KYOTO: CASUAL DRINKS

Bungalow Great drinking hole with a regular rotation of 10 Japanese beers on tap, and tasty side dishes. The Japanese chalkboard menu can be difficult to decipher though! *3-10pm Mon-Fri, from noon Sat & Sun*

Beer Bar Miyama 162 Intimate little dive bar on Ponto-chō with a good selection of Japanese craft beer; chatty bartenders make for an extremely friendly vibe. *5pm-1am*

Rocking Bar ING Cosy 2nd-floor drinking spot on Kiyamachi-dōri with cheap drinks and good grub. *7pm-5am*

Jam House Rock Bar Welcoming rock bar packed with vinyl records and a varied playlist to accompany the affordable beers and spirits. *7pm-3am*

WALK THE SIGHTS OF DOWNTOWN KYOTO

Kyoto is a great city for walking, and this atmospheric stroll takes in some of the contrasting and most interesting areas of Downtown Kyoto – if possible, aim for a late afternoon start so that you arrive at Ponto-chō in the evening to see it in all its glory.

Start your walk at the south entrance to the Teramachi Kyōgoku shopping street. This *shōtengai* (covered shopping street) is towards the southern end of historic **❶ Teramachi** (p70), and the eclectic mixture of shops is endlessly fascinating. Walk north, and then branch right onto the parallel Shinkyōgoku shopping street; here you will find **❷ Seigan-ji**, an old and pretty Buddhist temple.

Continue north and right onto Sanjō-meitengai and then Sanjō-dōri, soon taking another right onto **❸ Kiyamachi-dōri**. This wonderfully scenic street runs north–south alongside the Takase-gawa, a narrow tree-lined river, and is particularly beautiful at dusk, especially during the cherry-blossom season.

Follow it down to Shijō-dōri and head towards the bridge, taking the steps down to the **❹ Kamo-gawa** (p65). Where Paris has the Seine, Kyoto has its own famous river, and this is where joggers run in the mornings and evenings, locals walk their dogs and couples escape for a bit of romantic time. Take a short breather down by the riverbank – as well as people-watching, you may be able to spot some of the local birdlife, including herons hunting for fish.

If you've timed it well and dusk is near, then you can end the evening with a stroll through **❺ Ponto-chō** (p58), one of Kyoto's most atmospheric and lively entertainment districts. There are plenty of restaurants, bars and even clubs if you want to extend the fun into the night.

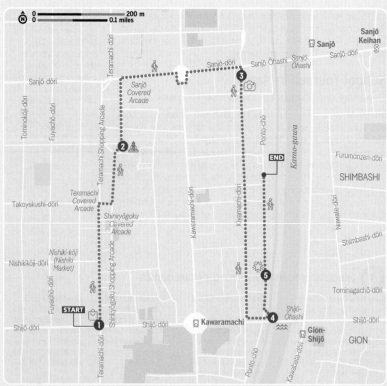

Bridge over Takase-gawa, Kiyamachi-dōri (p60)

visitors to learn something about this popular storytelling form. If you visit on a weekend or national holiday it's possible to have your portrait drawn by a professional manga artist, which makes for a really personalised and unique souvenir. It's easy to envisage hard core manga fans spending an entire day here flicking through the comics (and many seem to do just that), but for most casual visitors, an hour or so is enough time to see everything on offer.

A Way to Dye

Fabulous Fabric at Kyoto Shibori Museum

A small family-run museum a short walk from Nijō-jō, the **Kyoto Shibori Museum** (京都絞り工芸館) showcases the under-appreciated art of *shibori* (Japanese tie-dye). This is the only museum in Japan specialising in the craft, and the English-speaking guides are only too happy to help explain the intricacies of the process. There are many beautifully patterned fabrics on display, including kimonos and smaller

---

 EATING IN DOWNTOWN KYOTO: VEGAN & VEGETARIAN OPTIONS —————

Cafe Phalam Great choice of vegetarian and vegan dishes (gluten-free options too) at this homely and relaxed cafe; excellent coffee is sourced from Africa and South America. *9.30am-5pm* ¥

mumokuteki cafe Popular vegan restaurant with excellent tofu hamburgers and large and satisfying set meals. The queue system is a little confusing, but staff are helpful. *11.30am-4.30pm Thu-Tue, to 5.30pm Sat & Sun* ¥

Nijiya This welcoming vegan place has a varied menu of classic Japanese *izakaya* fare, all with a vegan twist, such as soy *yakitori* and vegan *gyōza*. *6-11pm* ¥¥

Ain Soph Quietly stylish and very foreigner-friendly vegan restaurant serving mouth-watering burgers, soy *karaage*, green curries and fluffy pancakes. *11.30am-4pm & 6-9pm* ¥¥

BEST GALLERIES & MUSEUMS

Kaleidoscope Museum of Kyoto
This one-room collection of colourful kaleidoscopes is tremendous fun, especially (but not only!) for kids.

Dohijidai Gallery of Art
Nice free-to-enter art gallery in the old Mainichi Newspaper Company building – now the Gear Theatre. Ever-changing exhibitions.

Hosoo Gallery
Stylish gallery show-casing Nishijin textiles, on the 1st floor above a shop. Sometimes hosts art and photo-graphy events.

Ōnishi Seiuemon Museum
Small museum with a collection of cere-monial teapots made by the Ōnishi family, masters of the craft since the 16th century.

Samurai Ninja Museum Kyoto
Experience-based museum about the exciting world of samurai and ninja, geared towards tourists with tours and hands-on activities.

Shinsen-en

cloths and garments; some items have so much intricate fine detail that they resemble paintings. You can also participate in a dyeing lesson for an additional fee, and this is a fun, hands-on way to learn about *shibori* and leave with your own personalised art piece.

Consuming Culture

Peruse Exhibits at the Museum of Kyoto

A decent option on a rainy day or if you have an hour or two to spare, the **Museum of Kyoto** (京都文化博物館), or more correctly the Cultural Museum of Kyoto, is home to exhibits spread across two buildings and multiple floors; the red-brick Meiji-era original building is architecturally interesting in its own right. The upper floors house temporary exhibits that can vary by theme tremendously – recent ones have included Studio Ghibli artwork and a surrealism exhibition. It is worth noting that touring exhibits can cover quite niche interests and require an additional entry fee (sometimes more expensive than the base fee for the museum), so it's wise to look up

 ACCOMMODATION IN DOWNTON KYOTO: OUR PICKS

Sora Niwa Terrace Kyoto
Sleek and luxurious hotel a short walk from Kyoto-Kawaramachi Station, offering indoor and outdoor hot spring baths and exceptional hospitality. ¥¥¥

Ritz-Carlton Kyoto
Downtown Kyoto's plushest hotel boasts wonderful mountain and riverside views, a pool and spa, and stunning design throughout, fusing Japanese tradition with modern pizzazz. ¥¥¥

Kakishibu-an Machiya
Spend a night in this gorgeously renovated *machiya*, featuring a stylish tatami-floored living room, an inner garden and wooden ceiling beams. ¥¥

Hanaya Ryokan
Quaint 100-year-old building offering very traditional and rustic rooms at a lovely quiet spot on Kiyamachi-dōri; breakfast included. ¥

what's on when you're in the city. There isn't a great deal of English around, but the amiable volunteer staff will try to explain things as best they can.

Garden of the Dragon Queen
Take a Short Detour to Shinsen-en

Just across the road from the southern perimeter of Nijō-jō (p56), **Shinsen-en** (神泉苑) is a small Buddhist temple and garden that dates back to the start of the Heian period (794–1185). Literally translating to 'sacred spring garden', Shinsen-en is all that remains of a once much larger palace and strolling garden that was built for Emperor Kammu when Kyoto first became capital city (the temple and small shrines at the current site are later additions), and it makes for a nice little stop-off if visiting the castle next door. The site is notable for its large pond with a pair of bridges, including a strikingly symmetrical vermilion one leading across to a central island – the shrine here is dedicated to a dragon deity that is said to reside in the pond. The bridge, pond, *torii* gate and shrine all combine to create a picturesque scene straight out of classic Japan – the garden is said to be the oldest surviving of all the many ornamental gardens in the city.

Taste the Seasons
Indulge in Fine Dining

The exquisite multicourse refinery of a *kaiseki* meal is more than just a fancy (and admittedly pricey) dinner out – it is a complete sensory experience, and one that, if your budget allows, should be tried at least once during your time in Kyoto – this, after all, is the city where this culinary art form traces its origins and has over the centuries been honed to near-perfection.

Located not far from the banks of the Kamo-gawa, **Kikunoi Roan** (菊乃井 露庵) is one of the best places to sample *kaiseki* dining in Downtown Kyoto. It is a cosy, intimate establishment, where the chef uses traditional techniques in a creative manner to construct delicate masterpieces using the finest seasonal ingredients. Each dish is a treat for the eyes and mouth, and the staff do their best to explain everything in English. Advanced bookings are pretty much essential, and be prepared to set aside three hours for the full belly-filling meal.

KYOTO & KAISEKI

Kaiseki (Japanese haute cuisine) or *kaiseki ryōri,* traces its origins back to the imperial courts of the Heian period, when Kyoto first became the nation's capital.

These multicourse banquets would be enjoyed over several hours and feature ornately arranged dishes of fish and vegetables, but traditionally no meat.

Seasonality is one of the key components, so the menu is almost always changing, but most meals start with *sakizuke* – a small appetiser. This will be followed by various small dishes including *wan-mono* (something served in a bowl, usually soup or possibly *chawanmushi,* a Japanese egg tart), fresh sashimi, grilled fish, and a rice dish towards the end, with something sweet to finish. Sake is the traditional *kaiseki* accompanying drink.

EATING IN DOWNTOWN KYOTO: QUICK BITES

Nishiki Warai Near the west end of Nishiki Market, this casual *okonomiyaki* place is cheap and cheerful, although non-smokers be warned that smoking is permitted. *11.30am-3pm & 5-10pm Mon-Fri, 11.30am-10pm Sat & Sun* ¥

Independants Quirky cafe/restaurant with an international vibe in the basement of an Art Deco building, serving up large salads, curries, pasta, paella and other non-Japanese fare. *Noon-11pm* ¥

Yasubee At this warm, welcoming and lively *okonomiyaki* restaurant the food is unassumingly good. One of the more afford-able places to eat on Ponto-chō. *4-10pm Wed-Mon* ¥

Gyoza Chao Chao Line up for the delicious and crispy fried *gyōza* at this popular downtown dumpling restaurant. Great as a pre- or post-drink snack; there's a vegetarian option too. *2-10.30pm* ¥

STROLL & EAT YOUR WAY AROUND DOWNTOWN KYOTO

Start the day early to beat most of the crowds at ❶ **Nishiki Market** (p68), Kyoto's biggest and most famous food market. There is a huge variety on offer, from gourmet goods and local speciality snacks to wonderful fresh produce.

It's then a short hop to ❷ **Daimaru**, Japan's best-known department store. There's a tremendous amount on offer, but the highlight for many is the basement food section, where the cakes, breads, fruit and *bentō* boxes are all of the highest quality.

You're not done shopping just yet though, as a 10-minute walk down Shijō-dōri brings you to ❸ **Takashimaya** (p59), the most luxurious department store in Kyoto. Browse the many high-end brands and then make a beeline for the basement food area, where you can pick up the finest sweet and savoury snacks, or whet your appetite for lunch.

Just across the road is ❹ **Tagoto Honten** (p71), a lovely restaurant offering exceptional yet affordable *kaiseki* (Japanese haute cuisine) meals in a peaceful setting. The use of seasonal ingredients and the chef"s creative skill will ensure this is a lunch to remember.

Following your feast, take a pleasant walk north to a cafe that's a favourite for locals, ❺ **Karafuneya** (p70). It does nice lunches and coffee, and those with a sweet tooth can try one of the huge selection of sundaes on offer – Japanese-style varieties include *matcha* (powdered green tea) and *azuki* (sweet red bean) with black sesame.

Finish your walk with a spot of tea; at the Kaboku Tearoom (p67) you can enjoy a fresh cup of *matcha*, or pop in next door to ❻ **Ippodō Tea** (p71), where you can shop for a host of tea-related products and souvenirs.

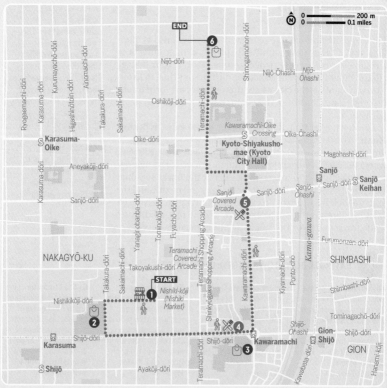

Geisha and *maiko* dance, Kaburen-jō Theatre

Dancing Geisha

Enjoy the Spectacle of Kamogawa Odori

If you're visiting Kyoto in the spring, then it's worth heading to the **Kaburen-jō Theatre** in Ponto-chō. During most of the month of May, here you can witness the *Kamogawa Odori,* an elegant geisha dance show that has origins going back to 1872. Performances are held three times a day and last just over an hour – tickets can be booked online.

Riverside Ramblings

Relax Along the Kamo-gawa

The **Kamo-gawa** (鴨川) is Kyoto's best-known river, and flows down from the mountains through the eastern end of the city, dividing Downtown Kyoto from Gion. If all the shopping and crowds of central Kyoto start to wear you down, then take a breather on the bank of the river – there are walking paths on either side, but the western riverbank has more places to

CONTEMPORARY THEATRE

Kyoto isn't all about ancient sites and centuries-old traditions; there is also a lively and fresh contemporary-arts scene thriving just beneath the surface.

Nowhere is this exemplified more than at **Gear Theatre**. Situated in an art-deco building near the Teramachi shopping district, the rip-roaring 90-minute steampunk shows here feature a heady mix of acrobatic dancing, mime, magic, juggling and illusions to create something supremely unique and exciting; what's best is that everything is non-verbal, so there is no language barrier to hinder the enjoyment.

In fact, it's best if you go in knowing as little as possible, so just buy a ticket (bookings available online) and enjoy a great evening of entertainment.

 DRINKING IN DOWNTOWN KYOTO: BARS & COCKTAILS

Bee's Knees Speak-easy-style cocktail bar with friendly service; innovative drinks and flavour combinations include *matcha* tiramisu. Get here early to avoid queuing. *6pm-1am Mon-Sat*

Nokishita 711 Reservations only at this cool and one-of-a-kind gin and cocktail bar, serving a sensory and creative drink and snack course with tasty flavour pairings. *Reservations from 2.30pm, 5pm, 7pm & 10pm*

Bar K6 Fashionable, modern bar overlooking the pretty Kiyamachi-dōri, and a favourite of locals and visitors. There's an impressive whisky selection and many excellent cocktails. *6pm-2am Wed-Mon*

Atlantis Classy Ponto-chō bar with an outdoor terrace overlooking the Kamo-gawa. Attentive service and English-speaking staff make it a great spot for late-night cocktails. *6pm-1am*

DOWNTOWN KYOTO'S BEST CLOTHING & FABRIC SHOPS

Mimuro
There is a huge range of high-quality kimono and *yukata* (light cotton kimono) on sale at this large shop, with English-speaking staff to help you make your selection.

Harajuku Chicago
Used clothing shop where you can pick up numerous bargains, including contemporary fashion and secondhand kimonos and *yukata* for very reasonable prices.

Erizen
Almost opposite Takashimaya department store, this is one of the best places in Kyoto to get measured up for a kimono.

BAL
This chic and sophisticated department store houses Japanese and foreign designer fashion, along with high-quality homeware goods.

Fujii Daimaru
A fairly small department store on Shijō-dōri offering modern fashion and affordable casual labels.

Tawaraya ryokan

sit. This is a popular place for couples, runners and locals to stroll, and can be great for a spot of people-watching. In the summer, children splash about in the shallows, and it is quite easy to see wildlife such as herons ducking for fish in the water. On warm evenings it's a lovely place to enjoy a riverside bentō or convenience-store beer.

Feudal-Era Inn

Discover the Secrets of Nijō Jinya

Tucked away on a small backstreet just south of Nijō-jō is one of Downtown Kyoto's most intriguing spots, **Nijō Jinya** (二条陣屋). This splendidly preserved and richly evocative private home once functioned as an inn for visiting feudal lords during the Edo period (1603–1868), and to guarantee the safety of these important guests, the building was kitted out with all sorts of unique features such as trapdoors and hidden escape routes. Visiting Nijō Jinya is a little tricky, as reservations for the daily one-hour tours (starting at 11.30am, 1.30pm and 3pm) must be made by telephone in Japanese, and the tours themselves are conducted entirely in Japanese.

 EATING IN DOWNTOWN KYOTO: NOODLES & SUSHI

Ippūdo Popular ramen place (there's often a queue), serving noodles in a rich pork-based broth; the *gyōza* set is good value and delicious. *11am-9.30pm* ¥

Honke Owariya Soba noodle shop in a wonderful historic building. The house special is *hourai soba* – stacked small plates of soba with various toppings. Expect to queue. *11am-3pm Wed-Mon* ¥¥

Tai Sushi Cosy and traditional sushi restaurant (cash only) with generous and outstandingly fresh portions. Choice of grilled fish dishes too. *5-10pm Fri-Wed* ¥¥

Isami Sushi Family-run establishment with bar seating and a couple of tables; high-quality sushi and sashimi is very reasonably priced. Reservations are a must. *11.30am-2pm & 5-8.30pm Fri-Tue* ¥¥

If you don't speak Japanese or have any Japanese-speaking friends at hand, it is possible to organise a free interpreter to join you on the tour – see the links on the website (nijyojinya. net) for details.

Hip Beats in Ponto-chō
Dance the Night Away in Kyoto's Party District

Kyoto may not have quite as raucous a nightlife scene as the likes of Tokyo or Osaka, but should you feel the urge to get your groove on, there are a few popular clubs downtown, mostly around the Ponto-chō area. **World Kyoto** is a friendly multifloored club frequented by locals and foreigners, with occasional big name DJs. **Kitsune Kyoto** is a lively spot boasting three floors and a good sound system and tunes. **Kyoto Chambers** offers hip-hop, house and club hits, and tends to be busiest on Fridays.

Slumber in Style
Spend a Night at Kyoto's Finest Ryokan

A Kyoto institution, **Tawaraya** is a fantastic traditional establishment and one Kyoto's best places to stay; some even go as far to say it's one of the finest ryokan in all of Japan. With a history spanning back three centuries, the whole place oozes atmosphere, but in no way feels dated or worn around the edges – quite the opposite in fact, with its truly exceptional decor, service, food and attention to detail, all befitting one of the premier lodgings in Kyoto. This does come at a price, however, and you will very likely need to book some months in advance, and even further ahead if you plan to come during one of the peak tourist periods (cherry-blossom season in spring and during the autumn leaf-viewing season).

If you are lucky enough to get a room reservation, you will be assured an unforgettable experience – this is the place people such as Steve Jobs, David Bowie and Marlon Brando stayed at during their trips to Kyoto. Rooms have their own private wooden bathtubs with garden views, and despite its extremely convenient location in the heart of downtown (within walking distance to two subway stations), it feels like a relaxing oasis of tranquil calm – check in early, relax and enjoy the old-fashioned ambience, while revelling in the exemplary service like pampered royalty.

BEST STATIONERY SHOPS

Japanese *washi* (handmade paper) and stationery is regarded as some of the best in the world, and makes for fabulous souvenirs.

Wagami no Mise
Also known as Morita Washi, this shop sells an excellent range of traditional Japanese *washi* paper and stationery products.

Hands Kyoto
This branch of the large variety store, formerly Tokyu Hands, stocks affordable gadgets, homeware, cosmetics, souvenirs and stationery.

Kamiji Kakimoto
Historic traditional paper shop with a fine selection of handmade *washi* paper and other unique stationery, incuding ornately patterned notebooks and calligraphy sets.

Rakushikan
Small shop on the eastern corner of the Museum of Kyoto, specialising in paper-craft products.

Kyūkyodō
An Aladdin's cave of traditional paper goods and stationery in Tera-machi; the stylish second shop nearby is architecturally impressive.

 DRINKING IN DOWNTOWN KYOTO: TEA & SWEETS

Kaboku Tearoom Watch *matcha* being whisked up at the counter, or choose from a variety of other teas at this tearoom next door to the famous Ippodō Tea. *10am-4.30pm*	**Zen Kashoin** Stylish and modern tearoom in a quiet corner of Downtown Kyoto; browse the attached gallery shop afterwards. *11am-6pm*	**Motoan** Situated in the Marukyū Koyamaen Teashop just southeast of Nijō-jō, this is a cosy rest stop after visiting the castle. *10.30am-5pm Thu-Tue*	**Maikoya Nishiki** Touristy tea-ceremony experience in the heart of central Kyoto where you can wear a kimono and learn about the way of tea. *9am-5pm*

Scan this QR code for a rundown of the shops (in Japanese).

TOP EXPERIENCE

Nishiki Market

A highlight of any foodie itinerary, Nishiki Market (錦市場) is a narrow, covered and always lively pedestrian shopping street, popular with locals and tourists alike. Crammed with over 100 shops, stalls and restaurants, and known colloquially as 'Kyoto's Kitchen', it is the place for seeing and sampling the many unique ingredients of Kyoto cuisine.

DON'T MISS

Tsukemono

Wagashi

Kyō-yasai

Yakitori

Tako-tamago

Dashimaki-tamago

Aritsugu

Historic Market

Nishiki Market has long been Kyoto's most famous and main food market, serving locals, professional chefs and high-end restaurateurs, and more recently tourists, who all come searching for the freshest local ingredients. The covered market street stretches for 390m (about five blocks) across the centre of town, one block north of and parallel to Shijō-dōri, from Teramachi *shōtengai* (covered shopping street) in the east to Takakura-dōri in the west, just a short hop from Daimaru department store. It is believed that there were stalls here from the 14th century, and it was certainly a fully fledged commercial district by the early Edo period, when it was established by the shogunate as a wholesale fish market. These days it has a mix of traditional shops – many of which have been run by the same family for generations – and more modern vendors, but it is this eclectic mix of wares and produce that makes the market such an interesting place to shop and wander around

Food & Wares

Showcasing unique Kyoto cuisine, this is the city's one-stop shop for traditional food items and local ingredients. Sample the sweet or sour crunch of *tsukemono* (Japanese pickles), fresh tofu made using age-old processes, delicately flavoured *wagashi* (traditional Japanese sweets), *kyō-yasai* (Kyoto vegetables), tea, fresh seafood and almost anything else you can imagine. It is a real assault on the senses, and can be a genuine culinary adventure; some shops have spaces for eating any purchased products and there are a smattering of proper sit-down restaurants. A few vendors sell takeaway items such as *yakitori* (skewered chicken), but be warned – walking and eating at the same time is strictly frowned upon.

One of the market's most popular and famous street foods is *tako-tamago;* these tiny red octopuses are cooked and marinated in a mixture of mirin, sugar and soy sauce, stuffed with a quail egg and skewered, and are a local savoury delicacy. Over the years the market has evolved somewhat, with kitchenwares and craft shops, and you will now find souvenir shops nestling alongside much older and more rustic shopfronts.

Shopping Highlights

One of the most famous foods on offer in the market is *dashimaki-tamago* (rolled egg omelette). A few shops sell this soft and moreish rolled egg cooked with *dashi,* and Miki Keiran is a specialist that also sells the utensils and fresh eggs if you fancy making your own. For something sweeter, try *manjū* at Fuka. These sweet and sticky buns are made from a *mochi*-like wheat gluten, then filled with *azuki*-bean paste – a traditional *wagashi* treat, they are often served with Japanese tea.

One real must-visit establishment is Aritsugu (p71), a legendary knife shop with a huge selection of blades, where some of the city's top chefs come to do their tool shopping. After making your selection, you can watch as the artisans engrave and hone it on a huge, round knife-sharpening stone.

ORIGINS OF KYŌ-YASAI

Kyō-yasai, or Kyoto vegetables, have a history stretching back centuries. As the former capital and home of the aristocracy, in Kyoto there was strong demand for high-quality produce, but as the city is mostly surrounded by mountains and some distance from the sea, it became imperative to source most food locally, and so the cultivation of unique *kyō-yasai* developed – still-popular varieties include the round-shaped *kamo-nasu* (aubergine).

TOP TIPS

- The market is narrow and can get very busy, so aim to visit early or later in the day for a more relaxed and leisurely experience, as well as a bit more personal space.

- Although most vendors are OK with it, do ask before taking photos of a shop or goods.

- Walking and eating at the same time is considered very uncouth; consume snacks in front of the shop or inside if there's the option.

- You're spoilt for choice of snacks and refreshments around the market, but for some of the city's heartiest ramen, Ippūdo (p66), is just around the corner.

DELVING DEEP AT NISHIKI MARKET

Asai Shinji is a fourth-generation tofu shop owner in Nishiki Market.

Nishiki Market has a rich history going back centuries, and that is why I think it is an attractive place for locals and tourists. In truth, most foreign visitors don't buy from my store, but they are very interested in the local produce, and I think most shop owners don't mind if people only come to look – just be respectful and don't get in the way of paying customers!

One of the unique points of the market is that all the shops here use well water from directly underground – the water is cool even in Kyoto's hot summers, and was like an early form of refrigeration!

Festival Fun
Join in the Revelry of Gion Matsuri

The **Gion Matsuri** is Japan's most famous summer festival, with an incredibly long history – it dates back to 869 – and takes place during the whole month of July. It features many events, including a spectacular procession of floats on 17 July called the **Yamaboko Junkō**, where a local boy is selected and paraded through the city as a divine messenger.

While the festival originates at Yasaka-jinja in Gion (hence the name), the main events mostly take place in Downtown Kyoto; roads are closed to traffic for the rand procession along a 3km downtown course. Two types of floats are pulled through the streets, the *yama* and the larger *hoko,* which are up to 25m tall, weight up to 12 tonnes and have wheels as big as people! For three nights before the main 17 July event, the numerous impressive floats are displayed and dotted around streets close to the Karasuma/Shijō intersection, so you can get a good look at them up close. In the evenings the roads are closed to traffic and are instead filled with throngs of people and stalls selling food and drink, all creating a lively festival buzz.

The main procession on the 17th takes place between 9am and 1pm, and as the course is so long, it's usually quite easy to find a good spot to watch from. There's also a more scaled-down procession held on the 24th, with similar festivities in the build-up to that too.

Downtown Shopping Arcade
Wander the Covered Street of Teramachi

One of Kyoto's most historic shopping streets, **Teramachi** (寺町) runs north–south for over 4km, passing through the heart of Downtown Kyoto. It has its early roots in the Heian period, but was remodelled in 1590 by Toyotomi Hideyoshi, who ordered that many Buddhist temples be moved to the area – hence the name (Teramachi literally means 'temple town'). It was in the Edo period when the street really began to flourish as a shopping district, with numerous craft and book shops opening here and selling their wares, and something of this artisanal tradition remains to this day.

 DRINKING IN DOWNTON KYOTO: CAFES & COFFEE

Cafe Bibliotic Hello!	**Tribute Coffee**	**Smart Coffee**	**Karafuneya**
Popular, hip cafe in a converted *machiya* (traditional townhouse) with bookshelves lining the walls. Good coffee plus sweet and savoury light bites. *11.30am-11pm* ¥	Quiet and relaxed space offering carefully made hand-drip coffee, best enjoyed with a simple plate of biscuits or Japanese sweets. *Noon-7pm Tue-Sun* ¥	Wooden-panelled coffee shop in the Teramachi shopping district. A great brunch spot; try the excellent pancakes or French toast. Very good coffee too. *8am-7pm* ¥	While the coffee is good, this cafe's real pull is its delicious sundaes, with Japanese twists including red bean and black sesame. *9am-10pm Sun-Fri, to 11pm Sat* ¥

Gion Matsuri

DOWNTOWN KYOTO'S BEST CRAFT SHOPS

Aritsugu
Some of the highest-quality and sharpest chef's knives and kitchen tools around. Staff offer advice and a personalised engraving service.

Zōhiko
Specialises in lacquer-ware, one of Japan's most beautiful crafts, with a range of elegant and traditional items.

Ippodō Tea
Old-fashioned tea shop selling some of Kyoto's best *matcha* and other tea varieties, plus tea-making accessories. There's a lovely tearoom in the neighbouring building.

Kyūkyodō
Long-established shop in the Teramachi shopping arcade, offering a staggering range of traditional Japanese goods.

Tsujikura
Small shop selling a colourful selection of beautiful *wagasa* (waxed-paper umbrellas) featuring both traditional and modern designs.

The section between Oike-dōri and Shijō-dōri is a covered shopping street known as a *shōtengai* – these are quite common in Japan and were once the commercial hubs of most towns and cities, although many are now in decline.

The Teramachi *shōtengai,* while retaining a slight old-fashioned charm, still has a vibrant feel, with a good mixture of new and old shops, and is a popular thoroughfare with both tourists and locals alike – it's a great place to spend an hour wandering, browsing and people-watching.

To the east and running parallel to Teramachi is another historical covered shopping street called **Shinkyōgoku** (新京極); this strip was once central Kyoto's main entertainment hub, with numerous theatres and comedy halls, but now caters more to tourists with its many souvenir shops and eateries.

 EATING IN DOWNTOWN KYOTO: FINE DINING

Kikunoi Roan
Exceptional *kaiseki* restaurant (p63) with attentive service and a creative take on seasonal dishes. *11.30am-1.30pm & 5-7.30pm Thu-Tue* ¥¥¥

Yoshikawa
This intimate restaurant has possibly the best tempura in Kyoto; counter seats allow you to see the chef at work. The lunch menu is recommended. *11.30am-1.30pm & 5.30-8pm* ¥¥¥

Tagoto Honten
Across the street from Takashimaya, this long-established restaurant offers affordable *kaiseki* lunches and dinner courses so you don't have to break the bank. *11.30am-3pm & 5-8pm Thu-Tue* ¥¥¥

Kiyamachi Sakuragawa
Refined *kaiseki* courses are served at this long-standing restaurant on the beautiful tree-lined Kiyamachi-dōri. Lunch is a much cheaper option. *Noon-2pm & 6-10pm Mon-Sat* ¥¥¥

Imperial Palace & Around

FIND HISTORY, GREENERY AND PEACEFUL NEIGHBOURHOODS

This large area of the city stretches from the southern end of the Imperial Palace Park up north all the way to Takara-ga-ike-kōen, encompassing wonderful parks, historic districts and ancient shrines.

Dominated by the Imperial Palace and its vast surrounding park and gardens, this area was once the political and ruling heart of Kyoto (and indeed Japan), but now it is more known as a tranquil and spectacularly green retreat in the centre of the city, just to the north of bustling downtown. The Imperial Palace Park is central Kyoto's largest park by far, and while it once drew dignitaries and the ruling elite, it now attracts a more varied crowd of picnicking families, weekend runners and tourists taking in the sights. The Imperial Palace itself was the seat of the imperial family for many centuries, while the neighbouring Sentō Imperial Palace was a retreat for retired emperors, and both remain grand monuments to Kyoto's historic importance, with fabulous gardens for visitors to enjoy.

While it is true that Kyoto's main tourist attractions and most famous spots tend to be dotted around the edges of the city, there are still plenty of things to see and do in the cluster of neighbourhoods in this relatively quiet and spread-out corner of Kyoto. To the west of the Imperial Palace Park is Nishijin, Kyoto's traditional textile-making district, while northwest is the Zen enclave of Daitoku-ji, a hidden sanctuary of mysterious temples and quiet paths. The two Kamo shrines – Shimogamo-jinja and Kamigamo-jinja – are among the oldest and most important Shintō sites in the whole of Japan and are also celebrated World Heritage Sites. Between them lies the Kyoto Botanical Gardens. A vast, relaxing oasis home to a plethora of native and exotic plants, it's a great escape for when you need to refresh your senses without leaving the confines of the city itself.

DON'T MISS...

DAITOKU-JI	IMPERIAL PALACE PARK	SHIMOGAMO-JINJA	NISHIJIN
Discover the many temples, pathways and exquisite Zen gardens of this self-contained temple district. **p78**	Relax and unwind among the luscious greenery and gardens of the Imperial Palace. **p75**	Get in touch with your spiritual side and learn your fortune at this ancient shrine. **p77**	Step back in time among the *machiya-* (townhouse) and workshop-lined streets of this evocative weaving district. **p81**

TOP TIP

Kyoto is one of the world's great food cities, but the sheer choice of establishments – particularly downtown – can at times make eating out a bewildering ordeal. For straightforward but reliable options, the restaurant floors of Takashimaya and Daimaru offer a good selection of high-quality eateries in a compact area.

Left: Shimogamo-jinja (p77); Above: Kyoto Botanical Gardens (p77)

WHY I LOVE THE IMPERIAL PALACE AREA

Tom Fay, Lonely Planet writer

I think what draws me most to this area of the city is the quiet, relaxed atmosphere (despite its mostly centralised location) and the sheer variety of sights on offer.

The Imperial Palace Park has an undoubted sense of history and understated grandeur, and yet is a place where joggers and families can casually revel in the resplendent greenery.

While rather spread out, the two Kamo shrines, Daitoku-ji, the Kyoto Botanical Gardens and the Nishijin textile area can all be reached by bicycle, and this is a wonderful way to get around – on a warm day it's a real joy to ride along the riverside bike path with lunch in your basket and interesting things to see wherever you stop.

IMPERIAL PALACE & AROUND

Kamigamo-jinja (1.3km)

Kitaōji

Kyoto Botanical Gardens

Kamo-gawa

Kitaōji-dōri

Funaokayama-kōen

Kuramaguchi-dōri

Shimei-dōri

Kuramaguchi

Karamaguchi-dōri

Izumōji-bashi

Tadasu-no-mori

Kamigoryōmae-dōri

KAMIGYŌ-KU

Teranouchi-dōri

Kamitachiuri-dōri

Dōshisha University

Demachiyanagi Shōtengai

Aoi-bashi

Imadegawa-dōri

Nakasuji-dōri

NISHIJIN

Yokoshinmei-dōri

Imadegawa

Kyoto Imperial Palace Park

Kamo-Ōhashi

Demachiyanagi

Ichijō-dōri

Sasayachō-dōri

Nakatachiuri-dōri

Chūkōin-dōri

Ōmiya-dōri

Demizu-dōri

Kōjinguchi-dōri

Jōfukuji-dōri

Shimotachiuri-dōri

Jingū-Marutamachi

Marutamachi

Marutamachi-dōri

Marutamachi-dōri

Marutamachi-bashi

Takeyamachi-dōri

Ebisugawa-dōri

Nijō-dōri

NAKAGYŌ-KU

Nijō-Ōhashi

0   500 m
0   0.25 miles

EATING IN THE IMPERIAL PALACE AREA: QUICK MEALS

Grand Burger Large juicy burgers on toasted buns, plus good sides. The quick, friendly service and quiet back-street location make this a local favourite. *11am-8.30pm Tue-Sat* ¥

Kanei Small place serving up excellent handmade soba noodles. There's little English, so ask for *zaru soba* (cold noodles) or *kake soba* (noodles in broth). *11.30am-2.30pm Tue-Sun* ¥

Sarasa Nishijin This cafe near Funaoka Onsen, built inside an old *sentō*, still retains the attractive mosaic bath tiles. Serves surprisingly hearty fare. *11.30am-9pm, to 10pm Fri & Sat* ¥

Manzara Honten Atmospheric bar in an old *sakagura* (sake brewery) with frequent live music – also serves good food. *5.30pm-midnight* ¥¥

Park Life
Stretch Your Legs in Kyoto Imperial Palace Park

Also known as Kyoto Gyoen National Garden (京都御苑), this enormous site is located almost slap bang in the centre of the city, and is home to both the Kyoto Imperial Palace and Sentō Imperial Palace. A green oasis of calm, **Kyoto Imperial Palace Park** is a lovely place to take a walk, picnic or people-watch, with forested pathways, wide gravel boulevards, landscaped gardens and grassy lawns that are great for frolicking and games. Beautiful at any time of year, the park is particularly popular in early spring during the plum (late February) and cherry-blossom (late March/early April) seasons. History buffs should not miss the former **Kaninnomiya residence** in the park's southwestern corner; this renovated and affluent old family home is often overlooked, but is free to enter and is enshrined within some wonderful gardens.

Palatial Splendour
Roam Like Royalty at Kyoto Imperial Palace

Near the middle of Kyoto Imperial Palace Park is the *Gosho* or **Kyoto Imperial Palace** (京都御所); this was the residence of Japan's imperial family until both the emperor and capital relocated from Kyoto to Tokyo in 1868. While the palace itself can't be entered, it takes about an hour or so to freely wander around the grounds and admire the grand buildings and sumptuous gardens. There are English-language signs dotted around explaining some of the history and details, but it's best to follow the free downloadable self-guided audio tour; otherwise there are free guided tours in English twice daily. The entrance is at the Seishomon Gate on the west side of the palace grounds.

Grand Gardens
Join a Guided Tour at the Sentō Imperial Palace

Across from and slightly less grand than the Kyoto Imperial Palace is the **Sentō Imperial Palace** (仙洞御所). Originally built in 1630 as a retirement residence for Emperor Gomizuno, it was subsequently used as a retirement home for later washed-up emperors, although the current structure dates back to

GETTING AROUND

The subway is useful for this part of the city; the Karasuma line provides decent access to most of the sights, including the Imperial Palace Park and the Kyoto Botanical Gardens, and conveniently connects directly to Kyoto Station. If you don't mind strolling a bit, then many other sights are within walking distance of a station. City buses will also tend to get you closest to the main attractions, especially those in the northwest, such as Daitoku-ji and Kamigamo-jinja; tourist information centres will help you out with bus routes and timetables. The sights are quite spread out in this part of town, but the streets are flat, so bicycle is also a great way of getting around.

Start bright and early with the runners and ramblers doing circuits in the ❶ **Imperial Palace Park** (p75), but feel free to take a more leisurely stroll through the beautiful sculptured gardens and verdant forests – join a tour of either the Imperial Palace or Sentō Imperial Palace for detailed historic insights.

Next, head west to walk back in time through the streets of ❷ **Nishijin** (p81), Kyoto's old-fashioned but still very much alive weaving and indigo-dyeing district. The narrow streets are a rabbit warren of *machiya* (traditional townhouses) and workshops, with locals going about their daily business, so stroll around and take it all in. After getting a good feel for the area, do a deep dive into the history and artisanship of the textile industry at the ❸ **Nishijin Textile Center** (p81). There are weaving demonstrations and kimono shows, plus plenty of fabric-related items to admire and buy.

The walk east past the park should build up your appetite for lunch at ❹ **Grand Burger** (p75), with its delicious and juicy burger sets complete with chunky chips and coleslaw – fill yourself up with a tasty side dish too. It's then a short walk northeast to the confluence of the Kamo-gawa and Takano-gawa; either cross by bridge or hop along the turtle-shaped stepping stones to ❺ **Kamo-gawa Delta**, where you can sit and people watch, especially as they splash around in the summer.

Finish by ambling northwards to reach the forested front approach of ❻ **Shimogamo-jinja**, one of Kyoto's oldest and most important Shintō shrines. Here you can buy an *omikuji* (fortune paper) to dip in the stream and reveal your luck for the year ahead.

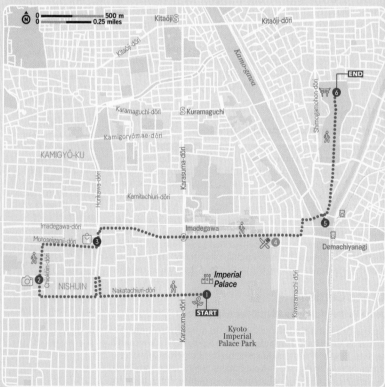

1867. The impressive strolling gardens do date back to the building's original construction, however, and can be viewed by joining a free tour (in Japanese, but with an English audio guide). Tours take place twice a day (10am and 1.30pm), take just over an hour and must be applied for in advance, either online (visit kunaicho.go.jp) or via the **Kunaichō**, the Imperial Household Agency, which has an office inside the northwest corner of the Imperial Palace Park – you need to be over 18 and have your passport with you.

Get Spiritual
Purify Your Soul at Shimogamo-jinja

A UNESCO World Heritage Site, this Shintō shrine dates back to the 7th century, making it one of the oldest and most important in Japan. Nestled close to the convergence of the Kamo-gawa and Takano-gawa, the **Shimogamo-jinja** (下鴨神社) main shrine is best approached along a path through the atmospheric **Tadasu-no-mori**, a forest where 600-year-old trees grow and where it is said lies cannot be concealed. A number of smaller shrines dot the site, including an intriguing one dedicated to rugby, while **Kawai-jinja** bestows visitors with beauty, **Aioi-no-yashiro** is for luck in love, and at **Mitarashi-sha** people wade through the nearby stream in the summer for purification and respite from the heat – you can dip your *omikuji* (fortune paper) in the water to reveal its hidden message too (use a translating app to decipher it!). City Bus 4 stops just outside the shrine, or it's a 15-minute walk from Demachiyanagi Station on the Keihan line.

Floral Fever
Refresh Your Mind at the Kyoto Botanical Gardens

A sprawling site covering 24 hectares and home to over 12,000 plants, trees and flowers, the wonderful **Kyoto Botanical Gardens** (京都府立植物園) are a must for those with green fingers, or anyone looking for a quiet few hours in a serene environment – all for only ¥200. There is a wild variety of areas to explore, meaning whenever you go something will be in radiant full bloom, and the enormous flagship conservatory is well worth the additional ¥200 entry fee for its fascinating botanical displays that take you on a whistle-stop tour around the world, from deserts to tropical rainforests and alpine biomes. The gardens tend to be skipped by most visitors to the city, so it is a great place to escape the crowds.

WHERE TO STAY IN THE IMPERIAL PALACE AREA

Kyoto Brighton Hotel ¥¥¥
A short walk from the Imperial Palace Park, it offers large rooms and refined luxury, with a free shuttle service to/from Karasuma-Oike Station.

Kyoto Garden Palace ¥¥
Directly across from the park, this is a relatively cheap but comfortable budget option, with bicycles for guests to use.

Rakucho Ryokan ¥
Basic old-style inn with clean and beautiful tatami-mat rooms and futons for sleeping; run by a lovely and helpful proprietor.

Guest House Bon ¥
Simple, homely and comfortable lodgings next to Daitoku-ji, also with free bicycle rentals.

Koiya Guesthouse ¥
Small, authentic and welcoming traditional residence with original fittings and a stunning interior garden; breakfast included.

DRINKING IN THE IMPERIAL PALACE AREA: CASUAL BARS

Mayday Coffee & Bar Enjoy cocktails and Japanese whiskies at this relaxed, cosy establishment; the bartender speaks good English. *7pm-1am Fri-Wed*

Bar Red Tails Squeeze yourself into this intimate bar with a big drink selection, and sip on reasonably priced cocktails created by the amiable bartender Hiroshi. *6pm-3am Wed-Mon*

Cavalletta A civilised yet in no way pretentious wine bar; savour rare vintages in a calm atmosphere – the food is wonderful too. *6pm-1am Fri-Wed*

Jittoku Atmospheric bar in an old *sakagura* with frequent live music – also serves good food. *5.30pm-midnight*

Scan this QR code for background information.

TOP EXPERIENCE

Daitoku-ji

A secluded Zen sanctuary in the heart of the city, Daitoku-ji (大徳寺) is a joy for those willing to walk and explore a little, as this sprawling, walled temple complex is a haven of peaceful sculpted landscapes and rock gardens, and exquisite Zen architecture. As it is a little out of the way, Daitoku-ji is rarely overrun with visitors.

DON'T MISS

Daisen-in

Zuihō-in

Ryōgen-in

Ōbai-in

Kōtō-in (if open)

Hōshun-in Bonsai Garden

Kazariya

The Main Temple

Daitoku-ji is the head temple of the Rinzai sect's Daitoku-ji school of Japanese Zen Buddhism. Located at the eastern end of the complex, the headquarters were founded in 1319, burnt down during the Ōnin War a century later, were rebuilt and later developed associations with the art of the tea ceremony and infamous warlords such as Toyotomi Hideyoshi. The impressive main buildings are not usually open to the public (although they can be glimpsed through the pines), but a number of the surrounding sub-temples are – what's more, they're all quite distinct from one another, making the district well worth a thorough exploration. Note that separate entry fees are required for each temple.

Daisen-in

Open year-round and adjacent to the main Daitoku-ji temple building, **Daisen-in** is particularly famed for its small and sublime rock gardens, which represent a high-point of *kare-sansui* (dry landscape) design – there are plenty of English explanations to help you make sense of it all. The temple structure itself also features the oldest known *tokonoma* (alcove), a key feature of tatami rooms in traditional Japanese buildings to this day, while its highly valued *fusuma* (sliding doors) are worth a peek too. Be warned that photography is strictly forbidden here, but this allows you to more thoroughly immerse yourself in the moment. You can sip green tea and eat sweets in the cosy tearoom afterwards.

Glorious Gardens

Clustered in the southeast corner of the complex are three more sub-temples you can enter. **Zuihō-in** is the first of these, and has unusual origins in that it was founded by Christians in 1535. Its wonderful main garden was designed in the 1960s, however, and features pebbles raked into striking patterns resembling ocean waves – in the smaller garden behind the main hall try to spot the rocks arranged in the shape of a crucifix. Next door is **Ryōgen-in**, a quiet temple with handsomely arranged gardens of both moss and stone varieties; one of which (Totekiko) is said to be the smallest rock garden in the country. The temple itself houses a few treasures, including a gun believed to be the oldest in Japan, dating from 1583. The last of this cluster is **Ōbai-in**, a temple with extensive and varied Zen gardens, which are especially picturesque in the autumn and should not be missed.

Tucked away on the western side of the complex is **Kōtō-in**, home to arguably one of the finest Zen gardens in the country, although it was closed to visitors at the time of writing – if it is open during your visit then it is something of a must-see. The garden is entered via a long flagstone path over a carpet of moss and through swaying bamboo forest, passing through three gates before reaching the inner sanctum – a truly transformational experience. If you are interested in the art of bonsai, then the **Hōshun-in Bonsai Garden** is a must with its collection of over 50 miniature trees, including a remarkable Japanese yew that is over 800 years old.

TEMPLE FOOD

There is an excellent *shōjin-ryōri* (Zen Buddhist vegetarian cuisine) restaurant called **Izusen** on the grounds of Daiji-in, in the southern section of Daitoku-ji. *Shōjin-ryōri is* the traditional food of Buddhist monks, with the beautifully presented seasonal and delicious small dishes consisting of vegetables, tofu, mushrooms and rice. Courses are not super-cheap (around ¥4000 to ¥5000), but are well worth it for the excellent vegetarian food and overall experience.

TOP TIPS

- The temple complex can be entered from all sides and the main gate (Sōmon) is on the southeast side of the complex; there's an information booth here where you can pick up a map showing all the different sub-temples and which ones are currently open to the public.

- The most atmospheric and beautiful approach to the main temple is along the 200m walkway from the south (Nammon) gate.

- Enjoy the traditional atmosphere of Kazariya (p81) on the north side of the temple; this centuries-old rustic teahouse has long been one of Kyoto's best spots for *aburi-mochi* (grilled and skewered rice-flour cakes).

Kamigamo-jinja

Rewind Time

Pay Homage at Kamigamo-jinja

One of a pair of shrines in this part of the city (referred to as the Kamo shrines, along with Shimogamo-jinja), and constructed even before Kyoto itself was founded, **Kamigamo-jinja** (上賀茂神社) is another celebrated UNESCO World Heritage Site up in the city's northwestern quarters.

Established in 679 and dedicated to Raijin, the deity of thunder, the numerous shrine buildings – including the impressive *haiden* (worship hall) – were built between the 17th and 19th centuries and are exact replicas of the original structures. Wandering around should take less than an hour and Kyoto City Bus 4's final stop is here; otherwise Kitayama Station is a 15-minute stroll away.

DRINKING IN THE IMPERIAL PALACE AREA: COFFEE SHOPS

13F Coffee Stylishly renovated and arty townhouse with a friendly feel; it opens early, so it's good for your morning caffeine fix. *7am-6pm Tue-Fri, to 9pm Sat* ¥

Wife & Husband Cosy out-of-the-way coffee shop like something out of a Ghibli movie, offering riverside picnic-set rentals if you book in advance. *10am-5pm, closed irregularly* ¥

Tasuku Coffee Minimalist and under-stated coffee joint brewing high-quality seasonal beans; it's a great stop-off or takeaway place if cycling along the Kamo-gawa. *7am-4pm Tue-Sat* ¥

Kamogawa Cafe Laid-back and airy cafe a couple of blocks east of the Imperial Palace Park, serving single-origin beans and tasty light meals. *Noon-9pm Fri-Wed* ¥

Fabulous Fabric

Learn About Traditional Weaving in Nishijin

This small district to the northwest of Kyoto Imperial Palace Park is famous as the city's traditional textile-making quarter. Spread over several blocks, the streets of **Nishijin** (西陣) are filled with *machiya* (traditional townhouses) and have a real old-fashioned feel, making it a great place to wander.

There are a number of small museums and galleries that showcase the area's long-standing weaving industry, but most tourists head to the **Nishijin Textile Center** (on the southwest corner of the Horikawa-dōri and Imadegawa-dōri intersection) to watch weaving demonstrations, see how kimonos are created and maybe purchase something. **Orinasu-kan** is a much quieter and more evocative workshop, museum and shop where you can see the elegant fabrics and craft-making process up close.

Take a Bath

Soothe Yourself in the Waters of Funaoka Onsen

Kyoto is not a city blessed with many hot springs, but **Funaoka Onsen** (船岡温泉) is one of the best places for a rejuvenating soak. This quaint old *sentō* (public bathhouse) gives bathers plenty of options, with an outdoor bath, a cypress-wood tub, herbal waters, an ice bath, an electric bath and a sauna, among others.

It's open from 3pm until 11.30pm daily (from 8am on Sundays), with towels to buy or rent. If you have inked skin then you'll be pleased to know that this bathhouse is also tattoo-friendly; find it on Kuramaguchi-dōri nestled behind some large rocks.

Baths are gender-segregated; use the showers or washbowls to wash beforehand, being careful to rinse off any soap suds, and take a small towel to protect your modesty or to dry off a bit afterwards.

BEST TRADITIONAL WARES

Aizen Kōbō
Beautiful *machiya* workshop offering high-quality handmade indigo-dyed items, crafted by the same family for generations.

Nishijin Textile Center
Slightly touristy but plenty to see, with kimono shows, crafting demonstrations and a 2nd-floor shop selling various garments.

Sawai Shōyu
Historic soy-sauce maker in a grand old wooden building two blocks west of the Imperial Palace Park. A good place for foodie souvenirs.

Demachi Futaba
One of Kyoto's oldest and most popular traditional confectionery shops, specialising in sweet and chewy *mochi*; *mame-mochi* bean rice cakes are the signature item.

Raku Museum
Small but interesting pottery museum, although the entry fee is a little expensive if you only have a passing interest.

 EATING IN THE IMPERIAL PALACE AREA: CAFES & SWEETS

Toraya Karyō Kyoto Ichijō Tearoom-cafe with a cool yet traditional vibe just west of the Imperial Palace Park. Tasty Japanese sweets and *matcha* options, plus picturesque garden views. *10am-5.30pm* ¥

Papa Jon's Light and airy cafe a short walk north of the Imperial Palace Park. Reasonably priced and varied menu; the pizza and especially the cheesecakes are exceptional. *11am-7pm Wed-Mon* ¥

Kazariya One of two charming, rustic sweet shops at the eastern entrance of Imamiya-jinja; both have been serving skewered and sticky *aburi-mochi* for generations. *10am-5pm Thu-Tue* ¥

Kamo Mitarashi Chaya Extremely popular cafe and the birthplace of *mitarashi-dango* (small, round skewered rice dumplings covered in a sweet soy-sauce glaze). *9.30am-5.30pm Thu-Tue, to 6pm Sat & Sun* ¥

Above: *Maiko* performance; Right: Kiyomizu-dera (p98)

DON'T MISS

GION
Immerse yourself in the geisha culture of Kyoto's famous entertainment district.
p86

KIYOMIZU-DERA
Take in the views from the wooden veranda at one of Kyoto's most iconic temples.
p98

CHION-IN
Make a pilgrimage to this vast temple complex and still-thriving Buddhist hub.
p90

SHŌREN-IN
Escape the crowds to reflect at one of Kyoto's finest yet blissfully quiet temples.
p85

SANJŪSANGEN-DŌ
Explore the magnificent Buddhist temple housing 1001 statues of the deity Kannon.
p88

KŌDAI-JI
Visit this Zen temple with stunning sculptured gardens designed by masters of the art.
p85

Gion & Southern Higashiyama

KYOTO'S MOST POPULAR AND SIGHT-PACKED DISTRICT

If you only had one day in Kyoto then visiting this area would be top of the agenda. Here you will find geisha districts, world-famous temples, and picturesque streets and back alleys straight from old Japan.

For many visitors to Japan, Kyoto is synonymous with geisha, ancient temples and teahouse-lined streets, and Gion and Southern Higashiyama is the district where these classic symbols of the city can all be found in abundance.

Stretching along the foot of the low-lying Higashi-yama (Eastern Mountains) range, which buffers the east side of the city, and confined between Shichijō-dōri and Sanjō-dōri, this area is packed with remarkable sights at almost every turn.

Gion is Kyoto's famed traditional drinking and entertainment quarter, where beautiful kimono-attired geisha and *maiko* (apprentice geisha) may be spotted skirting along the backstreets before slipping down a narrow alleyway and into an upmarket teahouse for an evening appointment, usually involving drinking and dance performances for well-heeled guests. Even if you don't have the budget or connections for an evening of full-on traditional geisha entertainment, there are more affordable means to experience a taste of the culture, and Gion's old-fashioned lantern-lit streets are almost impossibly charming, especially in the evenings, and particularly during cherry-blossom season.

Moving out of Gion and edging east towards the mountains, the attractions switch from the earthly to the sacred. Southern Higashiyama is crammed with some of the city's best-loved temples such as Kiyomizu-dera, a celebrated World Heritage Site and possibly Kyoto's best-known temple, whereas the sprawling temple com-plex of Chion-in is always a hive of religious activity. But there are also more secluded spots nearby that are relatively little-visited and so retain much of their serene charm, including the delightful Shōren-in, a lovely forest temple nestled in the literal shadow of its bigger neighbours.

Above all, this is the Kyoto of picture books and postcards, where wonderfully preserved wooden *machiya* (traditional townhouses) line the old-fashioned streets, world-class restaurants and rustic tearooms can be found tucked away on quiet back lanes, and narrow cobbled alleyways reward impromptu strolling.

GION & SOUTHERN HIGASHIYAMA

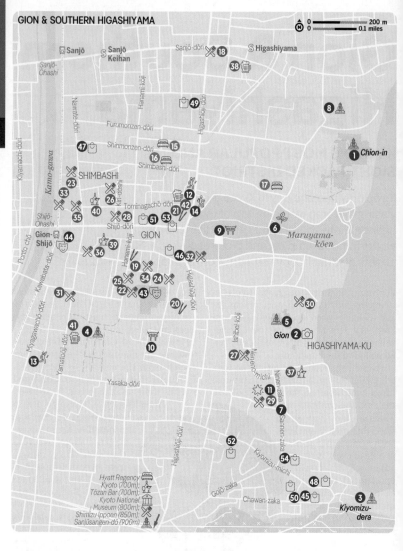

DRINKING IN GION & SOUTHERN HIGASHIYAMA: BARS & COCKTAILS

Tōzan Bar Soak in the warm ambience of this elegant bar in the Hyatt Regency Kyoto, specialising in cocktails, Japanese whiskies and premium Kyoto sakes, plus local beers. *5-11pm*

Gion Finlandia Bar Stylish, minimalist bar in an old Gion house; there's no menu – tell the bartender what you'd like, whether that's a high-end cocktail or a single malt. *6pm-2am*

Bar Kohaku Sophisticated cocktail bar at the Park Hyatt Kyoto with amazing city views. Slightly pricey, but there are few finer places for evening drinks in Kyoto. *4-11pm*

Rock Bar Crunch Exceptionally friendly and cosy rock and metal bar tucked away in Gion, with cheap drinks. Patrons are encouraged to choose the playlist. *7pm-2am Mon-Thu, to 5am Fri & Sat*

Hidden Retreat

Escape the Crowds at Shōren-in

Located just a stone's throw to the north of Chion-in and tucked away behind a wall of giant camphor trees, **Shōren-in** (青蓮院) is a peaceful temple and one of Kyoto's most overlooked gems. Enjoy a meditative wander through the stunningly scenic Zen garden with its pond, moss lawns and bamboo grove – its forested corners become a riot of colour in the autumn, although it is a delight in any season. For a truly memorable and calming experience, participate in a formal tea ceremony in the temple's tearoom, held at certain times during the spring and autumn (check the website).

Landscaped Beauty

Admire the Exquisite Gardens of Kōdai-ji

Lavish in design, **Kōdai-ji** (高台寺) is a temple of the Rinzai sect of Zen Buddhism, but it is the extensive and immaculate gardens, designed by some modern masters of the art, that draw most people here; one is a rock garden of raked gravel, said to represent the ocean; the other is a beautifully sculptured *tsukiyama*-style garden with a pond, grassy knolls, decorative rocks and picture-perfect trees. Established in 1606 by Kita-no-Mandokoro – the wife of Toyotomi Hideyoshi – this temple was built as a memorial to the great man. Up on the hillside you can find two tea-rooms, one of which was designed by the tea master Sen no Rikyū.

GETTING AROUND

The private (non-JR) Keihan line is a key artery in and out of the city, with stops all along the western edge of the district; Gion-Shijō Station is a great base for exploring the area.

You can also make use of the subway; the Tōzai subway line connects downtown Kyoto with the northern end of the district – simply hop on or off at Higashiyama Station. For the most direct access, Kyoto City buses service all of the main sights in the area, but they can be a bit busy and slow, particularly at peak times. The area is very walkable, however, and this enables spontaneous discoveries too.

 ACCOMMODATION IN GION & SOUTHERN HIGASHIYAMA: OUR PICKS

Sangen Traditional-style Japanese inn just off Ninen-zaka with a rooftop open-air bath, city views and outstanding breakfasts. ¥

Hyatt Regency Kyoto Modern five-star hotel in a peaceful neighbour-hood, with a minimalistic yet traditional aesthetic. One of the city's best bars and excellent restaurants. ¥¥¥

Hotel Mume Relaxing riverside boutique hotel in the heart of Gion, with stylishly appointed rooms and wonderful, attentive service. ¥¥

Indigo House Gion Beautifully restored *machiya* featuring a mix of modern amenities and rustic fittings, on a quiet street but within easy walking distance of the main sights. ¥¥

Scan this QR code for further information.

TOP EXPERIENCE

Gion

Gion (祇園) is Kyoto's famed and much-visited geisha district and traditional entertainment quarter. Its atmospheric streets are crammed with wooden-latticed *machiya*, shops, restaurants and *ochaya* (teahouses), and it's a place where there's always the chance of glimpsing a *geiko* (the Kyoto word for geisha) or *maiko* on the way to their next appointment.

DON'T MISS

Hanami-kōji

Shimbashi

Gion Corner

Entertainment District

Gion originally grew as a drinking and entertainment district due to its proximity to Yasaka-jinja; *ochaya* were built to cater for visitors to the shrine, and in the mid-18th century Gion was officially developed as Kyoto's teahouse quarter. Geisha and *maiko* would provide evening entertainment for teahouse patrons, and the district blossomed as Kyoto's main nightlife hub, with over 500 *ochaya* at its peak.

Main Street

Hanami-kōji is Gion's main pedestrian thoroughfare and one of Kyoto's most picturesque streets, running north–south a few blocks east of the Kamo-gawa – simply walk east from the bridge at Gion-Shijō Station (along Shijō-dōri/Route 186) and in a few minutes turn onto the paved street branching south. Immediately it feels like you've been transported back to late Edo- or Meiji-era Kyoto, with beautiful wooden *machiya* lining the streets, atmospheric roadside lanterns and even a conspicuous lack of overhead power cables.

The large, imposing red-walled building is Ichiriki-tei, a 300-year-old teahouse that's one of Gion's highest-end establishments and strictly invitation only. You can follow the foot traffic southwards (this is a popular approach to the temples and sights of Southern Higashiyama), but it's worth veering off the main road to explore some of the enchantingly pretty back alleys and side streets, where every turn feels like it could lead to a hidden teahouse, secluded private garden or rustic Michelin-starred restaurant.

Picturesque Scenes

There are a few spots in Gion that are arguably even prettier than Hanami-kōji, and are usually far less crowded too. Walk up the northern section of Hanami-kōji (on the north side of Shijō-dōri) and branch off at the third left – this leads to a remarkably picturesque area called **Shimbashi** (or Shirakawa Minami-dōri); here you can wander along the flagstone-paved streets lining the Shirakawa ('White River') and soak in the old-fashioned atmosphere – in the evenings it looks like something from a film set.

During cherry-blossom season the streets are enveloped in bouquets of pastel pink and are stunningly pretty (though this does bring in the crowds). Most of the attractive *machiya* in this area house expensive restaurants and exclusive clubs, but it's a great place for an evening stroll without spending a single yen. Slightly further north are two narrow streets running east–west; Shinmonzen-dōri and Furumonzen-dōri. These are both lined with quaint old houses, antique shops and art galleries, and are worth a look too.

See the Sights

One of the great joys of Gion is simply wandering around and seeing where the roads take you. As the sun sets there's always the chance of a fleeting glimpse of a *geiko* or *maiko* as they slip by; their beautiful attire and striking makeup does always make an impression. To experience an evening's entertainment in the company of a geisha usually costs serious money and requires deep connections, but at the annex theatre at **Gion Corner** (p95) you can get a taste of geisha dancing and other cultural mainstays in the daily hour-long evening shows.

THE MAKING OF A GEISHA

The first geisha (at least in the form as we know them today) began to appear at around the turn of the 18th century, emerging from a tradition of courtly entertainers, but for the increasingly wealthy emergent merchant classes. Not to be mistaken for sex workers, they were (and still are) highly trained in arts such as singing, dancing and playing the *shamisen* (a three-stringed instrument resembling a lute).

TOP TIPS

- Gion is Kyoto's famous geisha district, but there have been cases of tourists crowding around and hassling these (usually) young women for photos – be polite and keep your distance. Also, following a well-publicised 'tourist ban', some streets and alleyways in Gion are now closed to non-residents to protect the privacy of locals, so pay attention to any signs.
- Dinner in Gion doesn't have to be an expensive affair – head to Gion Danran for delicious and affordable *teppan-yaki* (hot plate) dishes.
- Early evening is the best time to experience the magic of Gion, when the roadside lanterns are lit up and geisha may be seen.

TOURISM TROUBLES

Kyoto is one of the world's most-visited cities, and with Japan now in a tourism boom following the COVID-19 pandemic, visitor numbers are only likely to increase. But this large influx of people has been the cause of some issues around the city, most notably in Gion, where there have been instances of unruly tourists hounding geisha and *maiko* in the district's narrow streets, as well as taking photos of them without consent.

There have also been problems with tourists trespassing on private property, to the extent that the local government has now implemented a ban on non-residents entering certain streets – multilingual signs clearly indicate the prohibited areas. So be respectful and pay attention to your surroundings when exploring.

Ninen-zaka

Sacred Statues

Marvel at the Unique Wonders of Sanjūsangen-dō

One of Kyoto's most remarkable sights and a definite must-see, **Sanjūsangen-dō** (三十三間堂) is a temple founded in 1164 and a place that impresses visitors immediately with its 120m-long temple hall, said to be the longest wooden structure in Japan. Inside is even more mesmerising, however, as 1001 statues of Kannon (the Buddhist goddess of mercy) line up to face you. In the centre of the hall sits a large, wooden 1000-armed statue of Senju-Kannon, carved in 1254, and flanking her on either side are 500 smaller but still human-sized statues – all in all, it makes for an awe-inspiring sight.

EATING IN GION & SOUTHERN HIGASHIYAMA: JAPANESE PUBS

Gion Yuki Short red curtains signal the entrance to this lively *izakaya* (Japanese pub-eatery); fish features heavily on the menu and sake is the tipple of choice. *4-9.30pm Mon-Sat* ¥¥

Bamboo Relaxed *izakaya* on Sanjō-dōri with counter seating and a wide range of staples such as sashimi, tempura and *nabe* (hot pot). *5-11pm* ¥¥

Mamoriya A stone's throw from the Kamo-gawa, this welcoming *izakaya* has a large (English) menu; it's great place for late-night food or drinks. *5pm-2am Mon-Sat* ¥¥

Siba *Izakaya* with hearty, unpretentious fare, quirky and cosy counter-seating, random clutter and a background soundtrack of swirling jazz tones. *6-11pm* ¥¥

Cultural Landmark
Go for a Stroll Around Yasaka-jinja

Also known as Gion Shrine, **Yasaka-jinja** (八坂神社) has mysterious origins, but was founded over 1000 years ago at least and is certainly one of Kyoto's most famous shrines – its distinctive vermilion gate is impossible to miss just beyond the streets of Gion and below the wooded slopes of the Higashiyama hills. Yasaka-jinja is open 24 hours a day and is a pleasant and atmospheric place to wander around after dark or at sunrise, but has a more bustling feel most of the time, with nearby stalls making it a good spot for some Kyoto street food. In cherry-blossom season it is particularly lively, and likewise in July, when it plays host to **Gion Matsuri** (p70), one of the most famous summer festivals in Japan.

Dress Up
Stroll Around in a Kimono

Renting a kimono and wandering around Kyoto like a geisha for the day is an increasingly popular activity for foreign visitors, and at **Rental Kimono Okamoto** you can do just that. Located next to Yasaka-jinja, they have a wide selection of garments, and will dress customers and do their hair for a reasonable price – there are traditional outfits for men available too. After getting dressed up, customers can then spend an hour or two wandering around all the nearby famous sights in almost full geisha garb, with pretty photo spots to be found around almost every corner. Make a booking in advance online.

Scenic Streets
Step into the Kyoto of Yesteryear at Ninen-zaka and Sannen-zaka

Just down the hill from Kiyomizu-dera are two of Kyoto's most quaint and scenic streets, **Ninen-zaka** (二年坂; Two-Year Hill) and **Sannen-zaka** (三年坂; Three-Year Hill), both named after the ancient imperial years when they were created. Lovingly preserved wooden *machiya* line both of these winding and narrow pedestrian walkways, with the rustic shopfronts giving the whole place a charming ambience, even if it can get busy at times. Come for a late-night stroll to experience the district at its atmospheric best.

QUIRKY KYOTO

At the southern end of Gion lies one of Kyoto's oddest sights, **Yasui Konpira-gū**. In front of this small and ancient Shintō shrine is a large stone covered with paper slips, so that it resembles a shaggy mop of hair. It's known as the '*enriki/enmusubi* stone', and it is customary to buy a slip of paper, write your name and wish on it, and then, paper in hand, crawl through the hole in the stone from front to back to bind your current relationship and make it stronger – or go the opposite way if you want to break some connections and end one.

EATING IN GION & SOUTHERN HIGASHIYAMA: NOODLE DISHES

Yagura Noodle specialist in Gion, across from Minamiza; choose from soba or udon bowls, or the *omakase* (chef's choice) – three small dishes from the daily specials. *11.30am-8.30pm* ¥

Mimikou Relaxed udon restaurant with plenty of tasty variations, including curry udon. The vegan and vegetarian options are veggie-packed and very good too. *11.30am-3pm & 5-8pm* ¥

Hisago In the middle of the Southern Higashiyama sightseeing district, this is a great spot for a light lunch, with a choice of noodle or rice dishes. *11.30am-4pm Tue-Thu, Sat & Sun* ¥

Gion Duck Noodles Hidden down a nondescript narrow alley, this small ramen joint serves noodles with succulent duck meat in broth. *11am-9pm* ¥

Scan this QR code for further information.

TOP EXPERIENCE

Chion-in

A sprawling hillside site of grand and imposing buildings and attractive courtyards, Chion-in (知恩院) is the head temple of the Jōdo school of Buddhism, the largest Buddhist sect in Japan. Always bustling with activity, Chion-in is the place to get a glimpse of Kyoto's spiritual underbelly, or simply marvel at the fabulous architecture and rare cultural treasures.

DON'T MISS
Sanmon gate
Miei-dō
Seishi-dō
Daishōrō
Hōjō Garden
Yūzen Garden
Kuromon

Buddhist Beginnings

The origins of Chion-in go back a long way; it was established in 1234 at a spot where the monk Hōnen, the founder of Jōdo Buddhism, taught and eventually fasted to death. Jōdo Buddhism (literally meaning 'pure land' Buddhism) is based on the premise that salvation can be had by anyone with faith in the Buddhist deity Amida – until that point, Buddhism was reserved for only literate monks and aristocrats, and so this new sect became very popular with the masses, and still has millions of adherents to this day.

Main Gate

The scale and grandeur of Chion-in impresses on first sight, especially if you approach and pass through the two-storey **Sanmon gate**, the largest wooden temple gate in Japan. The gate is so large, in fact, that its interior houses a worship hall, veranda and some fine Buddhist artwork, although they are only very occasionally open for viewing.

Temple Structures

Beyond the gate and up the stone steps lies the immense **Miei-dō** (main hall) – dating back to 1639 and measuring 35m wide and 45m long, it houses a sacred image (called the *miei*) of the temple's founder Hōnen, and the building serves as the religious heart of the complex. At various times of the year the Miei-dō is abuzz with worshippers and chanting monks – if you're lucky enough to be visiting during a ritual service then the ebbing rhythms and tones of the Buddhist mantras really add to the otherworldly atmosphere. The main hall was restored in recent years and is a mixture of Japanese architecture with some Chinese elements. A path heading east leads to the **Seishi-dō**, the oldest building in the complex, built in 1530. The corridors connecting the main hall to various subsidiary buildings contain 'nightingale' floorboards that squeak when walked on, an ingenious design to detect intruders.

Temple Bell

Chion-in's 70-tonne, 3.3m-high bell (known as the *Ōgane* – literally 'large bell') was cast in 1636 and is one of the largest temple bells in Japan. It is only rung twice a year; in April during Hōnen's memorial service, and on New Year's Eve, when it is struck 108 times by a team of 17 monks as they ring in the new year across Kyoto. It is housed in the **Daishōrō**, or Great Bell Tower, which also dates back centuries, to 1678.

Gardens

Two gardens can be found in the temple grounds; the **Hōjō Garden** surrounds the Kohōjō (small guesthouse) and is a beautiful space centred on a pond; it is said to have been designed in the early Edo period by a monk named Gyokuen, who had connections with the master garden designer Kobori Enshū, and was created to highlight the changes of the seasons. The more modern **Yūzen Garden** is next to the Sanmon gate and contains contrasting rock and pond gardens, as well as two teahouses. Each garden requires a small additional entry fee.

CURIOUS WONDERS

Chion-in houses seven 'wonders', although some of these are off limits to visitors. Two of the most curious are the *wasuregasa*, a forgotten umbrella left in the eaves of the Miei-dō, said to protect the temple from fires, and the *uryūseki*, a large rock near the Kuromon (Black Gate), where a deity is said to have descended and gourds sprouted from it overnight.

TOP TIPS

- For a more rewarding and atmospheric experience, aim to visit either early in the morning or late in the afternoon to avoid the tourist busloads.
- The main hall has numerous little details to spot; look for doorstoppers shaped like cicadas and turtles.
- The busiest times for worshippers are around O-Bon (in August) and at Higan-e (during the equinox of March and September), and at other festivals related to the temple's founding.
- Time your visit to coincide with a meal at nearby **Kikunoi Honten** (p94), one of Kyoto's finest *kaiseki* (Japanese haute cuisine) restaurants – allow a few hours, and book in advance.

THE CHANGING FACE OF GION

Masako Okasa, owner at kimono-rental shop Mugen in Gion.

Gion has changed over the years; it remains atmospheric and beautiful, but it's now much quieter at night.

Gion used to be Kyoto's famed drinking quarter, but most of the *nomiya* (drinking establishments) have now closed – young people don't want to pay the prices many of those old places used to charge.

In contrast, there are now far more people around Gion in the daytime, and kimono-rental companies like mine are proving popular with domestic and international visitors.

This part of Kyoto has so many attractions; the temples and World Heritage Sites are world class, but don't forget the simpler pleasures, such as enjoying *matcha* or *wagashi* in a beautiful spot.

Geisha Dances
Take in the Spectacle of Miyako Odori

If you don't have the cash (or connections) for an evening's entertainment with a geisha at an exclusive teahouse, then catching a geisha dance performance may be the perfect compromise. **Miyako Odori** is probably the most famous, with dazzling 45-minute shows throughout April at Gion Kōbu Kaburenjō Theatre. **Kyō Odori** is another option at the same time of year, while **Gion Odori** can be watched at Gion Kaikan in November.

Pretty in Pink
Take a Breather in Maruyama-kōen

A favourite spot for locals and tourists alike, **Maruyama-kōen** (円山公園) is a lovely park up the hill behind Yasaka-jinja that offers plenty of green spaces, ponds and paths for ambling, and is one of the most popular places in the city for cherry-blossom viewing in the spring. The park's crowning glory is a tall *shidare-zakura* (weeping cherry tree), which is lit up at night and looks like something out of a fairy tale. The park is a great place to while away an hour or so, munching on a few snacks and people-watching.

Drop in for Tea
Learn the Art of Beverage Making

The tea ceremony, or *sadō/chadō* (literally 'the way of tea'), is a deep-rooted cultural activity, with each of its element adding to the overall aesthetic experience. As the home of refined culture, Kyoto is the perfect place to try it. **Camellia** is located in a beautiful old house just off Ninen-zaka, and here you can experience a simple yet elegant ceremony with an English-speaking host who explains each element of the art form in clear detail. The price includes a bowl of *matcha* (powdered green tea) and a Japanese sweet.

Another good option in the same area is **Tea Ceremony Nagomi**, where guests can learn all about the history of tea and learn the process for themselves.

 DRINKING IN GION & SOUTHERN HIGASHIYAMA: CRAFT BEER

Beer Komachi Tiny, casual bar dedicated to the promotion of Japanese craft beer, with a rotating roster of seven beers on tap and good food and sake. *5-11pm Wed-Fri & Mon, 3-11pm Sat & Sun*

Yamaneko Stylish little standing bar with eight craft beers on tap, plus more than 50 sake varieties. There's seating on the 2nd floor. *5-11pm*

Shalara Craft Beer A lovely relaxed spot for a beer after a day of sightseeing, with plenty of brews on tap, plus ciders and good food. *Noon-10pm Wed-Sun*

Beer Stand 336 Tiny standing beer bar at the bottom of the main drag up to Kiyomizu-dera, with beer- and sake-tasting menus. *11am-7pm*

ATMOSPHERIC WALK THROUGH GION

This walk is best in the late afternoon and heading into dusk, as the lanterns give an atmospheric glow to Gion's streets; however, the walk can be enjoyed any time of day.

Starting at Gion-Shijō Station, head east along Shijō-dōri to admire the magnificent facade of ❶ **Minamiza**, Japan's premier kabuki theatre. Continue onwards a few blocks and turn right onto ❷ **Hanami-kōji**. Gion's most famous street, it's been wonderfully preserved and is lined with traditional *ochaya* (teahouses). The large, imposing red-walled building is Ichiriki-tei, a 300-year-old teahouse and one of Gion's highest-end establishments.

Walk southwards and keep your eyes peeled for *geiko* and *maiko* ambling by if it is early evening. In a few minutes you will see the Gion Kōbu Kaburenjō Theatre, otherwise known as ❸ **Gion Corner**. Come here for the famous geisha dance of the Miyako Odori

in April and October, or hour-long evening cultural shows at other times.

Continue southwards until the road veers off to a gate – this is one of the entrances to ❹ **Kennin-ji**, the oldest Zen temple in Kyoto, and much of the grounds can be freely entered.

After having a look around, follow the narrow streets eastwards and you'll soon reach ❺ **Yasui Konpira-gū**, one of Kyoto's most curious little shrines; the 'power stone' in front of it has a small hole that you can crawl through to get good connections in your life and break some bad ones.

From here, you can retrace your steps (or find your own way) back up Hanami-kōji, and then north to the quaint cherry-tree-lined streets of ❻ **Shimbashi**. If you arrive around dusk, the lanterns give the neighbourhood a fantastical aura. End your walk back at Gion-Shijō Station.

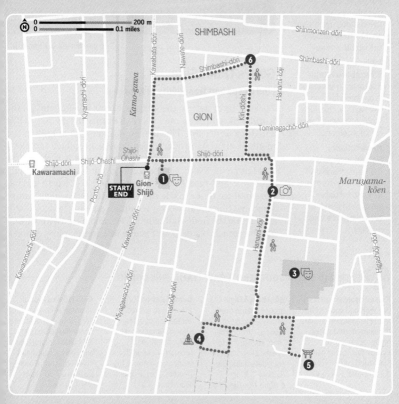

KYOTO'S BEST CERAMICS & CRAFTS

Asahi-dō
This specialist of *Kyōyaki-Kiyomizuyaki* (Kyoto-style pottery) has been operating since 1870 and has a huge selection.

Imamura
A treasure trove of hand-painted pottery, run by a lovely, friendly woman; find it on an unassuming backstreet near Kiyomizu-dera.

Kyoto Jizō-dō
Charming pottery and ceramic shop with lots of affordable, attractive items, directly across from Kyoto Higashiyama-sō on the street leading to Kiyomizu-dera.

Ichizawa Shinzaburō Hanpu
Bag-making specialist in business for over 100 years, with a wide range of canvas bags in many colours.

Miura Shōmei
Operating for over 120 years, this Gion institution is the place to come for paper lanterns of the kind seen in Kyoto's finest ryokans.

Zen garden view, Kennin-ji

Gion's Quiet Side

Find Peace and Tranquillity at Kennin-ji

Located right next to the vibrant streets of Gion and all the worldly pleasures on offer there, **Kennin-ji**（建仁寺）is like a little oasis of calm. This temple was founded in 1202 by the monk Eisai (who introduced Zen Buddhism and tea ceremony to Japan after his study trips to China), and it is the oldest Zen temple in Kyoto. The peaceful grounds are surprisingly extensive and mostly free to enter, but it is worth paying the small fee to see inside the main buildings, which feature some magnificent artwork, including a striking image of twin dragons on the Hōdō Hall ceiling. The temple's moss and gravel gardens are also a delight if you're in a contemplative mood.

EATING IN GION & SOUTHERN HIGASHIYAMA: FINE DINING

Kikunoi Honten Located in a secluded spot not far from Maruyama-kōen, this Michelin-starred *kaiseki* restaurant is one of Kyoto's finest, with exemplary food and service. *11.30am-1pm, 5-8pm ¥¥¥*

Gion Karyō High-quality yet not overly expensive *kaiseki* cuisine – the counter seats enable you to see the chef crafting each delectable dish. *11.30am-2.30pm, 6-10pm Thu-Tue ¥¥¥*

Sumibi Kappo Ifuki Private and refined three-hour courses showcasing the best of Kyoto cuisine, located in a beautiful wooden *machiya* in the heart of Gion. *5-11pm Wed-Mon ¥¥¥*

Gion Mikaku Award-winning family-run Wagyū-beef specialist operating in Gion since 1929; outstanding food and service from head chefs and staff. *Noon-2.30pm & 5.30-10pm Tue-Sun ¥¥¥*

Cultural Time Machine
Masterpieces of Art at Kyoto National Museum

The city's most illustrious art museum, **Kyoto National Museum** (京都国立博物館) was founded in 1895 as an imperial repository for the art and priceless treasures of Kyoto's many shrines and temples, and the original red-brick main hall building has recently been restored. It is a fantastic place to get an overview of the whole gamut of Japanese art throughout the ages, with collections encompassing everything from sculptures and hand scrolls to ceramics, archaeological findings and feudal-era paintings. The temporary exhibits are always worth checking out as well (visit the website to find out what's on).

Ceramic Centre
Delve into the World of Pottery

Kyoto is renowned for its ceramics, but if you want to do more of a deep dive rather than simply window shopping, then head to **Asahi-dō** (朝日堂), a renowned pottery shop in the Kiyomizu pottery district. Founded in 1870, it specialises in hand-thrown and hand-painted 'Kyō Ware', and at the pottery salon on the 2nd floor you can relax with a coffee as you admire their limited-time exhibitions. Just down the road at the Kura Art Salon, events are sometimes held where you can see master artisans demonstrating their skills – see their website for details.

Theatre Night
Experience a Smorgasbord of Kyoto Culture

If a three-hour kabuki performance sounds like too much, but you still want to sample a slice of Kyoto's rich cultural heritage, then a ticket for a show at Gion Kōbu Kaburenjō Theatre, otherwise known as **Gion Corner**, may be just for you. These one-hour evening performances are aimed at tourists, but include a mix of tea ceremony, bunraku (classical puppet theatre), ikebana (flower arranging), *kyōgen* (ancient comedy plays) and *kyōmai* (Kyoto-style dance) among others – tickets can be purchased online in advance. In April and October, the main Gion Kōbu Kaburenjō next door is also the place to come to watch the famous Miyako Odori, Gion's most celebrated geisha dance event.

KYOTO'S BEST SOUVENIR SHOPS

Yamashita
Rustic shop on Sannen-zaka selling cheap and tasty traditional Japanese pickles, ideal as souvenirs or a quick snack.

Kurochiku
Big store in Gion with a large choice of modern and traditional small items (stationery, ceramics and trinkets).

Honke Nishio Yatsuhashi
Bustling traditional sweet shop offering free green tea and samples of many varieties of *yatsuhashi*, a Kyoto delicacy made from rice flour, sugar and cinnamon.

Ayanokōji Gion
This shop has helpful staff and lots of locally made and Kyoto-themed wallets, bags and more.

Hararyōkaku
Historic condiment maker on Shijō-dōri; come here for Japanese black pepper and spice mixes, which can be used to enhance ramen and hot pot.

EATING IN GION & SOUTHERN HIGASHIYAMA: SPECIALITY RESTAURANTS

Gion Uokeya U Sample the succulent and sweet umami of perfectly grilled conger eel at this Michelin-starred *unagi* (eel) restaurant – reservations are usually a must. 11.30am-2pm, 5-8pm Tue-Sun ¥¥

Chikumo A unique *teppan-yaki* restaurant where most items are skewered before serving. Courses include a wide range of meat, seafood and vegetables. 5.30-10pm Mon-Sat ¥¥¥

Gion Tempura Koromo High-end, intimate tempura restaurant with varied *omakase* menu and exceptional, friendly service; wash everything down with the pairing sake. 5-10pm Wed-Fri, 11.30am-3pm & 5-10pm Sat & Sun ¥¥¥

Gion Danran Unpretentious *teppan-yaki* restaurant run by a lovely couple, offering hearty and affordable Kansai favourites such as *okonomiyaki* and *yakisoba*. 5-10pm Thu-Tue ¥¥

STROLL THE SIGHTS OF SOUTHERN HIGASHIYAMA

From Gojō-zaka bus stop, walk up Gojō-zaka slope, and at the first fork in the road veer right, continuing up Chawan-zaka (Teapot Lane), famous for its pottery shops.

You'll soon arrive at ❶ **Kiyomizu-dera**, the World Heritage Site where you can soak in the views from the huge wooden veranda and purify yourself at the sacred springs of Otowa-no-taki.

Next, walk downhill along Kiyomizu-michi, and at the first main junction take a right down the paved steps of the wonderfully quaint ❷ **Sannen-zaka**, leading onto Ninen-zaka. Then (a few doors before Starbucks), on the left, you will find ❸ **Kasagi-ya**, a fantastically rustic old teashop where you can enjoy some tea and traditional *wagashi* (sweets).

After refreshments, stroll down to the end of Ninen-zaka, zigzagging left then right and then north to ❹ **Kōdai-ji**. The main draw at this exquisite temple are the magnificent sculpted gardens, and there are tearooms if you want to spend more time admiring the views.

From Kōdai-ji walk north along pretty ❺ **Nene-no-michi**; follow it right then take a quick left to stroll down to ❻ **Maruyama-kōen**, a pleasant park with an iconic *shidare-zakura* cherry tree at its centre – mesmerising in the spring.

Make a quick detour west to the vivid vermilion gate and structures of ❼ **Yasaka-jinja**, one of Kyoto's most recognisable shrines and starting point of the Gion Matsuri. Back at the park, head northwards and you'll soon arrive at ❽ **Chion-in**; its extensive grounds and impressive temple architecture are usually awash with religious activity.

If time allows, pop in to ❾ **Shōren-in** next door; this delightfully peaceful temple is often overlooked, and so retains its Zen-like ambience. It's then a short walk down to Higashiyama Station.

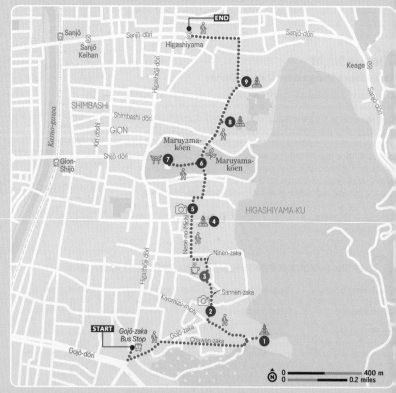

KYOTO'S MARVELLOUS MACHIYA

Machiya are the traditional wooden townhouses that were once ubiquitous throughout Kyoto, with most remaining examples dating back to around the late Edo or Meiji periods.

Typical Kyoto *machiya* (or *kyō-machiya*) are latticed and narrow, with the street-facing side originally used as a shopfront, and the living quarters tucked deep at the back, typically with a small enclosed garden called a *tsuboniwa*.

Many of Kyoto's *machiya* have been destroyed or rebuilt over the years, but a good number still remain and have been lovingly restored, some now functioning as guesthouses – a stay in one is a memorable way to sample a slice of traditional city life.

Kasagi-ya

Traditional Drama

Enjoy a Night of Theatre

Located in the heart of Gion, **Minamiza** (南座) is Japan's oldest kabuki theatre. The current building dates back to 1929, although there has been a theatre here since the 1600s, meaning it is regarded as the birthplace of this unique form of theatrical drama. Even if you struggle to make any sense of it helps to do a little reading up beforehand to add some richness to the experience. Tickets can be booked online in advance at kabukiweb.net.

EATING IN GION & SOUTHERN HIGASHIYAMA: CAFES & SWEETS

Kagizen Yoshifusa One of Kyoto's best-known and oldest sweet shops, with a lovely tearoom. One of the specialities is not a sweet but *kuzukiri* ('transparent arrow-root noodles'). *9.30am-6pm Tue-Sun* ¥

Kasagi-ya Traditional Japanese sweets, desserts and *matcha* in a lovely, and surprisingly quiet, rustic setting on the thoroughfare to Kiyomizu-dera. *10am-5.30pm Wed-Mon* ¥

Shimizu Ippōen Popular but low-key establishment around the corner from Sanjūsangen-dō. Great for a mid-afternoon *matcha* parfait or fluffy *kakigōri* (shaved ice) on a sweltering summer's day. *11am-5pm Tue-Sun* ¥

Zen Cafe Contemporary and minimalist cafe serving traditional Kyoto refreshments and tea/coffee, with an electronic reservation system, but the wait is rarely long. *11am-6pm Tue-Sun* ¥

Scan this QR code for further information.

TOP EXPERIENCE

Kiyomizu-dera

One of the city's most revered World Heritage Sites, Kiyomizu-dera (清水寺) is a temple with over 1200 years of history. Founded at the site of a holy spring, it has long been a place of pilgrimage and is famed for its impressive 13m-high wooden veranda, Buddhist art collections and a shrine for those seeking luck in love.

Historic Landmark

DON'T MISS

Hondō

Zuigu-dō Hall

Otowa-no-taki

Jishu-jinja

Niō-mon

Sai-mon

Sanjū-no-tō

The temple dates back to 778 and was built at a spot known as the Otowa Waterfall, from where the name Kiyomizu-dera ('pure water temple') derives. It was originally associated with the Hossō sect of Buddhism – one of the oldest schools of Japanese Buddhism – and most of the buildings in this extensive temple complex have burned down numerous times, so the current structures are reconstructions dating from 1633.

Glorious Gates

Most visitors arrive at the temple at the foot of the Niō-mon, a magnificent two-storey vermilion gate crammed with intricate artisanship, which towers at the top of some stone steps – it's an iconic and popular spot, so you'll need to visit very early or late in the day to experience it without the crowds. Nearby, Sai-mon is the equally impressive West Gate, and this is one of the best sunset-viewing spots in the city.

Main Hall

Kiyomizu-dera's main hall (Hondō) houses the temple's most sacred object of worship, an 11-headed and thousand-armed Kannon figure. The main attraction for most, however, is just outside the hall; stand on the magnificent stage-like *hinoki* veranda, which towers almost four storeys above the forested hillside – it is supported by enormous wooden pillars, and as you enjoy the views it's worth taking a moment to consider that the entire construction was built without using a single nail.

Otowa-no-taki

Just below the veranda is Otowa-no-taki ('Otowa Waterfall'); its sacred spring waters flow as three separate streams, with each said to bestow a different benefit, namely a long life, success at school and luck in love. Use one of the cups attached to a long pole to drink from them, but be warned; drinking from all three is considered greedy.

Get Lucky In Love

Up to the left and behind the main hall is Jishu-jinja, a Shintō shrine where visitors come to pray to the deity of love and matchmaking. Here you will find two stones placed about 18m apart – walking from one to the other with your eyes closed is said to bring romantic success, but if you need assistance to complete the challenge then it is prophesied that you will also need help to find your true love.

Interesting Sights

It is worth spending some time to explore all corners of the temple complex – there is certainly enough to fill an hour. Northwest of the main hall is a hill where hundreds of small stone Jizō statues stand, and among the grounds you can see a couple of brightly coloured pagodas including Sanjū-no-tō. The intriguing Zuigu-dō Hall dates back to 1735 and houses deities for matchmaking and child rearing, while a hidden Buddhist image is said to hear the desires and aspirations of everyone who enters. Most interesting of all is the *Tainai-meguri*, a short tour into the sanctified bowels beneath the building where (for a small additional fee) you can experience the unnerving sensation of wandering around in a pitch black underground space, said to represent a mother's womb.

THE INNER SANCTUARY

Usually closed off to the public, the *naijin* (inner sanctum) and the *nainaijin* (innermost sanctum) are the most sacred areas of Kiyomizu-dera, with the latter where the principal deity of the temple is enshrined. During the Thousand-Day Pilgrimage event in mid-August, where prayers are said to be amplified one-thousand-fold, visitors are permitted to enter and pray to the Kannon statue therein.

TOP TIPS

- Three times a year (during cherry-blossom season, autumn-foliage season and at O-Bon in August) there are evening light-ups, when the buildings and trees are spectacularly illuminated (the last entry is at 9pm).
- The temple is generally open between 6am and 6pm, but do check beforehand, as times change seasonally and during special events.
- The nearest bus stops are Gojō-zaka and Kiyomizu-michi.
- There are plenty of options for traditional refreshments along the streets approaching the temple; one of the best is Kasagi-ya, a rustic teahouse and a fine spot for a sip of *matcha* (powdered green tea).

Northern Higashiyama

TEMPLES, ART AND TRADITIONAL VILLAS

Situated east of the Kamo River and north of Sanjō-dōri, northern Higashiyama is something of a Kyoto everyman. In places bustling, in others quiet and suburban, the area delivers big-name temples alongside less famous but equally alluring attractions.

In and around the Okazaki Park area in the south, there's enough to keep you busy for a full day. Start with Heian-jingū and its varied gardens, built in the 1890s to celebrate the 1100th anniversary of Kyoto becoming the capital. On the shrine's doorstep, you'll find a hub of museums and galleries, with sites like Kyocera Museum of Art and Kyoto Museum of Craft and Design together covering everything from contemporary international art to traditional local crafts. Then there's Murin-an – tucked down a side street across the road from Kyoto Zoo, it's a villa built by a Meiji-era politician that today is perfect for escaping the crowds for a garden stroll followed by tea and sweets.

Getting a little closer to the foothills of the Higashiyama mountains, Northern Higashiyama then reveals a mix of famous and almost-secret temples. That includes the UNESCO World Heritage Sites of Ginkaku-ji and Nanzen-ji, in between which you'll find Eikan-dō and its stunning autumnal scenery, plus the opportunity for a calming walk along the canal-side Philosopher's Path.

Heading further north, the upper reaches of Higashiyama become a peaceful residential area ideal for an off-the-beaten-path ramble. Temples like Enkō-ji, Shisen-dō and Manshu-in are worth a good walk for the quality and variety of their gardens, not to mention their architecture and traditional works of art. Nearby, the guided tour of Shūgaku-in Rikyū Imperial Villa is a candidate for the best free activity in Kyoto – a chance to peek inside the grounds of one of Japan's official imperial residences. Not that everything this far north is about tradition. You also have Ichijōji Ramen Street, which many ramen fans consider the best congregation of ramen joints in Kyoto, with almost 20 places serving up Japan's favourite comfort food.

DON'T MISS...

GINKAKU-JI	PHILOSOPHER'S PATH	KYOCERA MUSEUM OF ART
Take in the Zen gardens and historic architecture at one of Kyoto's most famous temples.	A canal-side stroll punctuated by cafes, galleries, temples, and seasonal cherry blossoms.	A sprawling museum home to an eclectic mix of contemporary and traditional art.
p104	**p107**	**p103**

TOP TIP

Grab the one-day bus-subway pass and you can cover much of northern Higashiyama in a day, just hopping on and off Kyoto City Bus 5. That route runs from Kyoto Station through downtown and then stops at Okazaki Park/ Heian Shrine, Nanzen-ji/Eikan-dō and Ginkaku-ji, and even goes all the way up to near Ichijōji and Shūgaku-in stations.

Left: Zen garden, Ginkaku-ji (p104); Above: Eikan-dō (p108)

EIKAN-DŌ
The fiery maples make this temple an autumnal must-see, especially when illuminated at night.
p108

NANZEN-JI
Visit this UNESCO World Heritage Site for stunning landscaping and priceless screen-door paintings.
p110

MURIN-AN VILLA
A quiet retreat where you can take *matcha* and sweets with views across a traditional garden.
p106

NORTHERN HIGASHIYAMA

See Inset (1.8km)

N   0 ———————— 400 m
    0 ———————— 0.2 miles

Inset

Takano-gawa

Kawabata-dōri

Kyoto Institute of Technology

Shūgakuin

Shirakawa-dōri

SAKYŌ-KU

32

7

Ichijōji

34

4

17

11

0 ———————— 400 m
0 ———————— 0.2 miles

30

Ginkaku-ji ①

15

6

16

Tetsugaku-no-michi (Philosopher's Path)

Higashioji-dōri

Yoshidahigashi-dōri

Shirakawa-dōri

Shira-kawa

24

Marutamachi-dōri

21

Marutamachi-dōri

29

Higashioji-dōri

5

Okazaki Park

Nijō-dōri

23

Kyoto Municipal Zoo

Shira-kawa

26

3

Biwa-ko Sosui Canal

10

14

9

Niōmon-dōri

33

22

27
31

12

25 28

8

19

2 Nanzen-ji

13

Sanjō-dōri Ⓢ Higashiyama

Shirakawa-dōri

Sanjō-dōri

Pedestrian Tunnel

HIGASHIYAMA-KU

HIGHLIGHTS
① Ginkaku-ji
② Nanzen-ji

SIGHTS
③ Eikan-dō
④ Enkō-ji
⑤ Heian-jingū
⑥ Hōnen-in
⑦ Ichijōji Ramen Street
⑧ Konchi-in
⑨ Kyocera Museum of Art
⑩ Kyoto Museum of Crafts and Design

⑪ Manshu-in
⑫ Murin-an
⑬ Nanzen-in
⑭ National Museum of Modern Art
⑮ Philosopher's Path
⑯ Plus 81 Gallery
⑰ Shisen-dō
⑱ Shūgaku-in Rikyū Imperial Villa
⑲ Tenju-an

SLEEPING
⑳ Guesthouse Waraku-an
㉑ Hotel Okura Kyoto Okazaki Bettei
㉒ Waka Heian Shirakawa Hotel

EATING
㉓ 58 Diner
㉔ And Bull
㉕ Blue Bottle
㉖ Breizh
㉗ Hatsune Sushi
㉘ Junsei
㉙ Kyoto Nama Chocolat
㉚ Omen
㉛ Sanmikouan
㉜ entenyu
㉝ hree Horses
㉞ Tsurukame

Museum-Hop in Okazaki Park
Contemporary Art and Traditional Crafts

Located between the main compound of Heian Shrine and its Grand Torii gateway, Okazaki Park has become a hub of museums and galleries. You could easily spend half a day here, but if you are short for time, go straight to **Kyocera Museum of Art** (京セラ美術館), directly east of the Grand Torii. Kyocera's main strengths are its size, eclecticism and ability to show leading Japanese and international artists; previous exhibitions have featured work from street artists like Banksy and Kaws, as well as others studying the influence of classicism on early Shōwa-era Japanese paintings.

If you have more time to spare, head across the road from Kyocera to the smaller **National Museum of Modern Art** (京都国立近代美術館), which features regularly rotating exhibitions that tend to focus on artists with a connection to Kyoto and the wider Kansai region. Set aside at least 30 minutes to head into the basement of the Miyako Messe Exhibition Centre for the **Kyoto Museum of Crafts and Design** (京都伝統産業ミュージアム). Although it only occupies a single floor, the permanent collection does an excellent job of highlighting 74 crafts traditionally produced in Kyoto, ranging from *Kyō-shikki* lacquerware to *Kyō-yūzen* fabric dyeing. In some cases this includes detailed explanations in English of production processes, while most days there will also be an artisan on site giving a crafting demonstration. Just don't plan any of this for a Monday: everything is closed.

A Celebration of Kyoto's Birth
The Gardens of Heian Shrine

Compared to most of Kyoto's temples and shrines, **Heian-jingū** (平安神宮) is a fresh-faced newcomer, built in Okazaki Park in 1895 to commemorate the 1100th anniversary of Kyoto's establishment as Japan's capital. From anywhere in the Okazaki Park area, you'll see Heian-jingū's **Grand Torii**, at 23m the tallest in the country when it was built. Without an admission fee you can pop inside the main compound to see a collection of vermilion-coloured buildings arranged around a vast courtyard – a smaller-scale replica of Kyoto's original imperial palace. If you are interested in traditional landscaping, however, pay ¥600 for a walk around the shrine's gardens.

Covering 3.2 hectares, the gardens are split into four distinct sections that together reflect the varied garden designs developed since Kyoto's establishment. They begin with the

THE JIDAI MATSURI

When Heian-jingū was built to celebrate the 1100th anniversary of Kyoto's foundation as capital, it came with a new festival: the Jidai Matsuri (festival of the ages).

Now considered one of Kyoto's 'big three' annual celebrations, along with the Aoi Matsuri in May and Gion Matsuri in July, this 22 October event features a costume parade from the Imperial Palace to Heian Shrine, with some 2000 people dressed up to represent various periods of Japanese history from the 700s to the Meiji Restoration of 1868.

It really is on a grand scale: once the procession is in full flow, it stretches 2km and takes five hours to complete, with the route chock-a-block with spectators.

EATING IN NORTHERN HIGASHIYAMA: OUR PICKS

Breizh A good spot for coffee and dessert or filling French crepes. Between Eikan-dō and the Philosopher's Path. *9.30am-7pm Sun-Wed, 9.30am-10pm Thu-Sat* ¥¥

Hatsune Sushi Tiny, counter-only place run by a friendly couple who serve excellent sushi sets. *11am-8pm Fri-Wed* ¥¥

Junsei *Kaiseki ryōri* courses centred on *yudōfu* (simmered tofu), served in a traditional-style building near Nanzen-ji. *11am-2.30pm & 5-7pm* ¥¥¥

58 Diner Americana vibes plus a menu that includes homemade burgers (and veggie burgers), pulled pork and local craft beer. *11am-9pm Tue-Sun* ¥¥

Scan this QR code for background information.

TOP EXPERIENCE

Ginkaku-ji

Ginkaku-ji (銀閣寺) translates as the Temple of the Silver Pavilion – an unusual name for a temple that has never been decorated with even an ounce of silver. Nevertheless, with its raked sea of sand, mossy pond garden and classic architecture, the silver-less Ginkaku-ji is still one of northern Higashiyama's shining lights.

DON'T MISS

Ginshadan

Kōgetsudai

Tōgu-dō

Scenic viewpoint

Kinkyōchi

Kannonden

The Roots of Higashiyama Culture

It's a common origin story for a temple in Kyoto, with Ginkaku-ji originally built as a retirement villa in 1482 by shōgun Ashikaga Yoshimasa, before being converted into a Zen temple upon his death. Prior to that transition, the villa was called Higashiyama Sansō. As well as being a residence, it functioned as a hub from where Yoshimasa's patronage helped to develop traditional arts and crafts: a cultural movement now referred to collectively as Higashiyama Culture.

Where's the Silver?

Upon becoming a temple, Higashiyama Sansō also underwent a name change, officially becoming **Jishō-ji**. As is often the case with Kyoto's temples, Jishō-ji is known primarily by its familiar name, Ginkaku-ji. That might strike you as odd, when you realise there's never been any silver on the temple. Why? There are a few theories. One is that Yoshimasa ran out of funding before the planned silver could be applied. Another is that Ginkaku-ji was a nickname of sorts to contrast it to Kinkaku-ji (the Golden Pavilion, p120), which was built by Yoshimasa's grandfather and served as an inspiration for Ginkaku-ji's design. Or perhaps it was because the Silver Pavilion was once partially coated in black lacquer that was said to emit a silvery shimmer. We will likely never know for sure.

The Ginshadan and Tōgu-dō

While Ginkaku-ji admittedly doesn't deliver the initial, blinged-out wow of the gilded Kinkaku-ji, the overall garden design and subtle architecture is just as impressive.

One of the first standout elements you'll encounter is the Zen garden at the start of the route around the grounds, featuring a raked 'silver sea of sand' called the **Ginshadan**. This is accented by a 2m mountain of sand known as the **Kōgetsudai** (pictured left), aka the moon-viewing mound.

As the pathway begins to turn right around the Ginshadan, look left and you'll see a building called the **Tōgu-dō**, set behind a landscaped pond. Capped by a roof shingled in cypress, the (off-limits) tatami-mat rooms here functioned as Yoshimasa's personal Buddha Hall but also his study, from where he is said to have met with artisans and intellectuals as Higashiyama Culture began to flourish.

The Kannonden

Just after the Tōgu-dō, you'll come to a fork in the path. Go left up the hill and you'll be rewarded with views over Ginkaku-ji and northern Higashiyama beyond, before the path winds its way down to the main path for an up-close view of the two-storey Silver Pavilion (Ginkaku), officially called the **Kannonden**. Design-wise, it mimics its golden relative at Kinkaku-ji in several ways. First, it's set behind a pond (called the Kinkyōchi), which catches its understated reflection. Like Kinkaku-ji, it's also topped with a phoenix sculpture and employs a mix of architectural styles. In the Kannonden's case, the first floor is a classical *shoin* residential style, while the second incorporates bell-shaped windows and wood-panelled doors like a Chinese temple.

OCHA NO I

Higashiyama Culture saw the creation of new architectural and landscaping styles that are reflected in Ginkaku-ji's design. It also saw the development of *chanoyu* (the tea ceremony). On the way up to the temple's scenic outlook, you'll pass one reminder of the latter – a small well called the Ocha no I, from which water was drawn for making tea.

TOP TIPS

● You'll only need 30 to 45 minutes at Ginkaku-ji but, for a longer adven-ture, you could combine it with a walk along the Philosopher's Path (p107).

● If you are hungry, head to nearby Omen (p106) for some *udon* noodles. There are also places to grab a snack or coffee on the street leading to Ginkaku-ji's entrance.

● The route up to the scenic outlook is inaccessible to strollers and wheelchairs, but the rest of the pathway is accessible.

● You'll also find an accessible toilet by the souvenir shop, just after the Kannonden.

● The admission fee is payable in cash only.

Minami Shin-en (South Garden), a stroll garden based on Heian era (794–1185) landscaping that's best known for weeping cherry blossoms that bloom pink in spring.

Jumping forward to the Kamakura era (1185–1333), the next area is the **Nishi Shin-en** (West Garden) and its early-summer irises. Keep following the pathway as it loops behind the shrine and next up is the **Naka Shin-en** (Middle Garden), where the pond garden traversed by stepping stones takes inspiration from the Muromachi era (1336–1573). The best, **Higashi Shin-en** (East Garden), is saved till last. Giving a nod to Edo-era (1603–1868) landscaping, it combines a large pond that's surrounded by seasonal blooms and crossed by covered wooden walkway, but also features the borrowed scenery of the Higashiyama mountains in the background – a trick employed to add a greater sense of scale to the garden.

Tea With a View

Take *Matcha* at Murin-an villa

Built just to the southeast of Okazaki Park (p103) in 1896 as the private residence of statesman Yamagata Aritomo, **Murin-an** (無鄰菴) is an excellent example of a Meiji-era house and garden, combining naturally styled landscaping with a traditional Japanese building, a two-storey Western-style house and a teahouse. From the tatami-mat floor of the traditional villa, you can take *matcha* (powdered green tea) and sweets, accompanied by an elongated view of the garden with the Higashiyama mountains functioning as *shakkei* (borrowed scenery) in the distance.

Before or after your tea, the garden itself offers a calming 10-minute stroll, taking in a babbling stream, stepping stones and lawns before the path circles back to the Western-style house. The 2nd floor here has been preserved as it was in 1903 – complete with a mix of traditional Japanese wall paintings and Western furniture – when Yamagata, Prime Minister Katsura Taro and other leading statesmen met to plan for the Russo-Japanese war.

Thanks to an admission limit of 15 people every hour, it's all extremely peaceful. That also means that while reservations aren't essential, they are highly recommended, especially in high season. They can be done in English via murin-an. jp, where you can also see whether there are any events on when you plan to visit. Among other things, on the second and fourth Wednesday of the month, English-speaking guides are on hand to give garden tours.

EATING IN NORTHERN HIGASHIYAMA: BEST NOODLES

Omen Stop here after Ginkaku-ji for thick udon noodles served with hot or cold broth and sides. *10.30am-5.30pm Mon-Wed & Fri, 10.30am-3.30pm & 5-8pm Sat & Sun* ¥

Sanmikouan Soba noodles and side dishes like tempura in an old townhouse overlooking a river. *11am-3pm & 5-8.30pm Tue-Sun* ¥

Tentenyu One of Ichijōji Ramen Street's most popular restaurants, it cooks up chicken broth ramen with a generous topping of *chāshū* (sliced roast pork). *Noon-10pm Thu-Tue* ¥

Tsurukame This Ramen Street favourite uses local *saikyō* miso in its ramen broth, and also serves *tsukemen* dipping ramen. *11.30am-2.30pm & 6-9.30pm Fri-Wed* ¥

WALK THE PHILOSOPHER'S PATH

This walk visits two of northern Higashi-yama's major temples, joined together by the Philosopher's Path (哲学の道), a mellow canal-side route that in spring is engulfed by pink cherry blossoms. Allow several hours, including the time at each stop.

Start at the Ginkaku-ji-michi bus stop and walk to ❶ **Ginkaku-ji** (p104), for its dry sand andmoss gardens, plus views over northern Kyoto. Then, from the end of the shop-lined approach to Ginkaku-ji, turn left onto the ❷ **Philosopher's Path**. This 2km route is named after Nishida Kitarō, a philosopher who is said have strolled here in contemplation to and from his office at Kyoto University. After following the path south for a few minutes, you could take a brief detour left to ❸ **Hōnen-in** (follow the signs), a peaceful temple worth a look for its thatched gateway and the gnarly tree roots and moss taking over its garden.

Back on the path, and continuing south, you'll come across several cafes and galleries, including ❹ **Plus 81 Gallery** (closed Tuesdays), where the frequently changing exhibitions cover contemporary art across a variety of genres. Afterwards, stop for a coffee or pizza at ❺ **And Bull**, grabbing a counter seat to people-watch along the path. At the southern end of the Philosopher's Path, turn right, then left for ❻ **Eikan-dō** (p108), home to attractive maples in autumn and a fine collection of painted sliding doors. Finally, a few more minutes south is ❼ **Nanzen-ji** (p110), where the highlights include a 17th-century Zen garden and an even bigger collection of painted sliding doors than Eikan-dō. Allow at least an hour here, but more if you decide to pay extra to visit any of Nanzen-ji's sub-temples – ❽ **Konchi-in** (p111) is arguably the pick of lot if you aren't gardened-out already.

From here it's a short walk to Keage subway station.

ZAZEN MEDITATION

If you are interested in some early-morning calm, head to Enkō-ji on a Sunday, when the temple runs *zazen* (seated meditation) sessions from 6am to 8am (¥1000).

They are conducted in Japanese, but are open to anyone, and also include a simple breakfast if you help to sweep the temple and weed the gardens – meditation in movement *(samu)* to complement the meditation in stillness *(zazen)*.

To book a spot, call a day or more in advance (ideally have someone call in Japanese).

Kyoto at its Autumnal Best

A Visit to Eikan-dō

When Kyoto's summer heat is finally replaced by the gentle days of autumn, **Eikan-dō** (永観堂) becomes one of the city's most picturesque temples, its maples turning a fiery red in November before carpeting the ground in early December. While that can mean crowds and a slow shuffle from photo op to photo op – especially if you come for the autumn evening illuminations – it's well worth the potential scrum.

That's not to say you shouldn't come at other times of year. Without the leaf-loving crowds, you can have a much more relaxing stroll around the pretty pond garden, before visiting the two-storey hillside pagoda for views back over the city. You'll also feel less rushed taking in the wonderfully creaking **Shaka-dō Hall**, with its inner courtyard garden surrounded by rooms displaying priceless sliding-door paintings.

Wander off Higashiyama's Beaten Path

Temple-Hopping in the Suburbs

A stroll around the far north of Higashiyama is an opportunity to take in lesser-known temples and seasonal sights, and to see what life looks like in a residential part of Kyoto largely untouched by tourism.

Starting with a 10-minute stroll east of Ichijōji Station (Eizan Railway), the first stop of note is **Shisen-dō** (詩仙堂), aka the 'hermit's villa', which was built as a retirement home by samurai-slash-scholar (and landscape architect) Ishikawa Jōzan in 1641. Perhaps not surprisingly for a man dedicated to studying Chinese classics, the defining feature here is a Tang Dynasty–style landscaped garden, where the defining view from the hermitage's tatami-mat floor is a carpet of white sand leading to azaleas pruned to look like distant, rounded mountains, set against a backdrop of maples.

Next up, a couple of minutes north of Shisen-dō, is **Enkō-ji** (圓光寺), which is well worth the admission fee for its gardens. The first you'll see is the Honryutei, a *karesansui* (dry-landscaped garden) using raked white sand and rocks to depict a dragon swirling through clouds. Beyond lies the moss-covered Jyū-gyū no Niwa with its pond and maples, then a small bamboo grove before steps lead up a hill to views over the city.

A DAY IN TAKAO

A similarly under-the-radar area for temple hopping is **Takao** (p122) in northwest Kyoto. Like the Ichijōji and Shūgaku-in area, Takao's three standout temples are especially attractive in autumn.

From there, head 15 minutes north to **Manshu-in** (曼殊院), on a well-signposted route that feels semi-rural thanks to the occasional rice paddy among the houses. Like Shisen-dō and Enkō-ji, Manshu-in's gardens become especially photogenic when the maples turn red and orange in autumn, but year-round the temple delivers a lovely combination of raked sand accented by mossy islets. Inside, you'll also find some beautifully painted sliding doors dating from the 17th century.

When you are done, walk 15 minutes west to Shūgaku-in Station (also well signposted) for the Eizan Railway.

Manshu-in

ICHIJŌJI RAMEN STREET

When visiting Ichijōji for Shisen-dō or Enkō-ji, also check out **Ramen Street** (ラーメン街道) on the opposite side of Ichijōji Station.

With roughly 20 cramped ramen joints dotting this otherwise plain suburban street, this is the best place to go ramen hunting in Kyoto. If you don't know where to start, pick somewhere with a queue – the universal sign of quality ramen.

Alternatively, tag on a visit to the nearby **Shūgaku-in Rikyū Imperial Villa**, although that usually requires a reservation at least several days in advance.

Peek Inside an Imperial Villa

A Tour of Shūgaku-in Rikyū

Spread over 54 hectares in the foothills of Mt Hiei, **Shūgaku-in Rikyū** (修学院離宮) was built in the 1650s as an imperial villa. Unlike many other Kyoto villas that became temples, Shūgaku-in is still an official imperial residence – one that can be visited as part of a free, guided group tour.

Lasting 80 minutes, the tour visits three main areas, divided by pine-lined pathways bisecting terraced rice paddies. At the Lower Villa is a tea-ceremony house looking onto a garden that uses Mt Hiei as borrowed scenery, while the Middle Villa includes glimpses inside the thatched Kyakuden pavilion. The tour then finishes with the Upper Villa's more modest Rinuntei and Kyūsuitei pavilions, from where you get expansive views across an islet-studded pond to the northern suburbs and distant mountains. To visit, it's highly recommended to book a spot online at sankan.kunaicho.go.jp. If you do try to drop by for a same-day tour, you'll need to bring ID, such as a passport.

 DRINKING IN NORTHERN HIGASHIYAMA: CAFES

And Bull Coffee and pizza are the main draws at this dog-friendly cafe on the Philosopher's Path. *10am-5pm Tue-Sun* ¥

Blue Bottle Single-origin brews, brunch plates and pastries are served in a charming 100-year-old building near Nanzen-ji. *9am-6pm* ¥

Kyoto Nama Chocolat Serves handmade chocolates and cake, with tea and coffee, in an old *machiya* townhouse east of Heian-jingū. *Noon-6pm Wed-Mon* ¥

Three Horses This riverside cafe south of Okazaki Park has breakfast sets, sandwiches, salads and plump scones. *9am-5pm Tue-Fri, 9am-6pm Sat & Sun* ¥

Scan this QR code for prices and opening hours.

TOP EXPERIENCE

Nanzen-ji

Built as a retirement villa in the late 1200s by Emperor Kameyama, before he become a monk and donated it to Buddhism, Nanzen-ji (南禅寺) would go on to develop into a sprawling Zen complex with multiple sub-temples. Today, it remains home to some of Northern Higashiyama's finest landscaped gardens and traditional works of art.

DON'T MISS

The Hōjō Garden

Kanō School Art

Sanmon Gate

Tenju-an

Nanzen-in

The Hōjō Gardens

Once the abbot's residence, the *hōjo* is the focal point of a visit to Nanzen-ji for two excellent reasons: a superb collection of screen door paintings and landscaped gardens. The latter are a mix of styles. The main **Hōjō Garden** is a *karesansui* (dry landscaped garden) believed to have been created by famed designer Kobori Enshū in the 1600s, with a bed of raked gravel said to represent a river, plus large and small rocks to depict a tigress and her cubs. Far more recent is the smaller Kohōjō Garden, a *karesansui* added in 1966, where the arrangement of stones forms the kanji character for 'heart' (心). Further inside the *hōjo* is the Rokudō-tei, a pretty, mossy garden built in 1967 that's packed with so much Buddhist symbolism it would need a full chapter to try and explain.

Edo-Era Art

Then there are the 17th-century paintings by Kanō school artists, displayed in a succession of rooms on the route through the *hōjō*. Peering into the rooms through viewing slits in the doors, the intricate artwork bursts into life as soon as your eyes adjust to the lower light. Tigers play in a bamboo grove against an elaborate gold-leaf backdrop, alongside exquisite images of cranes and delicate cherry blossoms. There are also glimpses of the daily lives of society's upper echelons – on one screen men play a board game in the shade of stylised pines; in another a lady discreetly breastfeeds an infant.

The Free Bits

The *hōjō* requires an admission fee (and it's absolutely worth it), but you can also take in a few sights at Nanzen-ji free of charge. Upon reaching the complex, the first is the mighty Sanmon gate, a 22m-high structure dating to 1628 that marks the entrance, though you don't actually have to go through it to enter. Between the Sanmon and Hōjō, another is the Hōdō (hall). The inside is off-limits to the general public, but if you crouch down and peer upwards through the mesh wire blocking the entrance (that's allowed – don't worry), a spectacular dragon painted on the ceiling is visible through the dim light.

Tenju-an, Konchi-in & Nanzen-in

Nanzen-ji also has some less-visited sub-temples to consider visiting. Of the 13, **Tenju-an** (天授庵), directly south of the Sanmon, is worth the admission for its pond garden, dry-landscaped garden, and vivid autumn maples – the latter the only time the temple gets busy.

The highlight at **Konchi-in** (金地院), southeast of the Sanmon on the way to Keage subway station, is a rock garden said to represent a turtle and crane, which you can contemplate in peace and quiet from a wooden deck. **Nanzen-in** (南禅院), tucked behind the distinctive brick aqueduct you'll see to your right as you walk to the Hōjō, is known for a mossy stroll garden designed around a heart-shaped pond filled with colourful carp. Like Tenju-an, it can get crowded during the autumn leaf season.

THE SUIROKAKU

What is an aqueduct doing in one of Kyoto's most important Zen temples? The answer is that it's here by necessity. Called the Suirokaku, it was built in the Meiji era (in the rather ancient-looking style of a Roman raised aqueduct) as part of a canal system used to bring fresh water into Kyoto from Lake Biwa in neighbouring Shiga Prefecture.

TOP TIPS

- Give yourself at least an hour to visit just the Hōjō, then an extra 30 minutes or so for each sub-temple you plan on seeing.
- You can pay ¥600 to go inside the Sanmon and up a steep set of stairs for views from its balcony, but you get similar city views for no extra charge when visiting Ginkaku-ji or nearby Eikan-dō.
- For a break, stop by the complex's teahouse for *matcha* (green tea) and *wagashi* (traditional sweet) served in a tatami mat room with garden views.
- Come early in autumn to beat the worst of the crowds, as things get busy because of the seasonal colours.

TOP TIP
You can walk large chunks of
northwest Kyoto, but there are also
handy public transport options. The
Keifuku Randen tram has stops near
Kitano Tenman-gū, Ryōan-ji, Myōshin-
ji, Ninna-ji, and TŌEI Kyoto Studio Park,
while Kyoto City Bus 59 runs between
Kinkaku-ji, Ryōan-ji and Ninna-ji, and
also connects to Kawaramachi and
Sanjō in the downtown area.

Above: Kōzan-ji (p123); Right: Buddha statue, Ryōan-ji (p115)

DON'T MISS...

KINKAKU-JI
Visit one of Japan's most
iconic historic sites, aka the
Temple of the Golden Pavilion.
p120

RYŌAN-JI
Contemplate the cryptic Zen rock
garden, then try a subtle Kyoto
classic: *yudōfu* (simmered tofu).
p115

KITANO TENMAN-GŪ
Browse the monthly flea market
at this shrine known for its autumn
maples and spring plum blossoms.
p117

Northwest Kyoto

LEGENDARY TEMPLES AND QUIET MOMENTS

Out of the way, the northwest is home to Kinkaku-ji and Ryōan-ji, two of Kyoto's most famous temples. It also offers a peaceful retreat from the hustle and bustle of downtown Kyoto.

Northwest Kyoto's two famous temples provide a stark contrast, Kinkaku-ji coated in a decadent layer of gold and Ryōan-ji's rock garden a masterpiece of cryptic, understated Zen landscaping. What they have in common is fame and UNESCO World Heritage status that together adds up to large crowds. But try not to judge this part of Kyoto just by some of the touristy shops and restaurants nearby, or by the crush on the buses from Kyoto Station. That would be doing the northwest an injustice.

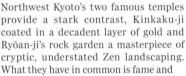

Walk a few minutes away from either Kinkaku-ji or Ryōan-ji and the crowds soon melt away, often replaced by opportunities to see moments of everyday Kyoto life, whether that's watching nursery school classes marauding in a local park or simply having a look through a local supermarket with no English signage in sight. Even though accommodation

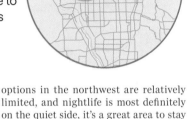

options in the northwest are relatively limited, and nightlife is most definitely on the quiet side, it's a great area to stay a night for anyone wanting to get a sense of normal, non-touristy Kyoto.

When Kinkaku-ji and Ryōan-ji have been checked off the to-do list, there are also plenty of less-heralded sights to explore in the northwest – the Nihonga art of Inshō Dōmoto, the under-visited gardens at Myōshin-ji, or a night at Ninna-ji for guest-only access to the early-morning prayers. You could even break from tradition with some family fun at the TŌEI Kyoto Studio theme park or hunt for bargains at Kitano Tenman-gū shrine's monthly flea market. Go even further off the beaten path and the northwest offers up the mountain valley village of Takao, which as a day trip brings the chance to see the Kyoto countryside and a collection of less-visited temples with rarely a bus tour in sight.

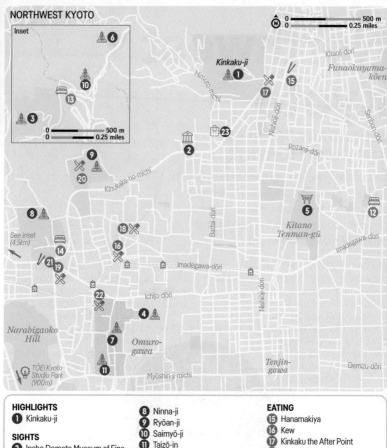

NORTHWEST KYOTO

Inset

Kinkaku-ji

Funaokayama-kōen

Kitaoji-dōri

Himuro-michi

Nishijin-dōri

Senbon-dōri

Rozanji-dōri

Kinukake-no-michi

Kitano Tenman-gū

Badai-dōri

Imadegawa-dōri

See inset
(4.5km)

Imadegawa-dōri

Nishiōji-dōri

Ichijo-dōri

Narabigaoko Hill

Omuro-gawa

Tenjin-gawa

Demizu-dōri

TŌEI Kyoto
Studio Park
(900m)

Myōshin-ji-michi

HIGHLIGHTS
1. Kinkaku-ji

SIGHTS
2. Insho Domoto Museum of Fine Arts
3. Jingo-ji
4. Keishun-in
5. Kitano Tenman-gū
6. Kōzan-ji
7. Myōshin-ji

8. Ninna-ji
9. Ryōan-ji
10. Saimyō-ji
11. Taizō-in

SLEEPING
12. Guesthouse Kioto
13. Momijiya Honkan Takao Sansou
14. Omuro Kaikan

EATING
15. Hanamakiya
16. Kew
17. Kinkaku the After Point
18. Okonomiyaki Katsu
19. Sanowa
20. Seigen-in
21. Soba Samon
22. Wonder Café

SHOPPING
23. Gallery Gado

 EATING IN NORTHWEST KYOTO: OUR PICKS

Hanamakiya The special here is *nishin* soba (buckwheat noodles topped with dried herring), although they also do *donburi* (dishes served over rice). *11.30am-5pm Fri-Wed* ¥

Seigen-in Within Ryōan-ji Temple, this tatami-mat restaurant serves *yudōfu*, a silky tofu simmered with vegetables and herbs. *11am-3pm Fri-Tue* ¥

Soba Samon A soba specialist near Ninna-ji's Niōmon gate, with options including soba in curry sauce or topped with tempura. *11am-2.30pm* ¥

Okonomiyaki Katsu Local's haunt specialising in *okonomiyaki* – a kind of savoury pancake that you cook at your own griddle table. *11.30am-1.30pm & 6-9pm Sat-Wed, 6-9pm Fri* ¥¥

Ryōan-ji

TEA CEREMONY INSIGHTS

Rie Kuranaka runs Koto (teaceremony-kyoto.com), which offers group and private tea ceremony experiences in English near Kinkaku-ji.

Tea ceremonies are full of subtle details, from the way we handle the utensils and serve the tea to the way a guest accepts and appreciates the teacup.

If you look closely, you'll see the cups we use have designs to match the time of year, but we also use deeper cups in winter to retain warmth and shallower ones in summer to help the tea cool.

The *wagashi* (traditional Japanese sweets) served with the tea are also seasonal, as is the design of the kimono we wear when performing a ceremony – although the latter is always simple and understated, so as not to distract from the beauty of the cups.

The Riddle of Ryōan-ji

Contemplate Kyoto's Most Enigmatic Garden

Originally the private villa of a local lord, **Ryōan-ji** (龍安寺) was repurposed as a Zen temple in 1450. Now with UNESCO World Heritage status, it's one of Kyoto's most recognisable sights, largely thanks to its small rock garden, which features a cryptic arrangement of 15 rocks on a rectangular patch of raked gravel.

Because it's so small, Ryōan-ji does leave mixed impressions. You could be done here in a blink of an eye, wondering why you didn't spend the admission on a good coffee instead, but sit down on the main hall's wood-deck viewing area to ponder the garden's meaning and Ryōan-ji comes into its own. That's partly because it was designed to function as a *koan,* or Zen riddle. From the wood deck, it's only possible to see 14 of the rocks from any given angle. Only those who have reached a state of enlightenment are said to be able to see all 15 – a number that represents completeness in Japanese Buddhism. The rest of us are reminded that our inability to see everything reflects our own human imperfection.

This walk combines two of Kyoto's most famous temples with a few roads less travelled, and will take roughly three hours, including time at each stop.

It begins at one of these iconic temples, ❶ **Kinkaku-ji** (p120), a three-storey gilded pavilion set in the middle of a landscaped pond garden.

After Kinkaku-ji, things briefly get arty. Walk five minutes southwest along Kinukake-no-michi street and you'll find wood-block print specialist ❷ **Gallery Gado**, then five minutes later comes ❸ **Inshō Dōmoto Museum of Fine Arts**, which is dedicated to the work of multi-genre, Kyoto-born artist Inshō Dōmoto.

Keep following the same road for 10 more minutes and you'll be at ❹ **Ryōan-ji** (p115). Originally a private villa with garden, this UNESCO World Heritage site became a Zen temple in 1450. There are several features, but it's the Zen rock garden that steals the

show – a small rectangle of raked gravel with an arrangement of rocks that some say represents a tigress leading her cubs across a river. You could also stop here for a *yudōfu* (simmered tofu) lunch at the temple's restaurant, ❺ **Seigen-in** (p114).

When you are ready, walk another five minutes southwest on Kinukake-no-michi and you'll get to ❻ **Ninna-ji** (p119). On a quick stroll around the grounds, you'll see a five-storey pagoda and a cherry blossom grove that blooms in spring. For a fee, there's also the Goten area with its near-palatial abbot's residence and landscaped garden.

Finally, from Ninna-ji's Niōmon Gate, wander southeast down route 101 to the ❼ **Myōshin-ji** (p122) temple complex. Most of the sub-temples in this peaceful enclave are off-limits, but among those open to the public ❽ **Taizō-in** (p122) is worth the admission fee for its gardens: one dry-landscaped and the other a small pond-stroll garden.

Momiji-en, Kitano Tenman-gū

Then there's the meaning of the design itself – something generations of academics have been unable to agree upon. The clustered placement of the rocks might be a depiction of a tigress leading her cubs across a stream, although other theories suggest they form a map of Chinese mountains or monasteries. To cap that, nobody knows for certain who designed the garden in the first place. Some people argue this is the work of legendary painter and landscape artist Sōami, who has been credited with the garden at another UNESCO World Heritage Site, Ginkaku-ji (p104). However, there is no conclusive proof. Throwing a spanner in the works is an unknown name researchers found carved into the base of one of the rocks.

Contemplation over, there is still a little more of Ryōan-ji to explore, with other garden features behind the main hall, a large pond dotted with islets, and a good lunch spot at **Seigen-in** (p114): with tatami flooring overlooking another traditional garden, it serves the Kyoto speciality of *yudōfu*, a silky simmered tofu.

Blossoms & Bargains
Kitano Tenman-gū's Market and Seasonal Blooms

Kitano Tenman-gū (北野天満宮), a shrine just a short walk from Kitano Hakubaichō Station on the eastern end of the Randen tram line, was built in 947 to honour the great scholar Sugawara no Michizane. Prayed to today at some 12,000

YUDŌFU

The prospect of eating plain tofu might sound unappealing, but give *yudōfu* (湯豆腐) a chance.

It's a Kyoto culinary classic. With its roots in plant-based Buddhist cuisine, in its simplest form *yudōfu* features blocks of silky *momen* tofu simmered in water with kelp, then accompanied with a bowl of rice and perhaps pickles, plus a *ponzu* (soy and citrus) dipping sauce. At Seigen-in in Ryōan-ji (p115), they also add a few greens to the pot, while in areas closely associated with *yudōfu,* such as Arashiyama (p124) and the streets around Nanzen-ji (p110), you also find restaurants serving it alongside multiple small, in-season dishes as part of a broader *kaiseki ryōri* course.

shrines nationwide, Michizane is worshipped as a god of agriculture, honesty, performing arts and, most importantly, academics. That latter part of Michizane's godly portfolio is why a steady stream of students (and parents) pass under Kitano Tenman-gū's towering *torii* gateways hoping for a little divine assistance with exams.

For travellers, however, there are many other reasons to give this sprawling shrine an hour or two. Firstly, there's the **Tenjin-san** flea market, held on the 25th of every month, which sees close to 1000 stalls fill the grounds and surrounding streets, selling antiques, crafts, food and all sorts else. Then there are seasonal highlights, such as the shrine's plum blossoms in spring and the fiery autumn maples in the **Momiji-en** garden.

Step into the Edo Era

Explore a Samurai-Period Theme Park

To walk into **TŌEI Kyoto Studio Park** (東映太秦映画村) is to enter a world of Edo-themed kitsch. More casually known as Eigamura, or movie village, this small theme park near Uzumasa Station is run by a film studio that, among other things, produces many of Japan's period dramas – movies and daytime TV series featuring brooding samurai and agile ninja.

The walk from the ticket booth into the theme park actually takes you by a few active movie lots. Then, once inside, things may not be as slick as Disney, but there's a good lineup of attractions well-geared to younger kids. That includes a ninja mystery house and indoor maze, as well as an obstacle course undertaken with a toy sword in hand. There's also a haunted house that genuinely could terrify kids, and an area called 'Escape the Castle' where you contort yourself through a succession of laser beam traps. To cap all that, there are also ninja shows, samurai costumes for rental and, if you come on a weekend, samurai-sword-fighting lessons.

One tip: if you are going for a few hours and plan to try all six of the paid attractions, it's cheaper to buy the ¥3900 day pass, rather than opting for the ¥2400 admission and then paying ¥500 to ¥600 extra for each attraction. It's also a cheaper to bring in a snack or two, instead of paying over the odds for the on-site restaurants.

DRINKING IN NORTHWEST KYOTO: CAFES & BARS

Kew Sleekly stylish cafe between Ryōan-ji and Myōshin-ji, known for its cream-filled doughnuts and moreish cheesecake. Reserve online to eat in. *11am-6pm Wed, Thu, Sat & Sun*

Kinkaku the After Point Casual spot near Kinkaku-ji for local craft beers, Japanese whiskies and well-made pastas – vegan options included. *11am-5pm Thu-Tue*

Sanowa Just southeast of Ninna-ji, Sanowa serves coffee and traditional Kyoto teas, plus desserts like *matcha* roll cake and *hōjicha* (roasted green tea) chiffon cake. *11am-6pm*

Wonder Café Full of retro toys and bric-a-brac, this eccentric cafe north of Myōshin-ji feels like a 1950s throwback. *11am-8pm Wed-Mon*

Pagoda, Ninna-ji

A Night at Ninna-ji

Stay at a UNESCO-Designated Temple

The third temple in northwest Kyoto with UNESCO World Heritage status, **Ninna-ji** is known for its five-storey pagoda, spring cherry blossoms and a complex called the Goten – a near palatial collection of buildings (plus garden) joined by covered walkways that was originally built as the abbot's residence. You can also stay here, in what's called a *shukubō* (temple lodging).

The accommodation – Omuro Kaikan (p123) – is just a simple, private tatami-mat room with a futon and access to shared toilets and small public bath, but it comes with an invitation to early morning prayers in the Kondō (main hall), an area usually off limits to the general public.

As candles flicker in the Kondō's gloom, you'll hear monks reciting sutras with a hypnotic, droning chant, before a senior monk delivers a brief sermon in Japanese. Outside, you'll probably pass more groups of robed monks reciting prayers in front of other temple buildings. That's then followed by breakfast back at the lodging – a plant-based meal centred on *yudōfu* (simmered tofu). One more bonus: guests get a free ticket to the Goten.

Scan this QR code for prices and opening hours.

TOP EXPERIENCE

Kinkaku-ji

With its gilded facade and positioning behind a traditionally landscaped garden whose pond catches its golden reflection, Kinkaku-ji (金閣寺) has become one of Japan's most recognisable sights. While that and its UNESCO World Heritage status can add up to crowds, this is one place you shouldn't miss: it's a must-see.

DID YOU KNOW?

Kinkaku-ji is one of 17 sites in Kyoto with UNESCO World Heritage status: all are jointly listed as the Historic Monuments of Ancient Kyoto.

The Golden Wow Factor

A visit to Kinkaku-ji doesn't take long to warm up. A minute after heading through the entrance, the gravel pathway opens up to one of the defining images of Kyoto: a golden pavilion seen across a pond that's designed to catch the pavilion's reflection.

Though there is nothing else quite like Kinkaku-ji in Japan, the temple's creation does follow a familiar story: originally it was part of the villa of 14th-century shogun Ashikaga Yoshimitsu, who requested its conversion into a Zen temple upon his death. Its official name, Rokuon-ji, was taken from part of Yoshimitsu's posthumous Buddhist name. Kinkaku refers only to the golden pavilion itself, with -ji (temple) added to create the temple's familiar name: the Temple of the Golden Pavilion.

The Golden Rebuild

In 1950, a novice monk called Hayashi Yōken sent shockwaves across Japan, when in the early hours of a summer night, he burned the Golden Pavilion to the ground. Despite being in financial ruin after WWII, the country embarked on a meticulous rebuild of its most iconic temple – a task completed in 1955. As for Yōken, he fled to a nearby hill and unsuccessfully attempted suicide before being caught by police. Just as the new Kinkaku-ji was unveiled, Yōken was given an early release on mental health grounds. He would die a year later from tuberculosis, although an embellished version of his story would be the focus of Yukio Mishima's novel, *The Temple of the Golden Pavilion*.

A Blend of Styles

The 1950s rebuild is loyal to the original pavilion, with each floor of the three-storey building using a different architectural style. The unadorned 1st floor, called the Hosui-in, uses *shinden-zukuri*, a style employed in 11th-century aristocrats' villas. The 2nd and 3rd floors are covered in pure gold leaf: the 2nd in a style called *buke-zukuri,* which is associated with warrior aristocrats, and the 3rd employing the style of Chinese Zen temples.

Beyond the Kinkaku

When you've had that initial view of the Kinkaku, the path partially loops behind the pavilion, offering up closer views of the shingled roof (made with 100,000 thin strips of water-resistant cypress) and the gold phoenix capping the temple like a star on a decadent Christmas tree. The path then takes in various small features: a waterfall, tiny shrine, and at one point the Anmintaku pond, with a central, mossy islet upon which sits a small stone pagoda. As it has never run dry, people have traditionally prayed here for rain.

Finish with green tea and a traditional sweet at the teahouse near the end of the route through Kinkaku-ji's grounds. If that's booked out, another place right outside the exit serves ice cream and tea.

THE GOLD BILL

About a decade after the 1950s rebuild was complete, Kinkaku-ji's gold leaf began to peel off and its black lacquering started to degrade. By the 1980s, a major renovation was needed, which saw builders re-cover the Golden Pavilion with 200,000 sheets of extra-thick gold leaf, weighing in at a whopping 20kg. The cost at the time? ¥740 million, or US$5 million.

TOP TIPS

- Make sure you carry some cash (a sensible thing to do anywhere in Kyoto), as the ticket office and teahouse accept cash only.
- Not including any time you might spend at the teahouse, Kinkaku-ji only takes 20 to 30 minutes.
- To get more out of the journey here, afterwards walk over to the other major northwest sight, Ryōan-ji (p115), 15 to 20 minutes southwest along Kinukake-no-michi street.
- Or, if you want to explore even more of northwest Kyoto on foot, start here at Kinkaku-ji, then follow the three-hour walking tour on p116.

KITANO ODORI

Immediately east of Kitano Tenman-gū, **Kamishichiken** is one of Kyoto's five traditional geisha districts.

Although it's far less busy than the more famous Gion (p86), Kamishichiken does come alive in late March to early April for its annual **Kitano Odori** festival, when the *geiko* (the Kyoto term for geisha) and *maiko* (apprentice *geiko*) put on twice-daily public shows featuring plays, dances and other performing arts they've perfected in their roles as traditional entertainers.

While seeing a genuine *geiko/maiko* performance is ordinarily an extremely expensive (and highly exclusive) event, Kitano Odori tickets start from ¥6000. The tourist information office at Kyoto Station can help you get hold of some.

SERG ZASTAVKIN/SHUTTERSTOCK ©

Behind the Walls of Myōshin-ji

Visit Secret Temple Gardens

You could easily spend an hour or three pottering around the **Myōshin-ji** temple complex. Hidden behind walled pathways, there are 46 sub-temples, most off limits but nevertheless offering tantalising glimpses of pretty courtyards and temple eaves. Those that are open are an antidote to the mobs at more famous temples. **Keishun-in** in Myōshin-ji's northeast corner has gardens that mix azaleas, maple and pines, plus a tea room serving *matcha* and sweets. **Taizō-in** in the southwest has one of Japan's oldest water-ink paintings and a pretty pond garden with weeping cherry blossoms.

Then there's Myōshin-ji's main hall (the *hattō*) in the centre of the compound, where the ceiling is decorated with a 12m-wide Indian ink painting of a menacing dragon by legendary artist Kanō Tan'yū.

You'll need to sign up for one of Myōshin-ji's guided tours (myoshinji.or.jp/english) to see that, and it's also worth checking its website for news about *zazen* meditation and calligraphy sessions. Since COVID-19 these are for large groups only, but that may have changed by the time you read this.

MORE KANŌ ART

Kanō Tan'yū also painted some of the screen doors on display at **Nanzen-ji** (p110) in Northern Higashiyama. The most famous is a screen of tigers playing in a bamboo grove.

Taizō-in

Guesthouse Kioto ¥
Private tatami rooms and a female-only dorm spread across two charming old townhouses near Kitano Tenman-gū. Has rental bikes and shared bathrooms. Breakfast is extra.

Momijiya Honkan Takao Sansou ¥¥¥
Traditional ryokan in Takao, with *kaiseki ryōri* dinners, public hot spring baths, and tatami mat rooms that come with a choice of futon or bed.

Omuro Kaikan ¥¥
No-frills lodgings in Ninna-ji Temple, with tatami-mat rooms, shared bathrooms, and guest-only access to morning temple rituals.

A Taste of Rural Kyoto

Spend a Day in Takao

In a mountain valley a 20-minute bus ride northwest of Ryōan-ji, a day in and around the village of **Takao** (高雄) is a lovely way to get a taste of Kyoto's natural side and slowly take in a collection of less-visited temples – all are especially beautiful when engulfed by autumn foliage in November.

Start with **Kōzan-ji** (高山寺), a UNESCO World Heritage Site spread over a cedar-clad hillside that's home to Japan's oldest tea field. It's also the home of what some argue is the first manga – a replica of this 12th-century scroll of animal images is on display in the temple's pretty Sekisui-in hall.

Afterwards, take the steep and winding walk into central Takao for two more temples. **Saimyō-ji** (西明寺), which is entered via a vermilion bridge over a river, has finely crafted wooden statues in its main hall and mossy stupas in its garden.

At **Jingo-ji** (神護寺), some visitors toss small *yaku-yoke* ceramic plates into the valley below to fend off bad luck. There are also a few simple restaurants nearby serving noodles and snacks, if you haven't packed food.

For a quiet night out of the city, you could even stay at traditional ryokan inn like Momijiya Honkan Takao Sansou (p123). Just book dinner too, as Takao has very little happening after dark. To get there, a JR Bus runs between Kyoto Station (bus stop 3) and Taganoo (60 minutes), which is a few minutes on foot from Kōzan-ji. On route, it stops at Ryōan-ji, Myōshin-ji and other points in northwest Kyoto. City Bus 8 also connects Takao (Takao or Taganoo stops) with Shijō Karasuma in downtown Kyoto.

Arashiyama & Sagano

GATEWAY TO KYOTO'S WESTERN MOUNTAINS

Arashiyama and Sagano have long been favoured as areas to escape to – with hillside temples, river boats to mess around in, gigantic culms of bamboo stroll beneath and tofu to taste.

From the earliest days of Kyoto, emperors and courtiers would sojourn to Arashiyama (嵐山, 'Storm Mountain'), a famed beauty spot in the city's far-western reaches. Painted with pink cherry blossoms or flame-red autumn maples, Arashiyama changes spectacularly with the seasons, a feat that inspired generations of poets, artists and aesthetes to wax lyrical on its natural good looks. An arena of forested mountains parts gracefully to reveal the rushing waters of the Ōi-gawa, a scene harmonised by the 155m-long 'Moon-Crossing Bridge' (Togetsu-kyō), Arashiyama's centre-piece. No wonder emperors had a habit of building temples and retirement villas in the vicinity, where they could flee the political intrigues of the capital and luxuriate in simpler pleasures: the turning of the seasons, or the moon crossing the clear night sky.

Nowadays, you can expect a relentless whirl of tourists, especially in Arashiyama's famous bamboo grove and along the main drag outside Tenryū-ji with its snack stalls and muscular rickshaw touts. But all you need to do is head northwards into Sagano (嵯峨野) and you'll soon leave the scrum behind – free to find your way along quiet rural lanes where sleepy temples grace the maple-strewn slopes, and antique teahouses beckon with crackling *irori* (hearths) and tasty meals.

Many travellers venture deeper into the mountains, embarking on scenic jaunts by sightseeing train and boat along the tree-studded Hozu-gawa valley. You could also cross Togetsu-kyō and hop on a train heading south to check out the imperial garden villa of Katsura Rikyū and the famous moss gardens of Saihō-ji, a World Heritage-listed Zen temple.

If you're considering staying in Arashiyama, there are some luxurious riverside ryokan perfect for a culture-rich splurge, and you'll have the area to yourself come evening. It's charming for a night or two, if a bit far from central Kyoto (half an hour by train) to make it a useful base.

DON'T MISS...

TENRYŪ-JI
Contemplate the 700-year-old landscape garden at Arashiyama's 14th-century Zen temple.
p134

ŌKŌCHI SANSŌ
Take in the views from from the hillside home and gorgeous garden of a silent movie star.
p127

SAIHŌ-JI
Rebalance your life energy in a whisper-quiet Zen temple with a famous moss garden.
p132

KATSURA RIKYŪ
Play at being royalty at this sublime garden villa built by an imperial prince.
p131

ARASHIYAMA & SAGANO

ANDRESGARCIAM/GETTY IMAGES ©

ellers short on time, aim to
n the area early – Tenryū-ji
t 8:30am. At a clip, you can
through Arashiyama's main
ons in half a day, then get in
nd zip across to Northwest
s big ticket sights, such as
nkaku-ji and Ryōan-ji.

Left: Sagano Romantic Train (p129); Above: Daijokaku, Ōkōchi Sansō (p127)

ARASHIYAMA BAMBOO GROVE

Walk beneath swaying spires of
bamboo in Arashiyama's most
ethereal natural attraction.
p127

YUDŌFU SAGANO

Treat yourself to a beancurd
banquet at this Zen-like
restaurant famous for tofu.
p129

SAGANO ROMANTIC TRAIN

Trundle through the river
valley on an old logging
railway.
p129

UKYŌ-KU

Osawa-no-ike

Enlargement

Torokko Saga

JR Saga-Arashiyama

Kurumazaki-jinja

Rokuōin

Hozu-gawa River Trip (15km)

Okura-ike

Torokko Arashiyama

Bamboo Grove

1 *Tenryū-ji*

Randen Saga

Kameyama-kōen

Arashiyama Monkey Park Iwatayama

Hozu-gawa

See Enlargement

Arashiyama

Sanjō-dōri

Katsura-gawa

Nakanoshima-kōen

Arashiyama

Saihō-ji (1.8km); Katsura Rikyū (4.2km)

200 m

HIGHLIGHTS
1 Tenryū-ji

SIGHTS
2 Adashino Nenbutsu-ji
3 Arashiyama Bamboo Grove
4 Arashiyama Monkey Park
5 Daikaku-ji
6 Fukuda Art Museum
7 Giō-ji
8 Jōjakkō-ji
9 Kameyama-kōen
10 Nison-in
11 Ōkōchi Sansō
12 Otagi Nenbutsu-ji
13 Seiryō-ji
14 Takiguchi-dera
15 Togetsu-kyō

ACTIVITIES
16 Hankyu Rental Cycle Arashiyama
17 Sagano Romantic Train

SLEEPING
18 Arashiyama Benkei
19 Arashiyama House Mama
20 Hoshinoya Kyoto
21 Suiran

EATING
22 Arashiyama Yoshimura
23 Cafe Dining Sera
see **6** Fukuda Museum Cafe
24 Hatoya Ryoyousha
25 Hiranoya
26 INITY
27 Kitcho Arashiyama
28 Kotoimo Honpo
29 MUKU
30 Muni Alain Ducasse
31 Nomura
32 Okina
see **1** Shigetsu
33 Shoraian
34 Yosiya
35 Yudōfu Sagano

DRINKING & NIGHTLIFE
see **6** % Arabica
36 Bread, Espresso and Arashiyama Garden
37 Muni La Terrasse
38 Sagano-yu

SHOPPING
39 Saga Tofu Morika
40 Tsuruya Kotobuki

DRINKING IN ARASHIYAMA & SAGANO: COFFEE SPOTS

% Arabica The second outpost of a craft-coffee chain, it's easily the most popular cafe in Arashiyama, so expect to queue. Killer river views. *9am-6pm*

Sagano-yu Taking photos is a no-no at this cafe in a former bathhouse, which is a pity because the interiors are really something. Coffee, *matcha* and simple meals. *11am-6pm*

Muni La Terrasse Fab river views at smart-casual cafe serving upmarket French patisserie. Pricier than % Arabica next door, but you won't have to queue. *7.30-10am & 11.30-4pm*

Bread, Espresso and Arashiyama Garden Delightful cafe in a 200-year-old farmhouse with Japanese-style tables, excellent coffee and brunch fare. *8am-6pm*

Moon Crosses the Bridge
Riverside Scenery at Togetsu-kyō

Arashiyama's iconic centrepiece is **Togetsu-kyō** (Moon-Crossing Bridge), so called by a 13th-century emperor who, while indulging in a spot of *tsukimi* (the quintessential Arashiyama pastime of moon-viewing) marvelled at how the moon in the night sky appeared to cross the low-slung wooden structure. A bridge has spanned the Ōi-gawa (which becomes the Katsura-gawa as it flows through Arashiyama) hereabouts since 836; the present 1934 structure is mostly concrete but clad in cypress wood for period effect. A prime photo spot is on the north shore outside the cafe % Arabica (ideally a selfie with designer latte in hand), or from a rowboat, which you can rent upstream from the bridge.

Beneath the Bamboo
Towering Stalks and Teeming Crowds

Though barely 200m long, there is something otherworldly about the **Arashiyama Bamboo Grove**, whether that's the great height and uniformity of the slender bamboo culms or the soft, eerie light filtering through them. Good luck getting those otherworldly vibes at peak times, though, as you join the crush of nations jostling for space at one of Kyoto's most hyped Instagram spots. Fortunately, there's nothing to stop you arriving at dawn or dusk to beat the crowds. You'll also find quiet (albeit smaller) bamboo groves in the nearby temple grounds of Takiguchi-dera and Adashino Nenbutsu-ji. Across town, the hillside shrine complex of Fushimi Inari-Taisha (p44) is another bamboo-viewing hot spot.

Samurai's Strolling Garden
Movie Star Mansion in the Hills

Like a Kyoto take on a Hollywood Hills mansion, the 1930s villa **Ōkōchi Sansō** was built by the late Ōkōchi Denjirō, a film star known for playing a sword-swinging samurai in *jidaigeki* (period dramas). Back then Kyoto was like the Hollywood of Japan's *jidaigeki* genre, producing hundreds of films a year. Set against the steep slope of Ogura-san, it's the gardens here that are the real star, meticulously crafted by Ōkōchi over 30 years, and lovingly maintained since his death in 1962.

PERFECT DAY IN ARASHIYAMA

Ayako Takemoto, Deputy Director of Fukuda Art Museum, @fukuda_art_museum

For the best views of nature I go to Kameyama-kōen and climb to the observation deck – it's a 10-minute walk up and always free of crowds.

My favourite place for snacks is Nomura. I love their warabi-mochi, a sweet, jelly-like dessert made from a type of fern. Then I'll wander over to sleepy Daikaku-ji. With its views of lakes, mountains and rice fields, it's like a scene from hundreds of years ago.

Next I'll shop for tofu made fresh that day at Saga Tofu Morika – you just simmer it in water infused with seaweed. Last but not least I'll have a coffee and sandwich at Fukuda Museum Cafe (p133) – we have Arashiyama's best outlook over Togetsu-kyō.

THE GUIDE

ARASHIYAMA & SAGANO

✕ EATING IN ARASHIYAMA & SAGANO: LUNCHTIME PICKS

Cafe Dining Sera	**INITY** Jamaican jerk	**Hiranoya** Round off a	**Arashiyama Yoshimura**
Homely hidden gem for tasty and affordable Japanese home-cooking, or go for a burger or steak. English menus available. *11am-4pm & 5-9pm Thu-Tue* ¥¥	chicken and rice in Arashiyama; Red Stripe beer and rum cocktails too. Find it next to the Arashiyama tram terminus. *11am-6pm Thu-Mon* ¥	Sagano temple safari with this time-warp Kyoto teahouse serving meal sets of *ayu* (sweetfish) over rice, miso soup and seasonal veggies. *11.30am-9pm* ¥	Enjoy tasty soba noodles and a million-dollar view over the Arashiyama mountains and Togetsu-kyō at this popular eatery. *11am-4pm Mon-Fri, to 5pm Sat-Sun* ¥

Jōjakkō-ji

A marked strolling route climbs up the crooked stepping-stone paths, teasing with new vistas at every turn. Up top you can gaze east towards Kyoto, or westwards to the green wall of Arashiyama's mountains – spot the tiny temple of Daihikaku Senkō-ji across the valley, the only visible speck of civilisation. The ticket price includes a bowl of *matcha* (powdered green tea) and a sweet, taken in the teahouse at the end of the walk. Look out for the open-air gallery showing stills of Ōkōchi Denjirō from some of his 200-plus movie roles. The entrance to Ōkōchi Sansō is just west of the Arashiyama Bamboo Grove.

On the Sagano Temple Trail

Hidden Gems and Hillside Retreats

You can spend a very pleasurable day in the area northwest of Saga-Arashiyama station simply by plotting a course between temples, which is particularly lovely during autumn foliage season when the whole area blazes amber and russet-gold.

Closest to the station, **Seiryō-ji** impresses with its grand scale and architecture, while over towards the mountains **Jōjakkō-ji** boasts lofty views, a garden of moss and azaleas, and a petite pagoda – spot the old straw sandals hanging from the temple's main gate, left as tribute by roving pilgrims. Close by **Nison-in** ('two deities temple'), dates back to the 9th century and houses a double bill of deities – two precious Kamakura-era Buddha statues side-by-side (Shaka on the right and Amida on the left), representing the beginning and end of life.

A little way north is is **Giō-ji**, which feels like a secret sanctuary with its perfectly formed moss garden. A former nunnery, the temple is named after a *shirabyōshi* (traditional dancer) called Giō, who committed herself here as a nun at age 21 after falling out of favour with her lover, a military leader of the late Heian period. **Takiguchi-dera**, another pint-sized temple opposite, has its own crowd-free bamboo grove.

Keep walking and you'll hit **Saga Toriimoto**, a charming heritage preservation zone of traditional lattice-fronted shops and thatched farmhouses. Here, **Adashino Nenbutsu-ji** is a temple with 8000 *nenbutsu* in the grounds – small stone statues honouring the souls of paupers who died without family to memorialise them. Their abandoned souls are remembered with candles each year in the Sentō Kuyō ceremony, held here on the evenings of 23 and 24 August. More moss-covered *nenbutsu* are on show at **Otagi Nenbutsu-ji**, many with humorous faces – these were mostly carved in the 1980s to rejuvenate the temple after it was devastated by a typhoon.

An outlier in the east, **Daikaku-ji** is a former imperial palace and a rare survivor from the Heian era. It retains a shapely Osawa pond, still revered as a spot for viewing the harvest moon. Temple halls have *fusuma-e* (screen door paintings) painted by artists of the prestigious Kanō school.

With is quiet lanes and light traffic, Sagano is perfect for laid-back cycling. You can get bikes for the day at **Hankyu Rental Cycle Arashiyama**, just outside Arashiyama Station on the Hankyu Line (south of Togetsu-kyō).

Rails Through the Valley
All Aboard the Love Train

Sit back and enjoy the views on this 25-minute jaunt along the high valley walls of the Hozu-gawa gorge. The **Sagano Romantic Train** trundles at a snail's pace, threading its way through forests and mountains and past heavy iron bridges, giving you ample time to enjoy the scenery through oversized windows. For a spot of mobile forest bathing, or for unimpeded landscape photos, book yourself on carriage 5, which is windowless and fully open to the elements.

The train departs from Saga-Torokko Station (just outside Saga-Arashiyama Station), or you can board at the subsequent stop of Torokko Arashiyama Station just past the bamboo forest. The final destination is Torokko Kameoka Station, from where you can take a bus to the Hozu-gawa River Boat Ride terminal and return by water. Alternatively, if you want to go back by train and you've had your fill of romance, walk to nearby Umahori Station and catch the regular fast service to Saga-Arashiyama.

During busy periods it's wise to book your Sagano Romantic Train tickets as soon as you arrive in Arashiyama; you can reserve a slot for later that day. Note that the train doesn't run in January or February.

SOY YOU THINK YOU KNOW TOFU

Tofu is culinary poetry in Kyoto, a city where time-honoured *tofu-ya-san* (tofu makers) are sought out by Michelin-starred chefs.

To make tofu, soybeans are soaked overnight in water, ground then boiled. The resulting soy milk then has a coagulating agent added to it, much like the cheese-making process.

Endlessly versatile, tofu can be boiled, baked, fried, steamed, frozen or eaten fresh.

In Arashiyama, *yudōfu* is a must-try. Traditionally a winter dish, cubes of tofu are simmered in water infused with *konbu* (seaweed), and served with a soy-based dipping sauce. Nutty, subtly sweet *Goma dōfu* is made with sesame seeds rather than soybeans, while *yuba* is a tasty tofu byproduct – the chewy skin that forms on the surface of simmering soy milk.

EATING IN ARASHIYAMA & SAGANO: TOFU TREATS

Yudōfu Sagano	Shigetsu Tofu stars	Saga Tofu Morika	Shoraian This elegant
Arashiyama's famous *yudōfu* (tofu simmered in a pot) is the centrepiece of tofu-themed lunch sets at this restaurant with a garden to rival Zen temples. *11am-5.30pm* ¥¥	at this vegetarian restaurant within the grounds of Tenryū-ji. The cuisine is *shōjin-ryōri*, the healthful fare of Buddhist monks. *11am-2pm* ¥¥	The best Kyoto restaurants buy their tofu fresh from this long-running shop just outside Seiryō-ji. *9am-5pm Thu-Tue* ¥	restaurant in a riverside villa serves *kaiseki* set menus with the emphasis firmly on tofu. Reserve on the restaurant's website. *11am-5pm Mon, Tue & Thu to 8pm Fri-Sun* ¥¥¥

Experience Arashiyama at its best on this 3km walk that weaves together intriguing temples and hidden gardens; allow at least two hours. After a short walk from Arashiyama Station, start at ❶ **Tenryū-ji** (p134) and take a moment to contemplate the 700-year-old pond garden. Can you spot the 'Dragon's Gate Waterfall' fashioned from weathered rocks? Exit the temple by the north gate and you'll pop directly into the ❷ **Arashiyama Bamboo Grove** (p127). Though barely 200m long, there is something magical about the eerie filtered light. Just past the bamboo you'll see the ticket booth for ❸ **Ōkōchi Sansō** (p127), a sublime hillside villa and garden built by an actor known for samurai films.

Take the lane north from Ōkōchi Sansō and after passing the lotus-filled pond of Ogura-ike you'll reach ❹ **Jōjakkō-ji** (p128), a forested temple that blazes ruby-red in autumn. Climb past the main halls and pagoda for panoramic vistas east towards central Kyoto.

Go straight from the front gate of Jōjakkō-ji and take the second left (north), and you'll soon arrive at ❺ **Nison-in** (p128; 'two deities temple'), so-called for its pair of wooden Buddha statues that represent the beginning and end of life. Keep going north past Nison-in and the next temple you'll reach is ❻ **Giō-ji** (p128). A former nunnery, this quiet sanctuary has a small but perfectly formed moss garden.

Continue along one of the loveliest lanes in Kyoto, past timber homes with gabled roofs, and after 1km you'll reach ❼ **Hiranoya** (p127), a teahouse that feels like it belongs to a different century. Relax over a lunch set featuring locally caught *ayu* (sweetfish). Climb up to the main road for buses into town, or find your own way back through the quiet lanes.

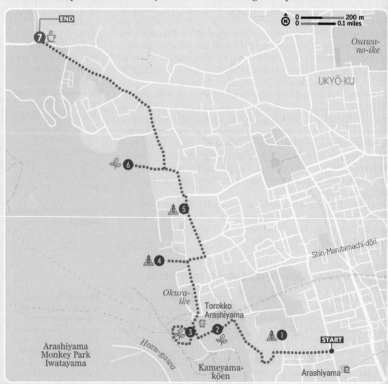

Katsura Rikyū

ALL HAIL THE HUMBLE TEAHOUSE

Classic Japanese *chashitsu* (teahouses), often found in stately landscape gardens like Katsura Rikyū (p131), might baffle you for just how poky, rough and rustic they appear.

Fashioned from mud and wood, and unadorned inside save for a flower arrangement or hanging scroll in the *tokonoma* (alcove), they embody an artistic vision that rejects grandiosity in favour of imperfection and impermanence.

Known as *wabi-sabi*, it's a philosophy that extends to the tools of the tea ceremony – misshapen clay cups are far more prized than precious porcelain. Teahouses and *sadō* (the way of tea) have had an outsized influence on modern Japanese art and aesthetics, from minimalism to the concept of *ma* (negative space).

Go With the Flow

Cruising the Hozu-gawa

Many a temple in Kyoto was built using felled trees floated down the frothing waters of the Hozu-gawa. In 1895, tourist boats took to the water and have been making the trip ever since.

It takes from 90 minutes to two hours, depending on water levels, to float the 16km to Arashiyama, helped along by rapids, oars, bamboo poles and well-honed banter from the avuncular four-person crew. The going is mostly slow and steady save for a few exciting stretches of white water, bumps and splashes. En route you might catch sight of deer and monkeys, and you're guaranteed to spot amusingly shaped rocks, which helps to distract from the hard bench seats. Boats are heated in winter and covered when it rains. You can take your own snacks and drinks on board. The departure terminal for the **Hozu-gawa River Trip** is a 10-minute walk from Kameoka Station, or a 15-minute bus ride from Torokko Kameoka Station for those taking the Sagano Romantic Train.

Imperial Garden Party

Play as a Royal Reveller

Prince Toshitada (1619–62) conceived the garden estate of **Katsura Rikyū** as a place to entertain his artist friends, which for folks of the early Edo period meant moon-viewing, tea ceremony, boat rides and the appreciation of nature and art. The garden's subtle features are a delight: paths narrow to make them appear longer; 'screen pines' block views to orchestrate a gradual reveal of the garden's highlights; and famous landscapes are

REGAL RESIDENCES OF KYOTO

Katsura Rikyū is one of several sightseeing spots operated by the Imperial Household Agency. This prized portfolio includes **Kyoto Imperial Palace** (p75), **Sentō Imperial Palace** (p75) and **Shūgaku-in Rikyū Imperial Villa** (p109).

LITERARY ARASHIYAMA

Not just renowned for its poetic beauty, Arashiyama also holds a place in the annals of classical Japanese literature.

Nonmiya-jinja, a small shrine just outside the bamboo grove, features heavily in Japan's most famous novel (and possibly the world's first), *The Tale of Genji*, written in the 11th century.

A brief stroll away is the former hermitage of the poet Mukai Kyorai, chief disciple of the haiku master Bashō, who visited the spot on three occasions. Called **Rakushisha** ('Hut of the Fallen Persimmons'), legend has it that Kyorai called it thus after waking one morning to discover a storm had blown down all the persimmons from the trees on his property.

Snow monkeys, Arashiyama Monkey Park

rendered in miniature, such as the 'bridge to heaven' sandbar of Amanohashidate in northern Kyoto prefecture. A quartet of teahouses reflects the rustic *wabi-sabi* fashion of the time, with humble *irori* (hearths) and framed views of neighbouring rice fields. The main villa buildings are considered masterpieces of Japanese architecture, admired in the recent past by such luminaries as Le Corbusier and Bruno Taut.

About 5km southeast of Arashiyama, Katsura Rikyū is easily reached by bus or train – Katsura Station on the Hankyū line is a 10-minute walk away. Visits are by guided tour only, with several slots in English each day, and you should pre-book through the Imperial Household Agency (sankan.kunaicho.go.jp), though they might have a few same-day tickets on the door. Passports are required to be shown on entry, with no children permitted under 12 years old.

Zen and the Art of Moss Maintenance
Seeking Balance in Saihō-ji

Exclusive even by Kyoto standards, **Saihō-ji**, otherwise known as Kokedera ('Moss Temple'), only opens for two hours each

EATING IN ARASHIYAMA & SAGANO: FINE DINING

Kitcho Arashiyama
Splurge on the meal of a lifetime at this legendary Kyoto *ryōtei*. Dishes resemble works of art, and are served in elegant private rooms. 11.30am-3pm & 5-9.30pm ¥¥¥

Okina Enjoy first-rate Kyoto cuisine, including local tofu, at this easygoing restaurant with a Michelin star. Lunch sets are great value. 11.30am-2pm & 5-8pm Thu-Tue ¥¥¥

MUKU On the south side of Togetsu-kyō, this contemporary hotel restaurant has set menus that showcase *dashi*, the stock fundamental to Japanese cuisine. 7.30am-3pm ¥¥¥

Muni Alain Ducasse The superstar French chef sources ingredients from all over Japan for this luxe restaurant with romantic views of the Hozu-gawa. 5.30-9pm ¥¥¥

day (10am to noon), costs ¥4000 to enter, and for decades you could only apply to visit by postcard...thankfully now there's an online form (intosaihoji.com/en/nichinichi/). It's worth it, however, not just because the famous moss garden is a haven of fairy-tale beauty, but also because the strict visitor limits are a boon to truly appreciating the atmosphere of a Zen temple. Visits begin by silently copying a sutra on paper in the *hondō* (main hall), a spiritual exercise that preps you to better contemplate the garden, said to contain over 100 different types of moss, which thrive in Kyoto's humid climate. A famous *karesansui* (dry landscape garden) overlooks the moss garden but is closed to visitors. Both were created in 1339 by Zen master Musō Soseki, the founding abbot and garden guru of Tenryū-ji (p134).

Saihō-ji is 15 minutes by bus from central Arashiyama – buses stop at the Kokedera Suzumusidera terminal right outside the temple.

Edo-Era Art by the River
Painted Screens and Hanging Scrolls

Opened in 2019, the impressively designed **Fukuda Art Museum** has two galleries displaying a world-class collection of *byōbu* (decorative folding screens) and *kakejiku* (hanging scroll paintings), together with regularly changing exhibitions on art from the Edo period to the present day.

The museum cafe, reserved for gallery visitors, offers charming views of Togetsu-kyō through floor-to-ceiling windows.

A Barrel of Monkeys
Mingle with Arashiyama's Macaques

Monkey-human relations are put to the test at the **Arashiyama Monkey Park**, a hillside nature reserve where visitors can get up close and personal with 100 or so snow monkeys (aka Japanese macaques), and even feed them from inside the safety of a hut. It's a sweaty slog up steep Iwatayama to reach the simians, but you'll be rewarded with a fine view for your efforts. The park entrance is just upstream from the southern end of Togetsu-kyō.

ENLIGHTENED EATING

Emerging from the need for Buddhist abbots to serve appropriate meals to high-ranking visitors, *shōjin-ryōri* （精進料理） is a traditional form of vegetarian cuisine that originated in monasteries and temples.

Shōjin means devotion or diligence, emphasising a disciplined and mindful approach to eating, rooted in the Buddhist principles of nonviolence.

Great care is taken over the meal's preparation, which excludes meat, fish and animal products in favour of tofu, *fu* (wheat gluten) and seasonal vegetables.

Flavours and seasonings are light but not bland, the goal being to achieve balance and spiritual alignment.

EATING IN ARASHIYAMA & SAGANO: STREET SNACKS

Kotoimo Honpo	**Yosiya**	**Tsuruya Kotobuki**	**Hatoya Ryoyousha**
Seek out this dessert shack for sticky *dango* – rice dumpling skewers in a sweet soy sauce glaze. It's just inside the path to the bamboo grove. *9.30am-6pm* ¥	Make a pit stop at this stall along the main Arashiyama drag for deep-fried skewers of *surimi* (fish paste) with cheese wrapped in *yuba* (tofu skin). *11am-5.30pm* ¥	Long-running sweet shop known for elegant *sakura mochi* – glutinous rice cakes wrapped in preserved cherry-blossom leaves. *9am-5pm* ¥	A little out of the way, but worth the walk for to-die-for *matcha* desserts including ice cream made from high-grade green tea. *11am-5pm Mon-Fri, from 10am Sat & Sun* ¥

Scan for monthly temple events and to book Shigetsu, the on-site vegetarian restaurant.

TOP EXPERIENCE

Tenryū-ji

A fitting centrepiece for beautiful Arashiyama, the Zen temple complex of Tenryū-ji (天龍寺) is a UNESCO World Heritage site and boasts one of the city's oldest and most celebrated landscape gardens. A morning stroll here, whether amid spring peach blossoms or ruby-red autumn maples, is an experience not to be missed.

DON'T MISS

Sōgenchi Teien

Dragon's Gate Waterfall

Hōjō (abbot's quarters)

Hattō (lecture hall)

Shigetsu Restaurant

Appease the Dragon

Established in 1339 and belonging to the Rinzai sect of Zen Buddhism, Tenryū-ji is one of Kyoto's leading Zen temples. Sprawled across a great swathe of Arashiyama, it boasted 150 sub-temples at its peak, though most of its lands were lost during the religious reforms of the Meiji era. Tenryū-ji was founded by Ashikaga Takauji, a warlord embroiled in the power struggles of Japan's Warring States period. In order to become shōgun, Takauji turned on his former ally, Emperor Go-Daigo. When Go-Daigo died a few years later, Takauji's brother had a vision of the late emperor as a golden dragon who had to be appeased. And so Tenryū-ji ('Temple of the Heavenly Dragon') was built to soothe the emperor's vengeful spirit.

Borrowed Beauty

Takauji appointed as founding abbot the Zen master Musō Soseki, a polymath who counted garden design among his talents, along with poetry and calligraphy. Though the temple buildings are newer constructions, **Sōgenchi Teien** (pictured left), Soseki's pond landscape garden, remains faithful to his 700-year-old design. One of Japan's first gardens to employ the technique of *shakkei* (borrowed scenery), Sōgenchi Teien blends the backdrop of Mount Kamayama into a living composition that centres on a pond sculpted to resemble the *kanji* (Chinese character) for heart. Take a moment to contemplate the garden view. Look for the **Dragon's Gate Waterfall** of weathered rocks beyond the water, and the 'carp stone' depicting a fish transforming into a dragon. It's said that if a koi carp can climb the mountain stream it will become a dragon, symbolising the attaining of enlightenment.

Grand Designs

Lost to fire no fewer than eight times over the centuries, Tenryu-ji's halls and constructions date mostly to the early 20th century. An extra ticket is needed to enter the main halls, threaded through the complex by ornate covered walkways. The **hōjō** (abbot's quarters) is a huge tatami space with sliding doors that frame the living canvas of Sōgenchi Teien. An enormous *fusuma-e* (sliding door painting) of a cloud dragon glares outwards towards the garden from the rear wall. Another giant beastie, known as the 'all-seeing dragon', looks down from the ceiling of the **hattō** (lecture hall), its eyes following you around the room. Viewable on weekends and public holidays, it was painted in 1997 to mark the 650th anniversary of Musō Soseki death.

A Meatless Feast

Tenryu-ji is one of a handful of Zen Buddhist temples in Kyoto with its own on-site restaurant. At **Shigetsu**, diners remove shoes and sit at low tables on tatami mats to savour healthful, meat-free repasts of *shōjin-ryōri,* the elegant cuisine traditionally served to important temple visitors – monks subsisted on much simpler fare. Food is served between 11am and 3pm. Book in advance via Tenryu-ji's website.

TENRYŪ-JI'S TREASURE SHIPS

To finance such an ambitious temple complex, Tenryu-ji's founding abbot Musō Soseki persuaded his backers to fund a trading mission to China. Two ships were sent across the East China Sea and came back loaded with religious and cultural goods. The resulting profits helped establish Tenryū-ji as the first-ranked temple in Kyoto's 'Five Mountains' system, a title it holds to this day.

TOP TIPS

- To skip the worst of the crowds, aim to arrive bang on 8.30am when Tenryū-ji opens.
- The north gate at the rear of the complex connects directly with Arashiyama's famous bamboo grove.
- On the second Sunday of the month at 9am (except February, July and August) Tenryu-ji hosts a free *zazen* meditation session, with no booking required.
- Though most sub-temples are closed to the public, take time to admire their exquisite front gardens.

Day Trips
from Kyoto

Choose your own adventure amid neon-lashed cityscapes, charming castle towns and an ex-capital even older than Kyoto. Kansai awaits.

You don't have to venture far from Kyoto to strike gold. Tame deer and a behemoth Buddha top the bill at nearby Nara, while electric Osaka seduces with more proletarian pleasures – bright lights, street snacks, offbeat bars and urban cool. Frankly it's so close to Kyoto you could make multiple trips. Compact Kōbe, a seaside charmer dotted with colonial relics, is perfectly proportioned for a day trip, and just along the rails sits Himeji-jō, Japan's finest castle. Dropping into a lower gear, sublime Lake Biwa beckons with a host of laid-back attractions easily reached by train from Kyoto, while the rural retreats of Ōhara and Kurama have long been favoured as places to escape the city.

Kasuga-taisha (p138)

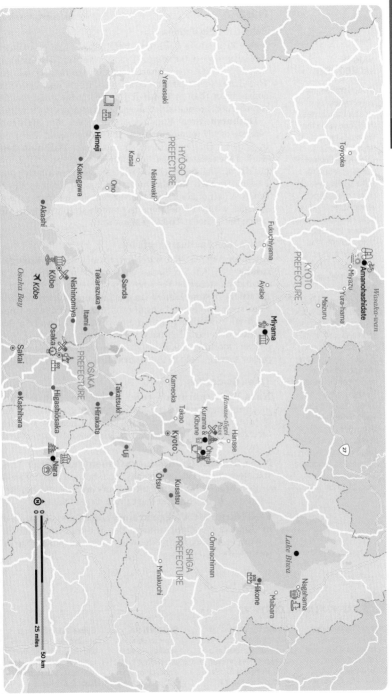

Yamasaki

Himeji

HYŌGO
PREFECTURE

Kasai

Nishiwaki

Ono

Kakogawa

Akashi

Osaka Bay

Kōbe

Kōbe

Nishinomiya

Itami

Takarazuka

Sanda

Osaka

OSAKA
PREFECTURE

Sakai

Higashiōsaka

Kashihara

Takatsuki

Hirakata

Nara

Uji

Takao

Kameoka

Kyoto

Kurama
Kibune

Ohara

Hanase-tōge
Pass

Hanase

Otsu

Kusatsu

Ōmihachiman

SHIGA
PREFECTURE

Minakuchi

Lake Biwa

Nagahama

Maibara

Hikone

Fukuchiyama

Ayabe

Miyama

KYOTO
PREFECTURE

Miyazu

Yura-hama

Maizuru

Wasaka-wan

Amanohashidate

Toyooka

27

N

0
0

25 miles

50 km

137

NARA'S SACRED DEER

Of all Nara's impressive sights, it's those adorable deer that often leave the deepest impression. Perfectly tame, some have learned to bow in return for *shika-sembei,* the deer crackers sold from vendors, while others tug and nibble at your clothes. The 1200 or so free-roaming silka deer are sacred to Kasuga-taisha, a shrine in the east of Nara-kōen.

One of the deities enshrined there is said to have ridden to Nara upon a sacred white deer, and ever since the deer of Nara have been protected as helpers of the gods. Though perhaps not divine, they are special – scientists have discovered Nara's deer possess a unique genotype not seen in other herds, reflecting their thousand-plus years of protection.

Nara

Behold the Big Buddha

Before Kyoto there was Nara (奈良), Japan's first permanent capital and one of the country's most rewarding destinations. The big sights are gathered in and around Nara-kōen (奈良公園), a park close to Nara's two stations, and they don't come bigger than at **Tōdai-ji** (東大寺), a Buddhist temple complex home to one of the largest bronze statues in the world.

Daibutsu (Great Buddha) sits just over 16m high and consists of 437 tonnes of bronze and 130kg of gold. Unveiled by Emperor Shōmu in 752, he's housed in the **Daibutsu-den** (Hall of the Great Buddha), one of the world's largest all-wood buildings. The approach to Daibutsu-den is similarly epic, passing through **Nandai-mon**, the biggest temple gate in Japan. A pair of fierce, 8m-tall Niō (temple guardians) stand sentinel, with yet more imposing temple statuary on display inside the adjacent **Tōdai-ji Museum**.

Nara's Most Spiritual Sanctuary

Established in 768 CE to watch over the new capital, **Kasuga-taisha** (春日大社) is Nara's most important shrine and a natural sanctuary on the edge of protected primeval forest. An avenue of stone lanterns marks the approach up through Nara-kōen, while hundreds of bronze lanterns dangle from the bright vermilion halls – these are lit twice a year for the **Mantōrō**, in early February and mid-August.

Every morning at 9am you can observe a *chōhai* (morning prayer service), held in the **Naoraiden** (Ceremony Hall).

Take a Guided Tour

Nara Walk (narawalk.com) Sign up for a three-hour morning tour around the main sights of Nara-kōen, run by professional English-speaking guides. Check the website for excursions to some of Nara's less-visited temples and sights.

Nara Student Guides (narastudentguide.org) This volunteer guide organisation has been showing international visitors around Nara since 1964. Tours are free and can last a full day. Book online at least three days in advance.

EGG Nara YMCA (egg-nara.org) Free tours of Nara led by 'English Goodwill Guides'. If you didn't book ahead, you might still see their volunteers soliciting outside Nara's two main stations.

EATING IN NARA: OUR PICKS

Mizuya Chaya Grab a snack at this lovely thatched-roof teahouse in a glade close to Kasuga-taisha. *11am-3.30pm Thu-Tue ¥*

Hirasō Try local dishes like *kakinoha-zushi* (sushi in persimmon leaf) and *chagayu* (rice porridge with green tea). *10.30am-8.30pm Tue-Sun ¥¥*

Sigenoi Nara Superior udon noodles in a side street close to JR Nara Station. *11am-9.30pm Thu-Tue ¥*

Gyōza no Ohsho Grab cheap *gyōza* (dumplings) and Chinese dishes from this chain with a branch near both Nara stations. *11am-10.30pm ¥*

Allow the best part of a day for this 6km walk taking in the main sights of Nara.

From Kintetsu-Nara Station, head east (you'll spot the sacred deer almost immediately), cross via the underpass to the northeast corner of the road then continue on to ❶ **Isui-en**. Savour the poetic beauty of this strolling garden, then navigate the quiet streets north of Isui-en to Tōdai-ji. Divert to ❷ **Nandai-mon** to check out the fierce Niō (guardian) statues, then join the throngs marching to ❸ **Daibutsu-den** to pay homage to Daibutsu (Great Buddha), holding court for more than 1250 years.

Exit to the east of Daibutsu-den and head up the hill to ❹ **Nigatsu-dō** for views across Nara Plain. Have a peek at the adjacent ❺ **Hokke-dō**, the oldest building in the Tōdai-ji temple complex, then take the path running south, passing the grassy slopes of Wakakusa-yama and down a set of steps towards forest.

Here you can stop for tea and sweets at ❻ **Mizuya-chaya** before continuing on to ❼ **Kasuga-taisha**, Nara's principal shrine, a vermilion beacon of colour garnished with lanterns.

Leave the shrine via its south gate and continue uphill to the sub-shrine of ❽ **Wakamiya-jinja**, passing several small shrines on the way. Retrace your steps towards Kasuga-taisha and take the path that leads down towards the centre of town. You'll pass first through ❾ **Ni-no-Torii**, a large Shintō shrine gate. Continue down the broad, wooded arcade to ❿ **Ichi-no-Torii**, another shrine gate. Cross the street and you'll soon see Kōfuku-ji's ⓫ **Five-Storey Pagoda**. Finish with a wander around the temple's grounds, then walk back to Kintetsu-Nara Station.

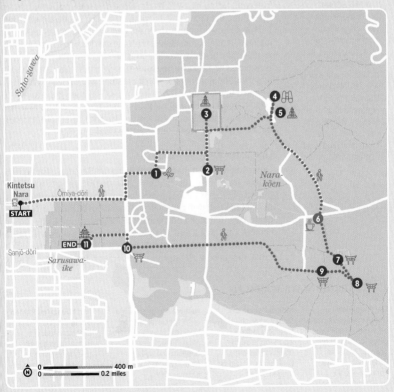

MASTERS OF PUPPETS

Once hugely popular in Osaka, *bunraku* is a performance art using near-life-sized puppets to tell dramatic tales of love, duty and politics.

Bunraku's most famous playwright, Chikamatsu Monzaemon (1653–1724), wrote plays about Osaka's merchants and the denizens of the pleasure quarters, and naturally theatres sprang up around Osaka's Dōtombori area to stage them.

A UNESCO-endorsed art form, *bunraku* performances can last for up to four hours, but theatres often sell tickets for just a single act. The **National Bunraku Theatre** stages tourist-friendly 'Bunraku for beginners' shows in summer, and has English audio guides.

Osaka

TIME FROM KYOTO **30 MINS**

Sights and Snacks of Dōtombori

Hop on a train at Kyoto Station and in just half an hour you'll be in Osaka (大阪), a high-rise urban playground geared to foodies, shoppers and party animals. More free and easy than Kyoto, Osaka has an infectious energy that fizzes through characterful neighbourhoods like **Dōtombori** (道頓堀). The 400-year-old *bori* (canal) that gives the area its name is a riot of glittering billboards, while running parallel is bustling Dōtombori street with its fabulous food signs – think giant octopuses, crabs, puffer fish and dragons. It's here that you'll see chefs deftly flicking rows of gooey, golf-ball shaped *tako-yaki* (octopus dumplings). **Ebisu-bashi**, a bridge over Dōtombori's canal, is a good place to start exploring. Dōtombori gets famously busy, so one way to sidestep the crowds is to hit the water on a **Tombori River Cruise**. Cruises last for 20 minutes and run on the half-hour. Get tickets from inside the Don Quijote Building – it's the one with a Ferris wheel on its facade.

Storm the Gates of History

Japan's most visited castle, mighty **Osaka-jō** (大坂城) is a testament to the awesome power and prestige of old Osaka. You can't fail to be awed by the *ishigaki* stone walls that make up the moats, gates and battlements – the beefiest stone slab is 11m wide, and many are inscribed with the crests of the 64 *daimyō* (feudal lords) tasked with the castle's construction back in 1620. The best way to view (and photograph) the battlements is aboard the **Gozabune Boat**, which cruises the inner moat every half-hour. From the water the stone walls rise up 34m high – almost like sailing through a canyon. Osaka-jō's graceful white *tenshu* (main keep) is actually a 1931 concrete rebuild housing a modern, multifloor museum leading up to an observation deck with lordly views out over the Osaka plain.

Lost in the Kita Labyrinth

Downtown Osaka divides into Minami (Japanese for south), where you'll find the bright lights of Dōtombori, and Kita (north), which is probably where you'll begin your adventure in Japan's third-biggest city. A multilevel maze of offices, department stores and thousands of restaurants, the action centres on Osaka and Umeda stations. Shoppers will be in department-store heaven: **Hankyū Umeda** has the city's most delectable *depachika* (basement food court), while

 EATING IN OSAKA: NOODLE FIX

Dotonbori Imai Try Osaka's famous *kitsune udon* (noodles in soup with fried tofu) at this peaceful haven in Dōtombori. *11.30am-9pm Thu-Tue* ¥¥

Kinryū Ramen Dōtombori institution serving noodles in a pork-bone broth (*tonkotsu ramen*). Look for the fibreglass dragon. *24hr* ¥

Nishiya A long-standing udon specialist, elegant Nishiya also serves hearty *nabe* (hot pot) dishes, tempura and sashimi. *11am-10.30pm Mon-Sat, to 10pm Sun* ¥¥

Most Deserted Ramen Bar in the World City execs and foodies queue up for superior spicy ramen at this office-block restaurant. *11am-10pm* ¥

Umeda Sky Building

SIGHTSEEING SAVER

If you're planning a packed day out in Osaka, consider purchasing the **Osaka Amazing Pass** (one day ¥2800), a tourist card that grants unlimited travel on city subways, buses and trains as well as free entry into more than 40 attractions including Osaka Castle, Umeda Sky Building, Tempozan and Hep Five Ferris wheels, plus a range of boat cruises.

Best of all, flashing the pass often lets you skip the queues. Buy it at metro stations, train stations and tourist information centres (osp.osaka-info.jp).

Daimaru Umeda, another retail giant, has official Pokémon and Nintendo stores on the 13th floor. **Hep Five** nearby caters to cut-price youth trends sold in tiny individual shops, with the added attraction of a giant red **Ferris wheel**. The Osaka Station area is also where you'll find the 173m-tall **Umeda Sky Building** (梅田スカイビル), Osaka's most iconic modern landmark. Designed by the same architect as Kyoto Station, it has been likened to a space-age Arc de Triomphe. The 39th-floor observation deck offers epic cityscape and bay views.

Hanging Out in Amerika-Mura

A magnet for Osaka's alternative crowd, **Amerika-Mura** (アメリカ村, literally 'America Town') is home to shops selling vintage denim, sneakers, baseball caps and vinyl records, along with quirky bars, clubs and music dives catering to every subculture going. So-called because this former warehouse zone started selling imported US fashions in the late 1960s and 1970s, 'Ame-Mura' today covers the area west of Shinsaibashi station all the way south to the Dōtombori canal. Head to tiny **Triangle Park**, a popular hangout, and often you'll see a parade of beautifully maintained sports cars, lowriders and motorcycles rumble on through. One block east is Ame-Mura's **Peace on Earth** mural painted in the 1980s, another local landmark. On the way you'll pass **Big Step**, a mall that houses a popular pinball arcade, **Silver Ball Planet**, on the 3rd floor.

 EATING IN OSAKA: LOCAL TASTES

Wanaka Wanaka's gooey *tako-yaki* (octopus dumplings) are some of the best in Osaka. At least 10 locations. *Hours vary* ¥	**Chibō** Grab a canal-view seat and try the house special Dōtombori yaki, with pork, beef, squid, shrimp and cheese. *11am-11pm* ¥¥	**Daruma** Try *kushi-katsu* – crumbed skewers of meat, seafood and veggies invented in Shin-Sekai back in 1929. *11am-10.30pm* ¥¥	**Takoyaki Umaiya** Family-owned since the 1950s, this *tako-yaki* joint was the first to make the Michelin guide. *11.30am-6.30pm Wed-Mon* ¥

OSAKA'S BEST TOURS

If you're short on time, an organised tour can be a great way to see more of the city and sidestep Osaka's main tourist trail.

Cycle Osaka (cycleosaka.com) Long-running outfit offering two-wheeled tours that go off the beaten track to explore lesser-known neighbourhoods. Fees include bicycle and helmet rental, water and food.

Osaka Food Tours (osakafoodtours. com) Offers a range of foodie-focused walking tours that mix history, traditional Osaka food (and alcohol), and plenty of local trivia.

Taste Osaka (tasteosaka.com) Hit the backstreets for a booze-fuelled tour of Osaka's nightlife or explore the underground arcades of Umeda on an afternoon eating tour.

JULIAN ELLIOTT PHOTOGRAPHY/GETTY IMAGES ©

Retro Vibes at Shin-Sekai

A gaudy entertainment district of shooting galleries, *pachinko* (vertical pinball) parlours and souvenirs, **Shin-Sekai** (新世界, 'New World') is a world away from the more rarefied refinements of Kyoto.

The fun centres on **Tsūten-kaku** (Tower Reaching Heaven), a 103m-tall mass of silver steel built in 1956. Shin-Sekai is also famous for *kushikatsu*, a blue-collar Osaka dish where skewers of meat, seafood or vegetables are coated in a panko crumb, deep-fried and served with a tangy dipping sauce. **Daruma**, now a major chain, started it all here back in 1929. The original (tiny) branch is in a small side alley and has an English menu. Shin-Sekai is also where you'll find **Spa World**, a seven-storey bathing complex offering a kind of hot-springs world tour – think Roman baths, Finnish saunas, Japanese cypress wood *onsen* and so on, together with communal swimming pools and water slides (tattoos forbidden).

Osaka's Tallest Building

Enjoy vertigo-inducing views of Osaka and the Kansai region from **Abeno Harukas**, Osaka's tallest building. The 300m-high César Pelli–designed giant has a free viewing

 EATING IN OSAKA: SUSHI AND SEAFOOD

Endo Sushi Start your day right with a delectable sushi breakfast at this century-old stalwart in Osaka's fish market. *6.15am-1.30pm* ¥¥

Yoshino Sushi In business since 1841, Yoshino specialises in Osaka-style 'pressed sushi' neatly formed using wooden moulds. *10am-2pm Mon-Fri* ¥¥

Sushiro Shinsaibashi Order sushi and beer from a tablet menu at this popular conveyer-belt chain originally founded in Osaka. *11am-11pm Mon-Fri, from 10.30am Sat & Sun* ¥

Kuromon Ichiba Food stalls at this historic covered arcade grill up tiger prawns, oysters, crab claws and more. *8am-6pm* ¥¥

Tsūten-kaku, Shin-Sekai

area on the 16th floor, but the best eye-candy is up on top-level Harukas 300 observation deck. You'll also find an **art museum** and the mammoth **Kintetsu department store** set over 16 floors. It's easy to tack on a visit here after exploring Shen-Sekai – simply stroll through **Tennōji Park**, perhaps making a stop at the **Osaka City Museum of Fine Arts**, due to reopen after renovations in 2025.

Go Full Mario at Universal Studios

One of Japan's best theme parks, 'USJ' got a huge boost in 2021 with the opening of **Super Nintendo World**, a Mario-themed zone of snapping piranha plants and magical mushrooms. It looks incredible, even if the **Mario Kart: Koopa's Challenge ride** fails to set the heart racing. For thrills try **Harry Potter and the Forbidden Journey**, a stomach-churning broomstick chase, or the frankly terrifying Jurassic Park coaster **The Flying Dinosaur**. Younger kids have gentler areas themed on Snoopy and Sesame Street, and the rollicking **No Limit! Parade** (2pm daily). The only drawbacks are that the rides are all in Japanese and queues can be hours long. To max out your visit, buy at least one 'Express Pass' set per person (on top of the park entrance fee) and a timed entry ticket to Super Nintendo World.

<aside>

HEAVYWEIGHT SLAPDOWN

For its combo of explosive spectacle, esoteric ritual and man-mountain athletes, watching sumo is an unforgettable experience. Every March the big boys come to Osaka for a 15-day tournament, held at Namba's Edion Arena.

In 2024, Osaka hailed a new hero in 24-year-old Takerufuji Mikiya, who became the first wrestler in 110 years to win the championship in his inaugural top division tournament. Despite being the lowest-ranked wrestler competing, Takerufuji triumphed in 13 of his 15 bouts at the Edion Arena, winning the Emperor's Cup.

Tickets (from around ¥4000) for Osaka's sumo tournament go on sale in early February and can be purchased online or as same-day tickets at the arena.

</aside>

THE GUIDE

DAY TRIPS FROM KYOTO

 DRINKING IN OSAKA: COOL COFFEE SPOTS

| **Brooklyn Roasting Company** Stick with the classics or indulge in an iced organic *matcha* latte. Hip, laptop-friendly spot with a lovely riverside terrace. *8am-7pm* | **LiLo Coffee Roasters** Choose from a selection of single-origin beans roasted in house. Clued-up, English-speaking staff. *11am-11pm* | **Mel Coffee Roasters** There's just enough room to stand in this tiny roastery serving some of Osaka's best hand-poured coffee. *10am-6pm Tue-Sun* | **Kissa Madura** An Osaka time-capsule, Madura rocks tulip chairs, mirrored walls, chrome trim and retro coffee. Smoking permitted. *9am-8.30pm Mon-Sat* |

Fishy Fun at Osaka Bay

If you've got the kids in tow, or you fancy some sea air, ride the metro to Osaka Bay, a slice of reclaimed coast that's home to the excellent **Osaka Aquarium Kaiyūkan**. A walkway winds between floors revealing marine species from the Pacific Rim region – penguins, butterflyfish, seals, otters, jellyfish, and Kai, a whale shark in the huge central tank. The 112m-high **Tempōzan Giant Ferris Wheel** soars over the aquarium, and you can set sail on a 45-minute cruise around the bay aboard the **Santa Maria**, supposedly a replica of Columbus' famous sailing ship. Little ones will love the **Legoland Discovery Centre** with its play zones, 4D cinema and interactive model of Osaka made from 1.5 million bricks, but note that adults can't go without a child in tow.

Use Your Noodle

Well over five billion servings of instant noodles are slurped up in Japan each year, a convenience food invented in Osaka by Momofuku Andō, founder of the Cup Noodles brand. At the wacky **Cup Noodles Museum Osaka Ikeda** you can see a replica of the wooden shack where he formulated his first batch in the 1950s, but the real highlight is the chance to make your own bespoke Cup Noodles pot to take away – the ultimate Japan souvenir. The museum is 20 minutes by train from Hankyu Umeda Station.

Himeji

TIME FROM KYOTO **90 MINS**

King of the Castles

Just 45 minutes from Kyoto Station if you take the shinkansen, the easy-going city of Himeji is famous for **Himeji-jō** (姫路城), the finest surviving castle from Japan's building boom of the late 16th and early 17th century. That's because it largely stayed out of trouble, avoiding conflict through the ages, including the bombing raids of WWII. It's also testament to the superb quality of the castle's construction, helping it withstand natural disasters like the Great Hanshin Earthquake. It takes about 1½ hours to follow the arrow-marked route around the castle. On the way you'll encounter many of the fiendish defensive features that belie the castle's graceful appearance: nearly 1000 gun and arrow notches; the disorienting, maze-like approach to the main keep with its narrow kill corridors; and hidden openings from which defenders could spring surprise ambushes. After visiting, check out **Kōkō-en** next door, a modern recreation of an Edo-era samurai residence with a lovely strolling garden.

DRINKING IN OSAKA: QUIRKY BARS

Bar Nayuta When you've found the hidden entrance, take a stool and let the bartenders wow you with bespoke cocktail creations. *5pm-3am*

Pink Elephant In a grungy Ame-Mura basement, this eclectic, music- loving dive extends a warm wel-come to travellers. *9pm-5am*

Cinquecento The name ('500' in Italian) is the price in yen of drinks at this easy-going, internationally minded bar. *8pm-5am Mon-Sat, to 3am Sun*

Leach Bar Inside the Rihga Hotel, elderly bartenders mix precise cocktails in 1960s bar. Old-school vibes. *4pm-midnight Wed-Mon*

Nunobiki Falls, Kōbe

At 5.46am on 17 January 1995, the Great Hanshin Earthquake struck.

The epicentre of the quake was just 20km away from Kōbe and the tremors lasted 20 seconds – but it was enough to topple expressways, road and rail bridges and destroy nearly 400,000 buildings.

Over 6000 people died and more than 30,000 were injured in Japan's strongest quake since the Great Kantō Earthquake of 1923 that devastated Tokyo.

You can learn more about the quake, its aftermath, recovery and legacy at **The Great Hanshin-Awaji Earthquake Memorial Disaster Reduction and Human Renovation Institution**. Dioramas and videos recreate the terrible scale of the disaster, and show how the earthquake proved a wake-up call for Japanese disaster prevention.

The castle is a 10-minute walk from Himeji station. Visit the tourist information centre in the station to meet local volunteer guides offering their services for free.

Kōbe
TIME FROM KYOTO **55 MINS**

Mansion-Hopping in the Hills

Long heralded as one of Japan's most attractive cities, the port of Kōbe (神戸) was one of the first places in Japan to open up to the outside world in the mid-19th century. Part of its appeal today lies in discovering historic traces of this cosmopolitan legacy, such as in the hillside enclave of **Kitano-chō** with its quirky colonial-era mansions. Two of the best residences you can enter are the red-brick **Weathercock House**, built in 1909 for a German trader, and the jade-green **Moegi House**, built in 1903 for the former US consul. The whimsy gets dialled up to 11 in the **English House**, where visitors don Sherlock Holmes outfits, while the eccentric **Ben's House** has a pair of stuffed polar bears collected by its former owner, a British aristocrat. Further up the hill, slate-clad **Uroko House** and the Tudor-styled **Yamate 8-Banjan** have gorgeous views down to the coast.

Step Out into Nature

In Kōbe you can step right off the shinkansen and on to hiking paths that whisk you up to some surprisingly tranquil beauty spots. **Nunobiki Falls** (布引の滝), accessed by a steep 400m path from Shin-Kōbe Station, cascades through a gorge into a picture-perfect pool hemmed in by forest. A more leisurely way to see the falls is by riding the **Kōbe Nunobiki Ropeway**, which glides upwards to the **Nunobiki Herb Garden**, a hillside attraction popular with Japanese families for its neatly pruned flowerbeds and city vistas.

MARBLED TO PERFECTION

Kōbe is famous for its top-class beef, considered by connoisseurs to be the world's finest.

What makes it special is the high level of marbling – essentially strands of intramuscular fat that give the meat the patina of marble. During cooking all that fat melts into the meat adding flavour and tenderness.

Contrary to popular belief, Kōbe cows are not massaged or played classical music, but the meat must fulfil strict criteria and come from a Tajima breed of Japanese black cow, born, raised and slaughtered in Kōbe's home prefecture, Hyōgo.

When ordering, splurge on the cut rather than the size, as the fat content makes Kōbe beef very filling.

KALPAPHOTO/SHUTTERSTOCK ©

Ski run, Biwako Terrace

Downtown Kōbe & the Waterfront

Downtown Kōbe is a compact, walkable grid of office blocks, hotels and covered shopping arcades. Pop inside the **Kōbe City Museum**, housed in a Greek-revival-style building from 1935, for the slick (and free) exhibition on the history of Kōbe, featuring interactive scale models of the foreign settlement. Also trading at Kōbe port were the Chinese who established **Nankin-machi**, Kōbe's Chinatown. Centred on China Sq with its decorative pavilion, it's a fun, colourful area for strolling and snacking. Down at Kobe's waterfront you'll reach **Meriken Park**, a harbourside plaza with fountains and attractions. The **Kōbe Maritime Museum** is crammed with highly detailed models of old ships, while the **Port of Kōbe Earthquake Memorial Park** commemorates the lives lost in Great Hanshin Earthquake (p145). A section of twisted dock has been left as it was after the quake.

 EATING IN KOBE: KOBE BEEF RESTAURANTS

| **Tor Road Steak Aoyama** Intimate, family-run *teppan-yaki* beef restaurant with just eight seats. Melt-in-the-mouth magic. *Noon-9pm Thu-Tue* ¥¥¥ | **Kōbe Gyūdon Hiroshige** Prime Kōbe beef is served as *gyūdon* (thinly sliced over rice) at this snug restaurant. *11am-3pm & 6-10pm Thu-Tue* ¥¥ | **Sai-Dining** Sizzlingly fragrant Kōbe steaks are cooked in front of diners at this stylish basement restaurant. *11.30am-2pm & 5-9pm* ¥¥¥ | **Daichi** A reliable standby for Kōbe beef served *teppan-yaki* style, with a range of differently priced cuts. *11am-3pm & 5-9pm* ¥¥¥ |

Lake Biwa

Castle Towns of the Eastern Shore

Just over Kyoto's eastern hills sits **Lake Biwa** (琵琶湖), Japan's largest freshwater lake. Eulogised in centuries past by Kyoto's poets and artists, modern development has sapped some of its lyrical charms, but there's still plenty to see and do along its 235km of shoreline, and it's all easily reached by train.

The small city of **Hikone** (彦根) is famous for its castle, which stands proudly atop Hikone-yama. Though tiny, **Hikone-jō** is considered a masterpiece, with its undulating gables and lashings of gold leaf and black lacquer framing the pure white plaster walls.

Another 25 minutes further round the lake by train is **Nagahama** (長浜), which has a lakeside castle, albeit a 1980s rebuild. The main reason for visiting is the charming historic quarter set **Kurokabe Glass House** (a former bank from 1900), which now showcases the delightful Nagahama custom of artisanal glassware. It's an easy-going place to stroll, and when it's time for a rest, grab a bowl of *yakisaba somen* (braised mackerel with noodles). Traditionally sent to married daughters by their parents at harvest time, it's Nagahama's signature dish. For liquid refreshment, **Nagahama Roman Beer** is a top-quality craft brewery, distillery and restaurant.

Ōtsu and the Western Shore

At the southern end of Biwa-ko, **Ōtsu** (大津) is just 10 minutes by train from Kyoto, and while you wouldn't guess it today, the city served (very) briefly as the imperial capital in the 7th century. Every August Ōtsu hosts a spectacular fireworks display, launched from barges on the water. Summer is also a popular time for lake cruises – the **Michigan** (biwakokisen. co.jp) is styled like an old-time paddle steamer.

Travelling clockwise from Ōtsu around the lake, the **Ukimidō** (Floating Hall) is Biwa-ko's premier Instagram spot for the way the temple building (constructed on a jetty) appears to float over the water.

More eye candy can be had at **Biwako Terrace**, high up in the Hira Mountains. Reached by the **Biwako Valley Ropeway** (a shuttle bus goes there from Shiga Station), there are hiking trails, restaurants and stunning views of Lake Biwa 1000m below, while in winter it transforms into a ski area.

Of several lowkey beaches on the western shore, one of the nicest and easiest to get to is **Omi-Maiko**, a winding belt of pebbly sand with fir trees for shade.

力

THE FORCE IS STRONG

Rooted in Japanese spirituality is the concept of 'power spots' – locations believed to possess spiritual energy or a strong positive aura. Japanese visit power spots to recharge their spiritual batteries; Mt Fuji is one, unsurprisingly, and so too is Lake Biwa, especially on **Chikubu-shima** (竹生島), a pint-sized island believed to be sacred since ancient times. On it you'll find **Hōgon-ji**, a Buddhist temple complex dedicated to Benzaiten, the goddess of all that flows – water, music, art, wealth and so on. Ferries depart for the island from Nagahama's port.

THE GUIDE

DAY TRIPS FROM KYOTO

 EATING IN NAGAHAMA: OUR PICKS

Yokarō A wonderfully atmospheric setting to try local favourite *yakisoba sōmen.* *10.30am-3pm Tue-Sun* ¥¥

Kyōgoku Sushi Experienced chefs make impeccable sushi sets at this traditional countertop eatery. *11am-9pm Wed-Mon* ¥¥

Nagahama Roma Beer Pair locally reared Omi beef with craft beer made on site, or go for traditional fish and chips. *11.30am-3pm & 5-9pm Wed-Mon* ¥¥

96 Cafe Take a break on the sunny terrace for soft-serve ice cream and simple lunch sets. *10am-5pm Thu-Tue* ¥¥

Ōhara

TIME FROM KYOTO **1 HR**

Hillside Hydrangeas and Temples

One of Kyoto's most popular day trips, the hillside farming town of Ōhara (大原) offers peace and quiet, a taste of rural Japan and a collection of fine temples. Famed for its autumn colours, hydrangea garden and stunning Buddha statues, **Sanzen-in** (三千院) is Ōhara's big draw. Tatami-lined halls open out to reveal **Yūsei-en,** a living canvas of plants, flowers, ponds and maple trees. A garden path leads down to **Ōjō Gokuraku-in** (Temple of Rebirth in Paradise), inside which is squeezed the Amida Triad – three sizeable Buddhist statues that are designated National Treasures. Among Ōhara's other temples, **Hōsen-in** has beautifully framed gardens and a 700-year-old pine. At **Jikkō-in** you can enjoy the view with *matcha* (powdered green tea) and a sweet. It's a 10-minute walk from Ōhara's bus stop to Sanzen-in.

Kurama & Kibune

TIME FROM KYOTO **50 MINS**

A Tale of Two Valleys

One of the most popular hikes close to Kyoto is this short mountain trail through old-growth forest connecting **Kurama-dera** (鞍馬寺), an 8th-century temple, with the riverside village of Kibune (貴船). Part of the fun is the dinky train journey from Kyoto, which trundles up the hillside through delightful scenery. From the mountain terminus at Kurama Station, it's a short walk to the main entrance of Kurama-dera. A steep path winds upwards through the temple precincts, shaded by looming cryptomeria trees, and connects with a trail across **Mt Kurama** to Kibune, around an hour's walk. Kibune is famous for the summer dining custom of *kawadoko,* in which diners sit on platforms installed directly over the rushing river. The food is mostly *kaiseki* (Japanese haute cuisine), but you can also find places doing *nagashi sōmen* (literally 'flowing noodles'), where diners 'catch' thin rice noodles flowing down a cold-water bamboo slide. Book ahead.

Miyama

TIME FROM KYOTO **80 MINS**

Farmhouses & Folk Museums

In the mountainous heartland of Kyoto Prefecture, Miyama (美山, literally 'beautiful mountains') is a scatter of rural hamlets joined up by quiet country lanes and dotted with sleepy temples and shrines. An easy day trip if you have a car,

---

A BIT OF A PICKLE

Surrounded by mountains and far from the sea, Kyoto evolved a culture of preserving food in the form of crisp, fresh-tasting *tsukemono* (Japanese pickles).

These can bought in hundreds of different varieties from vendors that set up shop in places like Ōhara.

Shibazuke is a Kyoto speciality, a salty-sour purple pickle made of cucumber, eggplant, *shiso* (perilla leaves) and ginger pickled in plum vinegar.

Senmaizuke is another Kyoto favourite – crunchy, sweet and sour slices of turnip brined in sweet vinegar and seasoned with *konbu* (kelp) and spicy pepper.

EATING IN KURAMA & KIBUNE: OUR PICKS

Yōshūji Hearty *shōjin-ryōri* (Buddhist vegetarian) set meals in an old Japanese farmhouse next to Kurama-dera. *10am-6pm Wed-Mon, to 3pm Sat & Sun* ¥¥

Aburaya-Shokudō Fuel up at this simple restaurant with generous bowls of soba noodles and tempura udon. *10am-8pm* ¥

Hirobun A good place to sample kawadoko 'above-river' dining, this hotel restaurant also serves nagashi sōmen noodles. *11am-3pm Thu-Tue* ¥¥

Hiroya Known for *ayu* (sweetfish), this is one of Kibune's oldest and most famous kawadoko spots. Reservations only. *10.30am-3pm* ¥¥¥

Kurama-dera

Miyama's star attraction is **Kayabuki-no-sato** (かやぶきの里), a collection of farmhouses notable for their traditional *kayabuki-yane* (thatched roofs). Most are private residences or operate as cafes and guesthouses. You can see inside one that has retained its rustic interior at the **Miyama Folk Museum**. The charming **Little Indigo Museum**, in another thatched-roof abode, is a gallery and workshop devoted to the practice of indigo dyeing. To learn more about life in the village, book a **Thatched Village Guided Walk** via the local tourist association (visitmiyama.com).

Amanohashidate

TIME FROM KYOTO **2 HRS**

Kyoto by the Sea

Go far enough north in Kyoto Prefecture and you'll hit sandy beaches, rocky inlets and the natural wonder that is **Amanohashidate** (天橋立, literally 'bridge to heaven'), a 3.5km-long belt of pine-shaded sand that snakes across the azure waters of Miyazu Bay. Observed from viewpoints on either side, it's hard to refute Amanohashidate's billing as one of Japan's top-three views. From the train station, you can take the chairlift up to **Amanohashidate View Land**, a viewpoint where it's customary to bend over and peer at the sandbar from between your legs to see a phenomenon called *hiryūkan* – it's supposed to resemble a flying dragon. The best way to cross the sandbar itself is by bike; rent them from the dock outside **Chion-ji**, a sleepy temple. **Hashidate Chaya** makes a lovely pit stop on the sandbar – try *asari don,* a dish of local boiled clams over rice. There are beach showers in the pine trees opposite if you want to take a dip. From the north side of the sandbar you can catch a bus (30 minutes) to the fishing community of **Ine-chō** (伊根町), notable for its traditional wooden stilt houses, or return across the bay by bike or sightseeing boat.

TANGO RAILWAY SIGHTSEEING TRAIN

A fun way to sojourn out to Amanohashidate is aboard the scenic Tango Railway.

From Kyoto, take a regular service to Nishimaizuru (1½ hours) then change on to the **Tango Aka-matsu**, a special tourist train service with window-facing seats that make the most of the fine scenery through Kyoto and Hyōgo prefectures. At certain points the train slows to take in the view, such as when traversing the 550m-long **Yuragawa Kyoryo Bridge**.

Tickets cost just marginally more than the regular fare, and there are two departures daily.

TOOLKIT

The chapters in this section cover the most important topics you'll need to know about in Kyoto. They're full of nuts-and-bolts information and valuable insights to help you understand and navigate Kyoto and get the most out of your trip.

Arriving
p152

Money
p153

Getting Around
p154

Accommodation
p156

Family Travel
p158

Health & Safe Travel
p159

Food, Drink & Nightlife
p160

Responsible Travel
p162

LGBTiQ+ Travellers
p164

Accessible Travel
p165

Overtourism
p166

Nuts & Bolts
p167

Language
p168

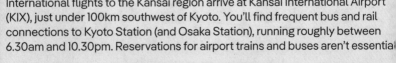

Arriving

International flights to the Kansai region arrive at Kansai International Airport (KIX), just under 100km southwest of Kyoto. You'll find frequent bus and rail connections to Kyoto Station (and Osaka Station), running roughly between 6.30am and 10.30pm. Reservations for airport trains and buses aren't essentia

Visas

Travellers from 69 countries, including Australia, Canada, New Zealand, the UK and the USA, can receive a free 90-day temporary visitor visa upon arrival. Other nationalities need to arrange visas prior to travel.

Wi-Fi & SIM

Kansai International Airport has several places where you can rent (and return) mobile wi-fi routers and SIM cards, including SoftBank Global Rental, WiFiBox and JAL-ABC.

Luggage

JAL-ABC (1F and 4F South) and Kansai Airport Baggage Service (4F North) both offer luggage forwarding services and storage at Terminal 1 of Kansai International Airport.

Currency

The 1st floor of Terminal 1 at KIX has currency exchange counters and automatic exchange machines, plus Seven Bank and Japan Post ATMs that accept international cards.

Kansai International Airport to Kyoto Station

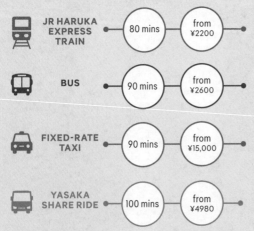

JR HARUKA EXPRESS TRAIN	80 mins	from ¥2200
BUS	90 mins	from ¥2600
FIXED-RATE TAXI	90 mins	from ¥15,000
YASAKA SHARE RIDE	100 mins	from ¥4980

BIOSECURITY

Don't be surprised when aeroplane staff start reeling off a long list of warnings about prohibited items and infectious diseases as you descend into KIX.

Japan takes avian influenza, African swine fever, foot and mouth, and other infectious diseases extremely seriously. Upon arrival, you'll need to complete a customs declaration form and hand it to officials who will likely ask a few questions. There are even dogs in the arrival area trained to sniff out animal products – almost all of which are prohibited. Being caught bringing in animal products can result in a fine of up to ¥3 million or up to three years in jail.

Money

CURRENCY: YEN (¥ OR 円)

ATMs

Banks, convenience stores, department stores and post offices have ATMs, but not all accept overseas cards. Japan Post machines and the Seven Bank machines in 7-Eleven convenience stores are the most reliable, usually accepting Amex, Cirrus, Diner's Club, Maestro, MasterCard, Plus and Visa cards. Seven Bank machines operate 24 hours a day, 365 days a year.

Card or Cash?

Credit cards are widely accepted in Kyoto, but there are still a lot of cash-only bars, cafes and restaurants. It makes sense to check before ordering anything or to carry cash. Temple admission is also often cash only. Visa, Mastercard and JCB are the most accepted cards.

HOW MUCH FOR A...

temple admission
from ¥500

Kyoto City Bus ticket
from ¥230

subway ticket
from ¥230

HOW TO... Save on Eating

Make lunch your main meal of the day, as you can fill up much more cheaply on lunch deals than on evening à la carte. You could also stick to simple one-dish dinners, such as noodles or *donburi* (dishes served over rice). For a super-cheap dinner, scour local supermarkets or department store food floors near closing, when items like *bentō* are heavily discounted. Bakeries and cafes are a lot cheaper than paying extra for a hotel breakfast.

Digital Payments

Smartphone payment apps like PayPay and Rakuten Pay are becoming increasingly common, with shops using them displaying signs by the cashier. IC travel cards Icoca, Pasmo and Suica can be used on trains, subways and buses, but also for shopping in convenience stores, supermarkets and newer vending machines.

FREE ATTRACTIONS

With admission to major temples and gardens usually costing upwards of ¥500, daily costs soon add up. You can save by targeting the best free attractions.

It costs nothing to stroll along Nishiki Market (p68) and the Philosopher's Path (p107) or to see Arashiyama Bamboo Grove (p127) and the rows of *torii* at Fushimi Inari-Taisha (p44).

The guided tours of Shūgaku-in Rikyū Imperial Villa (p109) and Kyoto Imperial Palace (p75) are also free – you just need to reserve these in advance.

CARRY CHANGE

If using buses without a pass or IC card, have change handy. The payment machine only accepts exact payment, though you can use it to break a ¥1000 note before paying.

Getting Around

With an efficient and far-reaching bus, subway and rail network, Kyoto is easy to get around. The city is also great fun to explore with a bicycle or on foot.

TRAVEL COSTS

Subway
from ¥220

One-day
subway-bus
pass
¥1100

Taxi ride
from ¥600

Kyoto City Bus

The City Bus network reaches most parts of Kyoto, with almost all journeys a flat ¥230 fare. Get on at the doors in the middle of the bus, then get off at the door by the driver, where you also pay – by either dropping the exact coins in the fare machine, scanning an IC travel card, or showing the driver your bus-subway pass.

Subway & Train

Kyoto has two municipal subway lines that cross in the heart of downtown. The Tozai runs east to west, while the Karasuma runs north to south, connecting with Kyoto Station. These are augmented by Japan Rail and four privately operated lines – Hankyu, Keihan, Kintestu and Randen – which are useful for visiting sights in the suburbs or further afield.

HEADED TO OSAKA?

The Osaka 1-Day Pass gives unlimited rides on the Osaka Metro and buses for ¥820 (¥610 on weekends/holidays), providing access to all of the city's eight subway lines. Of particular use is the Midosuji Line, which runs north–south, connecting major stops such as Shin-Osaka (where the shinkansen stops), Umeda (near JR Osaka Station), Namba and Tennoji. For information on other lines and discount passes, see subway.osakametro.co.jp/en/.

TIP

To navigate the bus network, pick up a route map from the bus station office on Kyoto Station's northside.

PUBLIC TRANSPORT ESSENTIALS

Prepaid IC Cards	For convenience, grab an ICOCA IC card. These rechargeable prepaid cards can be used to pay for subways, trains and buses just by scanning them on ticket gates and fare machines. They are also accepted in convenience stores and some other shops, or even newer drink vending machines. For a refundable ¥500 deposit, you can buy an ICOCA card at any subway or rail vending machine displaying the ICOCA logo and then recharge it at any machine with an IC charge (ICチャージ) option. Tokyo's Pasmo and Suica cards are also fully usable in Kyoto.
Correct Change	You'll avoid rolled eyes from locals if you are ready to pay your fare when you get off the bus. A subway-bus pass or IC card is quick and easy. If paying by cash, be aware that the fare machine only accepts the exact fare. You can, however, use a different part of the fare machine to break coins or a ¥1000 note...it just slows up the system a little.
Japan Travel by Navtime	This useful app has a public transport route planner, plus ideas for activities and guides on such things as how to exchange money or rent a car. There's a paid premium version that includes a six-hour rain radar, but the free version is more than good enough for navigating around Kyoto and beyond.
Driving	With good public transport, plus often congested roads and limited parking, exploring Kyoto by car isn't recommended. If you want to drive, however, you'll need to be at least 18 and to have an international driving licence. You can book rental cars online in English from Nippon Rent-a-Car and Nissan Rent-a-Car. And don't forget that Japan drives on the left.

Cycling

Kyoto is great for cycling. There are two options: rental or bike sharing. The website kyoto-bicycle.com details the procedures and prices for both in English and also lists rental shops, parking areas and road rules. For bike sharing, Koto Bike (kotobike.jp/en/kyoto) has flexible options, from 15 minutes to three days of use.

Taxis

You'll find taxis at stands by most stations and in busy areas, or you can flag them down. A red sign (空車) on the dashboard means the taxi is vacant, while a green sign (賃走) means 'occupied'. Average rates are ¥600 for the first 2km, then ¥100 per 250m, although this goes 20% higher late at night.

Walking

Basic precautions aside, Kyoto is a safe city to explore on foot. If you are used to walking a lot, most of the neighbourhoods in this book can be walked in full (or almost in full). You just need to use public transport to travel between neighbourhoods.

Accommodation

Ryokan

These traditional inns, featuring tatami-mat guestrooms, futon instead of beds, and communal baths, come in multiple price brackets. At the high end, expect exquisite Japanese dinners and highly attentive service, and in some cases a blend of contemporary luxury and traditional sensibilities. At the more budget-friendly end, you might have something closer to a guesthouse – traditional rooms but shared facilities.

Machiya

Kyoto's old townhouses, called *machiya,* make for a very characterful stay. Almost always full rentals, with no staff on site (though reachable by phone), they are an especially good option for groups and large families. They also tend to come with facilities for self-catering. *Machiya* specialists with English-language services include Machiya Residence Inn Kyoto (kyoto-machiya-inn.com) and Kyoto Machiya Collection (kyotomachiyas.com).

Business Hotels

Dependable and affordable, Japan's business hotel chains offer simple Western-style accommodation, with compact rooms typically aimed at solo travellers or pairs. At the most no-frills end are brands like Toyoko Inn and Route Inn, while smarter brands like Daiwa Roynet, Dormy Inn and Super Hotel often offer perks like rooftop hot-spring baths. All have free in-room wi-fi. Some include breakfast in the rate.

Guesthouses

A step up from a youth hostel, Kyoto's guesthouses are often in the same kind of old buildings as *machiya* rentals, making them a culturally immersive option (albeit one that can creak at night when someone goes to the toilet). Most offer a mix of dorms and private rooms, plus shared showers, toilets and common areas where you can meet other travellers.

HOW MUCH FOR A (NON-HIGH SEASON) NIGHT IN A...

business hotel
¥15,000/ double room

guesthouse
¥7000/person

midrange ryokan
¥20,000/ person

Capsule Hotels

Essentially sleeping pods stacked in rows on gender-separated floors, capsule hotels are a simplified budget option for single-night stays. These claustrophobic pods generally are furnished with a mattress, TV and a light, while baths and toilets are shared. There are usually curtains, not lockable doors, for privacy. There are also sleeker versions like First Cabin, which has a branch near Nijō-jō.

HIGH-SEASON ALTERNATIVES

In cherry blossom season (late March to mid-April) and autumn foliage season (late October to late November), room rates in Kyoto can double, yet still sell out months in advance. Beyond booking early and taking the financial hit, one alternative is to stay outside of Kyoto and train in each day. Osaka, which doesn't suffer such extreme high-season issues, is 13 minutes away on the shinkansen or just under half an hour on a far cheaper JR express train – and it's a fantastic city to explore in its own right.

AREA	ATMOSPHERE
Kyoto Station & South Kyoto	Great choice if planning trips from Kyoto Station to Osaka or elsewhere outside of Kyoto; not many major sights nearby, so you'll need to bus and subway a lot when exploring Kyoto. Busy, but not very atmospheric.
Downtown Kyoto	The best all-round place to stay in Kyoto: varied accommodation, dining, nightlife and shopping options, and excellent transport links to other major areas. A lively area that might feel too busy and touristy for some.
Imperial Palace & Around	Accommodation from budget up to luxury level; other than the Palace and Nijō-jō, most major sites will need a bus or subway trip; you'll also need to travel for the best nightlife and dining.
Gion & Southern Higashiyama	The main sightseeing areas, with Gion, Kiyomizu-dera and many other attractions within easy walking distance. Good accommodation and dining options, though less so than nearby downtown; can be swamped with tourists, especially in cherry-blossom season.
Northern Higashiyama	Has major sights like Ginkaku-ji and Nanzen-ji, plus less famous temples, peaceful strolls, museums and decent transport links. Fewer accommodation and nightlife options the further north you go (south of Okazaki Park is the most convenient).
Northwest Kyoto	Home to two star attractions: the Kinkaku-ji and Ryōan-ji temples. Mostly quiet and residential, with limited accommodation (beyond guesthouses), dining and nightlife; not very convenient for visiting other neighbourhoods.
Arashiyama & Sagano	Major sightseeing area home to the famous bamboo grove and Tenryū-ji. In the far west of the city, it's inconvenient as a base being busy with tourists during the day but then quiet at night, with a limited selection of dinner options.

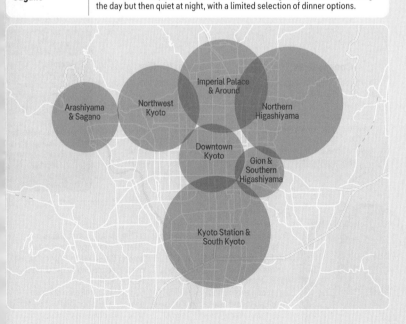

Family Travel

Whether it's the sushi, the temples or even the ninja, Kyoto's distinctive culture makes visiting as a family an unforgettable experience, especially if you add in a little modernity with a trip to Universal Studios Japan in Osaka or a jaunt on the bullet train. With a bit of prep and insider know-how, it can be relatively stress-free too.

The Essentials

Changing Department stores, malls and some stations have multipurpose restrooms with well-maintained changing beds.

Medical For doctors, dentists and other medical assistance, call the 24-hour Japan Visitor Hotline (050 3816 2787).

Supplies Japanese pharmacies stock essentials like nappies (diapers), baby formula and OTC medications, but the brands are almost always local and ingredients/instructions in Japanese. If possible, bring your own.

Eating Out

Family restaurants (aka *famiresu*) are a reasonably priced option that serve familiar Western dishes and kid-sized portions. For dinner, chain *izakaya* usually have no-smoking sections and can offer a mix of familiar flavours and local dishes, making them a good kid-adult compromise. To experience sushi, opt for a casual *kaitenzushi* (conveyor belt) restaurant – there's no need to stress about the kids being loud and the non-sushi items on the menu will suit picky eaters.

Concessions

Kids aged 12 and up typically pay adult rates for attractions and transport, including rail and bus passes. Children 11 and under usually pay 50% of the adult price, with those 5 and under often going free.

Breastfeeding

While breastfeeding in public in Japan isn't common, it isn't socially unacceptable if using a cover. For privacy, many mums head to baby/nursing rooms, which can be found in malls, department stores and most family-focused attractions.

KID-FRIENDLY ATTRACTIONS

TŌEI Kyoto Studio Park (p118)
Edo-era theme park with ninja- and samurai-inspired attractions geared to younger kids.

Kyoto Railway Museum (p48)
Driver training simulators plus a collection of classic trains ranging from steam engines to early bullet trains.

Kyoto International Manga Museum (p59)
Home to storytelling sessions, manga workshops and thousands of comics to read.

Sagano Romantic Train (p129)
A trundling, open-air train that delivers great views of Arashiyama.

FREE-RANGE KIDS

One thing that can be quite striking when visiting anywhere in Japan is how independent children are.

In residential areas and even on trains, it's normal to see primary- and secondary-school-aged kids travelling to and from school without adult supervision. Likewise, small children are allowed to go to the park to play without their parents.

One reason is that Japan has a relatively low crime rate, ranking among the safest countries on the planet, according to the Global Peace Index.

In schools, children are also given the responsibility of cleaning their own classrooms and taking turns with chores such as serving school lunches.

Health & Safe Travel

HEAT

The combination of heat and humidity makes summer sightseeing hard work in Kyoto, especially as the shrines and temples have little or no air conditioning. High temperatures remain above 30°C (86°F), and often loiter in the mid-to-high 30s, making heatstroke a major problem. Avoid going outside in the hottest hours, use hats and parasols, and hydrate frequently. Indoors, use air-conditioning and fans.

Quakes

Thousands of small earthquakes are felt in Japan annually, with occasional major events like the 9.0-magnitude Tōhoku earthquake in 2011. For emergency alerts and information on what to do in the event of an earthquake or other disaster, download the free, multilingual Safety Tips app (jnto.go .jp/safety-tips/eng/app.html). It also features useful language tips and guidance for getting medical care.

Emergency Help

For 24-hour English-language emergency consultation related to health and travel, call the Japan National Tourism Organization's Japan Visitor Hotline (050 3816 2787). Their online 'guide for when you are feeling ill' also lists medical institutions in Kyoto able to treat patients in English, plus information on where to buy insurance.

MEDICATION
You can bring a month's supply of prescription medications and two months of non-prescription medicines, but some meds aren't allowed.

INFOGRAPHIC: THE SHINDO EARTHQUAKE SCALE

Rather than the Richter scale, Japan measures earthquakes with the Shindo Intensity Scale, ranging from 0 (weakest) to 7 (strongest). If you turn on the TV immediately after a tremor, these are the numbers you'll see.

Shindo 3
Noticed by people in buildings and some who are walking.

Shindo 4
Startling.
Can wake you.
Felt by most.

Shindo 5
Difficult to walk.

Shindo 6–7
Can't stand.
Substantial damage.

Typhoons

Between May and October (especially August onwards), Japan experiences numerous typhoons. Generally, southern coastal regions bear the worst of the damage, but Kyoto can still be badly affected by heavy rain, strong winds and flooding, with transport and businesses disrupted. Do as the locals do: stay inside until the typhoon has passed.

CRIME RATES
Kyoto and Japan as a whole have a very low crime rate, with the national rate of robberies at 1.2 per 100,000 people (the USA is 81.4 per 100,000). Serious assault rates are similarly low. That doesn't mean travellers (especially women) shouldn't take basic precautions. Relatively prominent issues include sexual harassment towards women, including on busy trains.

Food, Drink & Nightlife

When to Eat

Chōshoku (7-10am) Except for cafes and family restaurants, not many places are open for breakfast.

Chūshoku (11am-2pm) Often set meals, but also the best time to get less-expensive sampler sets at high-end restaurants.

Yūshoku (5-11pm) Often features multiple dishes for sharing or multiple courses.

Where to Eat

Family restaurant Aka *famiresu*, these diner-like chain restaurants serve an affordable mixed menu

Izakaya Lively pubs with bites like *yakitori* and sashimi to pair with drinking

Kaitenzushi Low-cost sushi restaurants with conveyor-belt service

Kaiseki ryōri Japanese haute cuisine

Kissaten Old-fashioned cafes

Obanzai Like a home-cooked Kyoto tapas

Shōjin-ryōri Plant-based Buddhist cuisine

Tachinomiya Casual, smoky and no-frills standing bars

Teishokuya Budget-friendly places that focus on set meals (*teishoku*)

Yudōfu Specialises in simmered tofu

MENU DECODER

Ippin (一品) Appetizers/single dishes
Teishoku (定食) Set meal
Meibutsu (名物) Speciality
Chūmon (注文) Order
Tabemono (食べ物) Food
Sushi (寿司) Sushi
Sakana (魚) Fish
Niku (肉) Meat
Yasai (野菜) Vegetables
Dezāto (デザート) Dessert
Nomimono (飲み物) Drinks
Sake (酒) Alcohol
Nihonshu (日本酒) Sake
Bīru (ビール) Beer
Ocha (お茶) Tea
Aka wain (赤ワイン) Red wine

Shiro wain (白ワイン) White wine
En (円) Yen
Genkin nomi (現金のみ) Cash only
Zeikomi (税込) Tax included
Kaikei (会計) Bill/Amount due
Otsuri (お釣り) Change
Muryō (無料) Free
Arerugī (アレルギー) Allergy
Bīgan (ビーガン) Vegan
Bejitarian (ベジタリアン) Vegetarian
Seriakku-byō (セリアック病) Coeliac
Okosama Setto (お子様セット) Child's meal

HOW TO...

Pay the Bill

It depends on the restaurant or bar. In ramen shops and other low-cost eateries, you often choose your food and pay upfront at a vending machine that issues a meal ticket. In most places, however, you pay after the meal. Where the meal is quick and you aren't making repeated orders, you might receive the bill (to pay later) just after the food arrives. Elsewhere, staff will bring the bill when they know you've finished or once you've asked for it. To do that, say *kaikei* (bill) or just make an X with your index fingers. In more expensive restaurants, you can pay at your table, but it's more common to take the bill to the cashier by the exit. To split the bill, say *betsu betsu*. It's important to check beforehand whether the restaurant takes credit cards or other cashless payments. Some smaller or older places are still cash only.

HOW MUCH FOR...

kaitenzushi
¥2000

izakaya
¥4000

ramen
¥700

kaiseki
¥20,000

teishoku
¥1000

coffee
¥400

draught beer
¥500-700

HOW TO...

Order

Like paying the bill, ordering varies with the type of restaurant and meal. If you go for conveyer sushi (*kaitenzushi*), you can either grab items off the conveyor belt or use the touchscreen panel to order directly from the kitchen – the latter is fresher. At midrange sushi, à la carte and sets are usually available, but pointing to a picture of a set on the menu is the easiest option. At exclusive sushi restaurants, the service is *omakase* – the chef chooses what you'll be eating. Many mid- to high-end restaurants serving non-Japanese food will have some English on the menu.

Fast Fact

Common at high-end Japanese restaurants, *omakase* translates as 'I leave it to you'. The chef will serve whatever they think is most appropriate based on the season, the ingredients sourced that day, and any conversation they have with the guest.

Restaurants serving quick, cheap meals, such as ramen, *gyūdon*, and curry rice, often use a system where you select and pay for your food via a vending machine, which in turn issues a ticket that you hand to staff.

Chain *izakaya* and family restaurants frequently have touchscreen panels at the table or picture menus, both often with English. Independent *izakaya* can be much harder – they might have the menu written in Japanese only on strips of paper hanging on the wall. In that case, ask the staff what they recommend (*osusume wa arimasu ka*). Many lunchtime or *teishoku* places have replicas of their dishes in the window display, so if there's no English menu or picture menu, you can also go out and point. To grab the attention of staff at any restaurant, raise your hand and say *sumimasen* (excuse me).

ORDERING NIHONSHU

Whether you are out for sushi, *kaiseki* or an evening at an *izakaya*, there will be *nihonshu* (sake) on the menu. The easiest thing to do is ask for a recommendation and leave it at that, but if you want to pick your own, there are a few things to think about.

One is to decide how you want it served. Room temperature (*hiya*) and chilled (*reishu*) are common options, but in winter you could also have it warmed (*atsukan*). Next, do you prefer something sweet (*amakuchi*) or dry (*karakuchi*)? Then there are the grades – because not all *nihonshu* is made equal.

A regular cheap sake is *futsū* (standard), but for something finely crafted look for the word *junmai* (純米), the term given to

sake made with only rice, water, *kōji* mould and yeast.

If it's just *junmai*, it means the rice has a polishing rate of up to 60% (meaning up to 40% has been removed), so as well as the starchy centre of the grain, you'll also be getting some of the proteins and fats on the outer part of the grain in the brew. With *junmai ginjō* (純米吟醸), the polishing rate will be between 50% and 60%, with the resulting sake becoming a little less harsh.

Then comes the extra-pricey *junmai daiginjō* (純米大吟醸), which has a polishing rate of 50% or less, giving a very smooth finish. Remove the *junmai* from those labels and it means some brewers alcohol will have been added.

Responsible Travel

Climate Change & Travel

It's impossible to ignore the impact we have when travelling, and the importance of making changes where we can. Lonely Planet urges all travellers to engage with their travel carbon footprint. There are many carbon calculators online that enable travellers to estimate the carbon emissions generated by their journey; try https://www.resurgence.org/resources/carbon-calculator.html. Many airlines and booking sites offer travellers the option of off setting the impact of greenhouse gas emissions by contributing to climate-friendly initiatives around the world.

The Four Ss

Remember the Four S rule when it comes to ordering sushi: eating small, silver, seasonal and shellfish tends to be more sustainable. Also, skip the worst offenders: *unagi* (freshwater eel), shrimp and bluefin tuna.

Shop Secondhand

Kyoto's antique and flea markets are great for affordable, used souvenirs. The market at Tō-ji (p49) is worth a visit on the first Sunday and 15th of each month, as is the monthly flea market on the 25th at Kitano Tenman-gū (p117).

Manners Matter

You don't need to walk on eggshells at temples and shrines, but do follow the basic rules. Whether they are for removing your shoes or photography restrictions, locals take these rules seriously and they are usually well signposted.

Hiring a local guide can be a great way to get off the beaten path and mingle with Kyotoites. Booking directly also means more money ends up in local hands rather than with third-party sites.

The cherry blossoms of spring are beautiful, but coming to Kyoto in shoulder or low seasons instead helps to reduce the impact of overtourism. You'll find better deals, and fewer tourists, and have a more laid-back experience.

Sustainable Development Goals

The UN's Sustainable Development Goals (SDGs) are increasingly used by Japanese companies to highlight eco credentials. To weed out greenwashing, look for businesses that detail which of the SDGs they are targeting and steps they are taking.

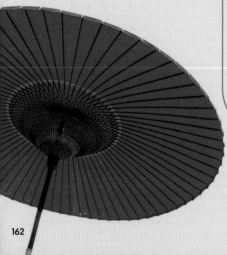

WATER REFILLS

To skip single-use plastic bottles, pack a water bottle and download the My Mizu app. With it, you'll be able to find free water refill points across Kyoto and elsewhere in Japan.

Plant-Based Traditions

Kyoto's traditional plant-based cuisine is excellent. Look for restaurants specializing in *yudōfu* (simmered tofu), such as Seigen-in (p114), or *shōjin-ryōri* featuring multiple small, in-season dishes. The latter can be found in Shigetsu at Tenryū-ji (p134), for example.

Go Indie

Instead of chain cafes, seek out Kyoto's excellent independent cafes. It's not just that you are supporting the local economy, but also that they tend to have more atmosphere, serve a better brew, and source their beans more ethically.

Save money and cut waste with end-of-day bargains on *bentō* boxes and other ready-made meals at supermarkets.

Many shops offer plastic bags (paid) and other packaging. Pack your own bag instead.

Animal Cafes

More and more animal cafes are appearing in Kyoto, but before visiting consider the stress the animals are under, and the poor reputation animal cafes have when it comes to neglect and animal care.

Kyoto Protocol

Kyoto famously gave its name to the Kyoto Protocol, an international agreement adopted in the city in 1997 with the aim of reducing carbon dioxide emissions. Eventually ratified by 192 parties, it has since been superseded by the 2015 Paris Agreement.

PEDAL POWER

For a low-impact way to get around and reduce the burden on Kyoto's crowded buses, rent a bicycle or use a bicycle share system; kyoto-bicycle.com has information on rentals, road rules and parking areas.

RESOURCES

moral.kyokanko.or.jp/en
Tips for sustainable travel in Kyoto

happycow.net
Vegan and vegetarian restaurant listings

japan.travel/en/ sustainable
JNTO's portal for sustainable travel in Japan

LGBTIQ+ Travellers

Kyoto is relatively low-key when it comes to venues and events specifically for the LGBTIQ+ community, but that doesn't mean the city is unwelcoming. Even though same-sex marriage is yet to be recognised in Japan, there are no laws against same-sex sexual activity and LGBTIQ+ travellers are unlikely to experience overt discrimination. And, with Osaka right next door, you aren't far from one of Japan's most vibrant LGBTIQ+ destinations.

LGBTIQ+ Venues

While the LGBTIQ+ scene in Kyoto pales in comparison to nearby Osaka, it's not entirely a wasteland. For bars, look to the neighbouring Kiyamachi and Ponto-chō areas, where among all the *izakaya* and restaurants you'll find **Bell Kyoto**, the lesbian-focused **Bar Look Me** (instagram.com/Lookmekyoto/) and the men-only **Azure** (azure-kyoto.info). For a bar that also does open-mic karaoke nights, there's Apple (apple1985.web.fc2.com). The biggest regular party is at Club Metro (metro.ne.jp), which despite not being a gay night club hosts the monthly Diamonds are Forever drag night.

PRIDE

Kyoto has a small Pride parade every spring and a smattering of minor events for a government-run Pride month in June, but the region's main Pride event takes place in nearby Osaka over two days in October. Called the Rainbow Festa, it attracts more than 20,000 people, with parades, music, food stalls and a mixture of events to celebrate the region's LGBTIQ+ community and promote diversity and acceptance.

Osaka's Gaybourhood

Near Umeda in Osaka, the Dōyama-chō district isn't exclusively for LGBTIQ+ venues, but it does have the greatest concentration of bars, clubs and restaurants for the community. That includes the foreigner-friendly bar **FrenZ FrenZY**, which is open to all – and once hosted Lady Gaga for a karaoke night.

CHANGING REPRESENTATION

LGBTIQ+ representation on Japanese TV has long tended to be focus on the stereotypically flamboyant, but several recent hit shows, such as the romantic comedy *What Did you Eat Yesterday?* (昨日何食べた) hint at change. Based on a successful manga series, it follows a middle-aged gay couple in Tokyo – one a lawyer, the other a hairdresser – in the process raising issues such as LGBTIQ+ rights.

RESOURCES

In Osaka, Pride Centre (pridecenter.jp) offers a safe space to all members of the LGBTIQ+ community, along with services such as counselling and educational seminars. The Osaka municipal government also runs the excellent Visit Gay Osaka website (visitgayosaka.com) for LGBTIQ+ travellers.

Public Affection

Regardless of sexuality or gender, Japanese people tend to avoid public displays of affection, even holding hands. While doing so is very unlikely to trigger abuse or hate speech, it can attract a few odd looks.

Accessible Travel

Kyoto is becoming more accessible, with an increasing number of businesses and the local government offering facilities such as multipurpose restrooms, wheelchair ramps and lifts. That said, traditional sights like temples and shrines can still be difficult to navigate.

Multipurpose Restrooms

You'll often find spacious multipurpose restrooms at stations, airports, malls, department stores, museums and some other public areas. They typically feature handrails, emergency call buttons, shower/sink for ostomate bag users, and multipurpose bed/mat.

RESOURCES

Accessible Japan (www.accessible-japan.com) is an excellent English-language resource, especially for getting around Japan in a wheelchair. It details accessibility information for many of Kyoto's major attractions.

Kyoto Universal Sightseeing (kyoto-universal.jp/en/) has info on accessible sights, model sightseeing routes and wheelchair rentals.

Airport

Kansai International Airport has loaner wheelchairs, personal mobility services and accessible toilets (with Braille information boards), among other facilities. For more details, visit kansai-airport .or.jp/en/service/bf or stop by the multilingual information counters in Terminal 1 (2F and 4F).

Accommodation

From budget business hotel to luxury property, modern hotels increasingly have one to a few barrier-free rooms, but older hotels and traditional ryokan often don't. Higher-range hotels typically offer better accessibility.

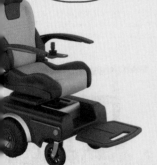

Wheelchair Size

Barrier-free facilities are designed for compact manual-electric Japanese wheelchairs, meaning overseas wheelchairs might be too wide for some ramps and lifts. Local rentals are possible through Accessible Japan.

Problematic Paths

The thick gravel pathways at many temples, gardens and shrines can be a major impediment for manual wheelchair users, anyone walking with a cane, and prams.

TACTILE PAVING

Found in stations and on pavements across Japan, Tenji Blocks are bright yellow markers to help those with partial vision and are also textured for cane users. The long lines on each block indicate direction, while the circles call out hazards.

Bus & Subway

Most Kyoto City Buses are wheelchair accessible but require the driver to set up a ramp for wheelchair users to get on and off the bus. The subway is fully accessible with lifts and has staff on hand if users need assistance boarding.

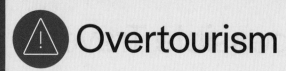

Overtourism

More tourists are good news for Kyoto's economy, but with 43 million visitors in 2022 as the city rebounded towards pre-COVID-19 tourist numbers, the city is once again feeling the strain of overtourism. Crowded buses, bars and restaurants; high-season lines for attractions; litter problems; and tourists disturbing the *wa* (harmony) have a growing number of locals calling for action.

ON THE BUSES

Kyoto's bus system often feels like it's creaking under the weight of overtourism, creating a degree of animosity towards travellers. That's why 2023 saw the local government do away with the one-day bus pass in favour of a one-day bus-subway pass, in the hope of spreading out tourist traffic better. To help ease the burden, you could try to avoid the peak travel times for locals during morning work and school rush hours (7-9am and 6-7pm).

Manners Matter

Another major focus of local authorities to date has been to promote good etiquette by foreigners (yes, despite only half a million of the 43 million tourists in 2022 being from overseas). In some cases, the near-ubiquitous manners posters state what should be obvious in any country, but they also offer a good rule of thumb for being respectful of locals. That's especially important when it comes to rules at temples and shrines, photography restrictions, and signs marking private property.

Hands-Free Sightseeing

A regular request on manner posters in Kyoto is to not bring large luggage on the buses and trains. Related to that, the city government has a website dedicated to hands-free sightseeing (hands-free.kyoto.travel) listing coin lockers, large luggage storage and luggage delivery services. At Kansai International Airport, you can have luggage delivered to your hotel in Kyoto with JAL ABC (jalabc.com).

Gion Restrictions

As of April 2024, certain private alleyways and side streets in Gion are officially off-limits to tourists, largely in response to tourists harassing geisha for photos. These restricted streets are well marked by multilingual signs. Be aware that there are ¥10,000 fines for anybody caught trespassing on private property. You can still visit Gion's main street, Hanami-kōji, but photographing geisha there isn't allowed without a permit.

WHAT'S NEXT?

When elected in 2024, Kyoto's mayor Matsui Kōji outlined several potential options for tackling overtourism. One would be to have higher public transport fares for non-residents; another the creation of a sightseeing bus route separate from the City Bus routes that locals use. There could even be smart bins installed, which when full would automatically let the municipal waste collection department know it's time to come and collect. Aimed more at domestic travellers, there might also be no-go driving zones for non-residents.

Nuts & Bolts

OPENING HOURS

Banks 9am-3pm Monday to Friday

Bars 6pm-midnight

Department stores 10am-8pm, with restaurant floors open longer

Museums 10am-6pm, often closed Mondays

Restaurants 11.30am-2pm and 6-10pm

Shops 9am-5pm

The Escalator Conundrum

Here's a local quirk. In Tokyo, people stand on the left side of escalators and walk up the right. Osaka does things the opposite way around. In Kyoto it isn't always clear cut, but the majority stick to Osaka rules: stand right, walk left.

Internet Access

Airports, stations, cafes, hotels and busy tourist areas often have free wi-fi, but it can be unreliable. Consider renting a mobile wi-fi router or buying a SIM card at the airport when you arrive.

GOOD TO KNOW

Time zone
GMT/UTC plus 9 hours

Country code
+81

Emergency number
119

Population
1.38 million

PUBLIC HOLIDAYS

There are 16 public holidays in Japan. Some businesses and nonessential services may be closed on public holidays and during the Obon (13-15 August) and year-end periods.

New Year's Day 1 January

Coming of Age Day 2nd Monday in January

National Foundation Day 11 February

Emperor's Birthday 23 February

Vernal Equinox Day 21 March

Showa Day 29 April

Constitution Memorial Day 3 May

Greenery Day 4 May

Children's Day 5 May

Marine Day 3rd Monday in July

Mountain Day 11 August

Respect for the Aged Day 3rd Monday in September

Autumnal Equinox Day 23 September

Sports Day 2nd Monday in October

Culture Day 3 November

Labour Thanksgiving Day 23 November

Electricity
100V/50Hz

Type A
120V/60Hz

Type B
120V/60Hz

Tap Water
Tap water is safe in Kyoto. For refill points, download the MyMizu app.

Bicycle Parking
Only park in designated zones or your bike can get impounded with a ¥3500 penalty.

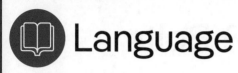 # Language

You can have a fantastic time in Japan's major cities without speaking Japanese, but even just a few phrases will help you make friends, attract smiles and advice from locals, and ensure you have a rich and rewarding travel experience.

Basics

Hello こんにちは
kon·ni·chi·wa

Goodbye さようなら *sa·you·na·ra*

Yes はい *hai*

No いいえ *ee·ay*

Please (when asking) ください
ku·da·sai

Please (when offering) どうぞ
dō·zo

Thank you ありがとう *a·ri·ga·tō*

Excuse me (to get attention)
すみません *su·mi·ma·sen*

Sorry ごめんなさい
go·men·na·sai

What's your name?
お名前は何ですか?
o·na·ma·e wa nan desu ka

My name is ...
私の名前は … です
wa·ta·shi no na·ma·e wa ... desu

How are you?
お元気ですか?
o·gen·ki desu ka

Fine. And you?
はい、元気です。 あなたは?
hai, gen·ki desu. a·na·ta wa

Do you speak English?
英語が話せますか?
eigo ga ha·na·se·masu ka

I don't understand.
わかりません
wa·ka·ri·ma·sen

Does anyone speak English?
どなたか英語を 話せますか?
do·na·ta ka eigo o ha·na·se·masu ka

Directions

Where's the ... ?
… はどこですか?
... wa do·ko desu ka

What's the address?
住所は何ですか?
jū·sho wa nan desu ka

Could you please write it down?
書いてくれませんか?
kai·te ku·re·ma·sen ka

Can you show me (on the map)?
(地図で)教えて くれませんか?
(chi·zu de) o·shi·e·te ku·re·ma·sen ka

Signs

Entrance	入口
Exit	出口
Open	営業中/開館
Closed	閉店/閉館
Information	インフォメーション
Danger	危険
Toilets	トイレ
Women	女
Men	男

Emergencies

Help! たすけて!
tasukete

Go away! 離れろ!
ha·na·re·ro

Call the police! 警察を呼んで!
kē·sa·tsu o yon·de

Call a doctor! 医者を呼んで!
i·sha o yon·de

I'm ill. 私は病気です
wa·ta·shi wa byō·ki desu

NUMBERS

1 一 *i·chi*

2 二 *ni*

3 三 *san*

4 四 *shi/yon*

5 五 *go*

6 六 *ro·ku*

7 七 *shi·chi/na·na*

8 八 *ha·chi*

9 九 *ku/kyū*

10 十 *jū*

DONATIONS TO ENGLISH

There are several – you may recognise futon, karaoke, tsunami, bentō box and manga, to name a few.

PRONUNCIATION TIPS

Japanese pronunciation is not considered difficult for English speakers. Unlike some other Asian languages, it has no tones and most of its sounds are also found in English.

Vowels

Vowels in Japanese can be either short or long. The long ones should be held twice as long as the short ones and are represented with a macron (horizontal line) on top of them.

Consonants

Most consonant sounds are pretty close to their English counterparts. Pronounce the double consonants with a slight pause between them, as this can change the meaning.

WHO SPEAKS JAPANESE?

10 Phrases to Sound Like a Local

How are you? げんき？ *gen-key*

I'm fine げんき *gen-key*

Delicious うまい *ooh-my*

That looks delicious おいしそう *o-ee-she-so*

You're kidding!? うそ？ *ooh-so*

See you later じゃあね *ja-nay*

Wow! すごい！ *su-goy-ee*

Excuse me すみません *su-mee-ma-sen*

Good luck がんばれ *gan-ba-ray*

OK? だいじょうぶ？ *dai-jo-bu*

10 Kansai-ben Phrases

How are you? もうかりまっか？ *mō·ka·ri·ma·kka*

I'm OK ぼちぼち *bo·chee bo·chee*

That's right そーやな *sō·ya·na*

Never mind かまへん *ka·ma·hen*

Don't/No good あかん *a·kan*

No/That's wrong ちゃう *cha·u*

Good ええ *ey*

Thank you おうきに *ō·ki·nee*

Really? ほんま？ *hon·ma*

How much? なんぼう？ *na·n·bou*

Japanese is spoken by more than 125 million people. While it bears some resemblance to Altaic languages such as Mongolian and Turkish, and has grammatical similarities to Korean, its origins are unclear.

Regional Dialects
- Eastern (Hokkaidō; east of the Japan Alps on Honshū)
- Western (Shikoku; west of the Japan Alps on Honshū)
- Kyūshū dialects (Kyūshū)
- Ryūkyūan dialects (Ryūkyū Islands)

Standard Language
- Tokyo dialect (whole country)

Japan ●

STORYBOOK

Our writers delve deep into different aspects of Kyoto life

Main hall, Ryōan-ji (p115)

A HISTORY OF KYOTO IN
15 PLACES

For almost 1000 years Kyoto was the ruling centre of Japan, where emperors and shoguns vied for power and control, great Buddhist sects rose up, and many of the mainstays of Japanese culture were born. Though no longer the capital, Kyoto remains the cultural heart of Japan. By Tom Fay

ARCHAEOLOGICAL EVIDENCE SHOWS that people have been living in the Kyoto basin since at least the Jōmon era (14,000–300 BCE). The first vestiges of a city began in 794 CE, when Emperor Kammu relocated the capital of Japan from Nara to Kyoto. Known as Heian-kyō, this new city was built as a replica of Chang'an, the capital of the Tang dynasty; it marked the beginning of the Heian era (794–1185) and the flourishing of Japanese culture as we know it, with the development of art and literature, and the increasing influence of powerful Buddhist sects.

It also saw the rise of the samurai class, with battles between their factions in later centuries culminating in widespread destruction to the streets of Kyoto during the Ōnin War (1467–77). Kyoto was eventually rebuilt by the famous samurai warlords Toyotomi Hideyoshi and later Tokugawa Ieyasu, who both worked to unite a country ripped apart by civil wars and the latter of whom established the shogunate in Edo (Tokyo). Kyoto prospered during the peaceful Edo period (1603–1868), with a new merchant class patronising the arts. The emperor and capital moved to Edo following the Meiji Restoration in 1868, and this signalled the start of the modern era. Kyoto was spared from major bombing in WWII, and its cultural treasures now attract millions of tourists every year.

1. Shimogamo-jinja
PRECURSOR TO THE CAPITAL

One of the oldest Shintō shrines in Japan, Shimogamo-jinja is one of the pair of ancient Kamo shrines (along with Kamigamo-jinja) that significantly predate the official formation of the city in 794. Shimogamo is the older of the two shrines by at least a hundred years, and was probably built in the 6th century. As the new capital grew up around them, the Kamo shrines were seen as crucial for protecting Kyoto (then Heian-kyō) from malign influences. The name is also a reference to the Kamo clan, who were the area's early inhabitants. Their descendants still live close by today.

For more on Shimogamo-jinja, see page 77

2. Fushimi Inari-Taisha
ODE TO OLDER TIMES

There are numerous Inari shrines in Japan, but this is the largest and oldest of them all. The hundreds of small shrines and fox statues among its precincts points to a deep history of spirituality and animism, and the many bright vermilion *torii* gates of Fushimi Inari hark back to an older time, when most of the ancient structures of Kyoto and Nara were painted a brilliant red. This has roots in Taoism, which came before before Buddhism reached its ascendency in Kyoto, and then the later development of *wabi* culture (an aesthetic of simplicity and understated imperfection) and its more muted tones.

For more on Fushimi Inari-Taisha, see page 44

3. Kiyomizu-dera

BUDDHISM GAINING GROUND

Kiyomizu-dera, one of Kyoto's most famous Buddhist temples, was established in 778, though most of the structures remaining today date back to its 1633 reconstruction. Originally associated with the influential Hōsso sect from the earlier Nara period, the construction of such an imposing temple hints at the increasing power Buddhism exerted over politics and the imperial court during the Heian period. Indeed, one of the reasons why Emperor Kammu moved the capital to Kyoto from Nara is because of the strong influence Buddhist monasteries were having on the government there.

For more on Kiyomizu-dera, see page 98

Lanterns, Shimogamo-jinja (p77)

4. Tō-ji

MONUMENT OF AGES

When it was constructed in 796, Tō-ji was one of only three Buddhist temples permitted in the newly formed capital. It is something of a generational time capsule, housing treasures from the Heian era, while the complex itself has buildings spanning the Kamakura (1185–1333) to Edo (1603–1868) periods. Tō-ji is often associated with Kōbō Daishi (also known as Kūkai), and the influential Buddhist priest and founder of the powerful Shingon sect was put in charge there in 823. Shingon would go on to have influence on other forms of Japanese Buddhism (Tendai, Shugen-dō and Zen), and have a broader influence on feudal-era art, crafts and aesthetics.

For more on Tō-ji, see page 49

5. Kyoto Imperial Palace

COURTLY RULE

The current Kyoto Imperial Palace – formerly the emperor's residence – dates from 1855. It was built to the east of the original and larger Heian Palace, which was the first and most important structure to be constructed in the new capital, and was the base from where the emperor ruled. However, following numerous fires and reconstructions during the Heian period, the palace's importance waned as emperors stayed at their secondary palaces. Many of these palaces were provided by the increasingly powerful Fujiwara family, who would go on to dominate the imperial court for centuries. The Heian Palace was eventually abandoned in the late 12th century.

For more on Kyoto Imperial Palace, see page 75

6. Yasaka-jinja

FLOATING FESTIVAL

Once called Gion Shrine, construction on this Shintō monument began as early as 656, and it became one of Kyoto's key religious sites during the early Heian era. It is now known as the principal shrine of the Gion Matsuri, Japan's most famous summer festival, which traces its origins back to the year 869 when a terrible epidemic swept the country. To appease the spirits believed to be responsible for the disease, the emperor instigated a Shintō ritual in which 66 pikes representing all the provinces of the country were carried in a procession. This would become an annual event, with the pikes eventually replaced by the much larger, decorated floats seen at the festival today.

For more on Yasaka-jinja, see page 89

7. Kennin-ji
ORIGIN OF ZEN

Founded in 1202, Kennin-ji is said to be Kyoto's oldest Zen temple. Its first priest was the Japanese Buddhist monk Eisai, who among other things is credited with introducing Zen to Japan following his trip to China from 1187 to 1191. Zen had been known in Japan much earlier, but it wasn't able to gain a foothold due to opposition from the powerful Tendai school of Buddhism. However, Zen would go on to have huge influence in Kyoto, as temples and gardens proliferated and the city became the Zen capital of Japan. Eisai also brought back something else from China that would further shape the culture of Kyoto: green tea.

For more on Kennin-ji, see page 94

8. Kinkaku-ji
GOLDEN FIRES

One of Kyoto's most instantly recognisable icons, Kinkaku-ji – the Golden Pavillion – started life as an aristocratic villa, until it was purchased by the shogun Ashikaga Yoshimitsu in 1397 and used as a retreat. It was converted into a Zen temple following his death. Its history hasn't been all peace and tranquillity, however; during the devastating Ōnin War (1467–77), which destroyed much of city, most of the temple buildings were burnt to the ground. It was burned down again in 1950 in an act of arson by a novice monk during a mental health crisis.

For more on Kinkaku-ji, see page 120

9. Ginkaku-ji
SYMBOL OF CULTURE

Officially named Jishō-ji, and in English known as the 'Temple of the Silver Pavillion', this beautiful complex was used as a retreat by shogun Asikaga Yoshimasa, who is said to have sat in contemplation in the gardens as the city around burned during the Ōnin War. The war signalled the start of the Sengoku ('Warring States') period, a century of civil risings and social upheaval. In 1490 work began on converting Ginkaku-ji into a Zen temple following the shogun's death, and its aesthetic beauty became a symbol of Higashiyama-bunka, a segment of culture that saw innovations in architecture, theatre and the arts.

For more on Ginkaku-ji, see page 104

10. Hongan-ji
TIME FOR A REBUILD

A few blocks north of Kyoto Station, the twin temples of Hongan-ji (east and west) belong to the Jōdo Shinshū school, the most popular form of Buddhism in Japan today. They have had a tumultuous history. During the 15th century the temple was attacked three times by warrior monks of the Tendai sect based on Mount Hiei. In the late 16th century, Oda Nobunaga, one of the main figures of the violent Sengoku period and the first great unifier of Japan, burnt the temple down. Hongan-ji was rebuilt by Nobunaga's successor Toyotomi Hideyoshi (1536–98), who reconstructed the war-torn city with new north–south roads, bridges and gates. Much of this blueprint is still present in the Kyoto of today.

For more on Hongan-ji, see page 47

11. Nijō-jō
INTO EDO

A striking symbol of the Tokugawa shogunate that came into power at the start of the Edo period (1603-1868), Nijō-jō was started by Tokugawa Ieyasu in 1601, although it was not completed until 1626 during the reign of his successor (Tokugawa Iemitsu). The castle was used as the Kyoto residence for Tokugawa shoguns, who ruled from Edo (present-day Tokyo) with the help of loyal *daimyō* (regional lords), though Kyoto was still home of the Imperial Court. The Edo period was characterised by economic growth, the start of Japan's isolationist policy, relative peace and a prospering of the arts and culture, especially in Kyoto.

For more on Nijō-jō, see page 56

12. Nishiki Market
COMMERCIAL SUCCESS

The peace and prosperity of the Tokugawa (Edo) period was accompanied by some

Kennin-ji (p94)

extreme policies, as Christianity was banned and Japan opted to cut itself off from the outside world. But there was a great expansion of the nation's cities: in Kyoto the population rose to 400,000 and remained steady for much of the period, and the city's artisans helped Kyoto became a production centre for luxury goods and a hub for crafts and the arts. The now-famous Nishiki Market has long been a thriving commercial district – many of the goods and fresh produce traded there today have origins harking back to this time.

For more on Nishiki Market, see page 68

13. Gion
ENTERTAINMENT AND ARTS

As well as economic growth, the Tokugawa era also saw the development of new art forms such as kabuki theatre, bunraku puppet-plays and wood-block prints, and Gion emerged as Kyoto's most prominent entertainment and geisha district. *Geiko* (the Kyoto term for geisha) actually have origins going back much further, but it was in the 18th century when the distinctive kimono-clad entertainers as we now know them first began working in the upmarket *ochaya* (teahouses) for the amusement of a new wave of merchant-class patrons.

For more on Gion, see page 86

14. Heian-jingū
HOMAGE TO THE PAST

The Meiji Revolution in 1868 was a colossal blow to the foundations of Japan. For the first time in centuries it restored power to the emperor, Japan's isolationist policy came to an end, and the country began to import Western ideas and technology as it embarked on a fast-track to industrialisation. It was an era-ending moment for Kyoto, as the the imperial court moved to Tokyo, and the city lost some of its merchants, scholars and artisans. Heian-jingū was one of the first big monuments of the Meiji era; it was built in 1895 to commemorate the 1100th anniversary of the city's founding, and was constructed in homage to Heian-era architecture – a poignant end to Kyoto's chapter as capital city.

For more on Heian-jingū, see page 103

15. Kyoto Tower
SYMBOL OF THE NEW

Thankfully most of Kyoto was spared destruction in WWII, and although Japan suffered great losses, in the following decades the country's economy boomed. Kyoto Tower was built in 1964 as a symbol of this rejuvenation, but its modern design caused consternation among those who thought Kyoto should do more to preserve its heritage. It was the same story in 1997 when the futuristic-styled Kyoto Station was opened to even fiercer criticism. It still divides opinion to this day in a city that wrestles with the issue of incorporating the new while conserving the old; just a few blocks from the station is where Rashōmon, Kyoto's original city gate, used to stand.

For more on Kyoto Tower, see page 46

MEET THE KYOTOITES

Kyoto has long been a city accustomed to hosting guests from other regions, and despite a reputation as being polite but reserved, Kyotoites have warm hearts when you eventually find a way in. TOM FAY introduces the people of his adopted home.

MANY STEREOTYPES CHARACTERISE the Japanese as hard-working, quiet and polite, and these stem from a societal expectation that seeks harmony, and a desire to 'fit in' and not upset the applecart. This is true to an extent, but when you consider all of Japan's many subcultures (from makeup-obsessed *gyaru* girls to throttle-thrashing *bōsōzoku* biker gangs), it is clear that people don't always aim to conform.

Stereotypes are spread by the Japanese themselves too: Kyotoites are famously described as refined but aloof, Osakans as talkative and friendly, and Tokyoites as uptight and unapproachable – but how much this rings true is a matter of opinion.

Kyoto is a of temples and shrines, but the vast majority of Japanese people are in fact not particularly religious; Shintō and Buddhism are both deeply ingrained in Japanese culture, but more in the form of well-practised traditions (Shintō weddings and Buddhist funeral ceremonies) than a pious belief system.

In Kyoto, as in much of Japan, society is rapidly ageing, as birth rates plummet and the population rate is on the decline. In the cities, this is noticeable by the sheer number of elderly folk out and about (many of whom remain remarkably sprightly) and a yearly decrease in class numbers

People of Kyoto

Kyoto has a population of just over 1.45 million people, making it the ninth-most populous city in Japan, and is the capital of Kyoto Prefecture (population 2.5 million). Outside of the city, much of the prefecture is rural and sparsely populated.

at schools. But in more rural areas – including large swathes of Kyoto Prefecture – the evidence is starker, with millions of empty houses *(akiya)*, boarded-up primary schools and shops, and farmland left to go fallow.

Much like the enigmatic meanings of Japanese gardens and temples, it is often said that Kyotoites themselves should not be taken at face value; you must peel back the ingrained levels of politeness and learn to read subtle clues in order to really understand their thinking. For instance, there is the famous example of *bubuzuke* (or *chazuke*), which is a staple Kyoto dish of hot tea poured on rice and eaten with pickles, typically served towards the end of the meal in *kaiseki* (Japanese haute cuisine). When visiting a Kyotoite's house and your host asks if you would care for *bubuzuke*, it should be taken as a sign that it is time to leave.

But Kyotoites have a rich heritage to be proud of, and as Japan goes forward and battles with issues such as an ageing society, population decrease and over-tourism, it will be a delicate challenge for the people of Kyoto to preserve their precious crafts, art forms and cultural legacy for future generations to enjoy.

KYOTO FROM (ALMOST) THE INSIDE

Although I will never be classed as a native Kyotoite, I live in Kyoto and have interacted with enough locals over the years to have some grasp of what it means to be born and bred in this city. Admittedly, I now call countryside Kyoto home, so I will never attain the cultured refinement reserved for Kyoto's urban elite.

Kyotoites take great pride in their heritage – Kyoto was, after all, the birthplace of Heian courtly customs and many of the traditional arts that still embody and define Japanese culture and society today. Perhaps it is a sense of custodial duty that can make Kyotoites come off as guarded (especially compared to their rambunctious Osakan neighbours), but I think it is more a case of them being proudly protective of their heritage. Kyoto is not a place that shuns outsiders; its secrets and nuances simply have to be unearthed and earned, and that's what makes it an alluring place to live.

177

Cherry blossoms
GUITAR PHOTOGRAPHER/SHUTTERSTOCK ©

THE SEASONS
IN KYOTO CULTURE

Seasonal expression is deeply woven into Japan's cultural fabric.
Nowhere more so than in the ancient capital Kyoto. By Rob Goss

WITH THE CHERRY blossoms of spring and fiery foliage of autumn, Kyoto's seasonal colours are among its biggest attractions. But embracing the seasons is also a cornerstone of traditional arts and the culinary world, the tea ceremony and haiku verse, and many other aspects of life in Kyoto.

Appreciating the Seasons
Looking at the natural world, the hanami (flower-viewing) parties of spring and kōyō (autumn foliage) are major events in Kyoto. Yet the city's parks, gardens, shrines, and temples are often designed to allow a broader appreciation of the seasons beyond spring and autumn. In February and early March, for example, Kitano Tenman-gū (p117) has some 2000 plum trees in bloom, signaling the first steps from winter to spring, while in late April and early May hanging wisteria add a violet contrast to the red-and-white architecture of Byōdō-in, the temple on the ¥10 coin (p51). In late May, the wooden framework of Shisen-dō's (p108) tatami mat hermitage almost acts like a picture frame for its sand garden and blueish-purple azaleas. That is a trick also employed at nearby Enkō-ji Temple

(p108), albeit with autumn colours held in view. The result is that whatever time of year you might visit Kyoto, there will be opportunities to appreciate the changing seasons and see how ingrained seasonality is in the culture of Kyoto.

The Tea Ceremony
Take a seat on the tatami-mat flooring of a tea ceremony room and you'll see the seasons reflected in many (sometimes subtle) ways. Perhaps the most noticeable expression is the room itself, which from late autumn to early spring typically features an iron kettle heated on a *ro* (a sunken hearth in the tatami). This is covered and replaced by a *furo* (brazier) placed on the tatami for the rest of the year.

Then come the finer details. The host's kimono will probably feature seasonal tones, although always with a simple, understated design that won't draw the guest's attention away from the more important seasonal design on the teacups. At Koto (p115) near Kinkaku-ji Temple, these cups change monthly, with motifs such as cherry blossoms, maples, and irises reflecting the changes taking place beyond the teahouse.

Culinary Seasonality

The tea served at tea ceremonies or in tearooms like that at Murin-An Villa (p106) is usually accompanied by traditional Japanese sweets called wagashi. These sweets themselves frequently express the time of year – whether that's because of the timely ingredients used or the shape of the sweet. In March, just as the cherry blossoms are contemplating their annual explosion of colour, a popular wagashi is sakuramochi, a pink-coloured rice cake *(mochi)* wrapped with a pickled cherry blossom leaf. Summer could be a refreshing mizu yōkan, a chilled confection made with red bean paste, agar, and sugar that is akin to a thick cube of jelly.

In Kyoto (and across Japan), there is also a tendency for chefs to focus on in-season produce, and something like kaiseki-ryōri takes that to different levels. Served in Kyoto at high-end restaurants such as Kikunoi Roan (p63), these multi-course meals, featuring a course of a dozen or so small yet beautifully presented dishes, are a fusion of culinary arts and seasonal appreciation. That might include seasonal motifs on the tableware and plate decorations, such as a maple leaf or sprig of budding blossom, but most importantly sees chefs aiming to draw natural flavours out of produce at the peak of its seasonality and freshness. With that, you can expect earthy matsutake mushrooms, Japanese chestnuts, and maybe snow crab in an autumnal kaiseki course, then perhaps bamboo shoots and firefly squid in spring. Another local delicacy, *hamo* (pike conger eel), is considered at its best in July, just after the rainy season has ended.

The Arts

Arguably most striking is how traditional art showcases the seasons. The screen door paintings at temples like Eikan-dō and Nanzen-ji (to name just two of many) include delicate representations of cherry blossoms and bare winter branches. Woodblock print artists have often focused on capturing Kyoto's distinctive seasonal faces – like Kawase Hasui's depictions of Kinkaku-ji and Kiyomuzu-dera blanketed with snow in winter. Head to the Kyoto National Museum (p95) and you'll see that trend continued across multiple genres of arts and crafts, including textiles and even ceramics.

A seasonal aspect is also integral to Japanese haiku, the short verse traditionally comprised of three lines of five, seven, and five syllables. There's even a word, kigo, that refers to the word or phrase in a haiku – whether related to the animal world, the earth, plants, observances, or even humanity – that gives us a sense of the season. That could be a reference to new rice in autumn or wild ducks in winter. Writing about Kyoto in the 1600s, the country's most famous haikuist, Matsuo Bashō, used a cuckoo to call to mind the renewal brought by spring: even in Kyoto / hearing the cuckoo's cry / I long for Kyoto.

The 72 Seasons

While the four seasons are frequently referenced in Japan, the traditional Japanese calendar was actually divided in 24 periods, each of which had three subdivisions of roughly five days each. Together, these 72 micro seasons detail the natural world's annual changes and have served as an inspiration for generations of artists. Due to changes to the climate, the old divisions no longer exactly match the current calendar of the natural world, but they still give us the opportunity to consider life through a wonderfully poetic lens. In early May, for example, you have a period called *kawazu hajimete naku* (frogs begin singing), immediately followed by *mimizu izuru* (worms surface). July sees warm winds blow *(atsukaze itaru)*, the first irises blossom (hasu hajimete hiraku), and hawks learn to fly *(taka sunawachi waza o narau)*. As the colours of autumn begin to fade at the end of November, we get perhaps the saddest of the 72 seasons: that's when rainbows hide *(niji kakurete miezu)*.

ROCKS & RAKED SAND
A GARDEN GUIDE

The embodiment of living history, Kyoto's gardens reveal Japan's profound and long-standing kinship with nature, beauty and spirituality. By Thomas O'Malley

IN KYOTO, IT can seem like you're never more than a few feet away from a lovingly tended garden. Here a precise whirlpool of raked gravel, there a pond fringed by delicate moss. You'll find them at Zen temples, royal palaces, Shintō shrine complexes and private villas. Some Kyoto gardens are arenas of beauty, designed to be enjoyed for pleasure's sake. Others are sacred spaces meant to inspire deep thought and introspection. Most are a bit of both. All are rich in symbolism and allusion, and taken together tell a story of Kyoto through the ages.

Hemmed in by forested hills, Kyoto is ideally suited to gardens. As well as plenty of wood and stone at hand, there are rivers, streams and underground springs, while the high humidity presents ideal conditions for growing moss, a key garden plant.

Japan's capital for over a thousand years, Kyoto's wealth and prestige meant no shortage of benefactors willing to invest in elaborate landscaping endeavours, while its ruling and religious classes designed garden spaces to reflect their own philosophies and aesthetic sensibilities. And that's before you factor in Japan's far

Strolling garden, Katsura Rikyū (p131)
BEIBAOKE/ SHUTTERSTOCK ©

A hōjō garden, Tōfuku-ji (p43)

older veneration of nature itself, investing rocks, trees, hills and forests with an animistic, god-like mystique.

Zen & the Art of Garden Design

Picture a Kyoto garden and you probably imagine a bed of whiteish-grey gravel or coarse sand raked into neat furrows, a few weathered rocks seemingly plonked down at random, and perhaps some green moss or a pruned bush. Known as *karesansui*

('dry landscape'), this type of garden is a fixture of Kyoto's Zen Buddhist temples, but the style had been around long before Zen established itself in Japan in the 12th century. Sand or gravel was used in gardens where water was scarce, and to symbolise purity at Shintō shrines. But when applied to Zen, raked gravel can be taken to represent flowing water or the ocean, or a concept even more abstract, such as emptiness or eternity.

Rocks, meanwhile, might represent islands or mountains from ancient Chinese mythology. In groupings of three, one tall and two shorter, they symbolise Buddha and his attendants. A group of rocks might be a waterfall, or a dragon taking flight. A tall rock next to a flat rock can represent the crane and the turtle, together embodying longevity and happiness. One soars to the heavens, the other swims to the depths, representing the unity of creation. Or those rocks might just be moments in time, thoughts in the mind, or simply there to draw you to the empty space in between. At Ryōan-ji (p115), the world's most famous *karesansui,* scholars have argued endlessly over what its 15 rocks might symbolise – baby tigers, mountain peaks, an abstract tree or nothing at all – but few would dispute their power to provoke thought and in turn aid meditation.

A TALL ROCK NEXT TO A FLAT ROCK CAN REPRESENT THE CRANE AND THE TURTLE, TOGETHER EMBODYING LONGEVITY AND HAPPINESS.

Resisting interpretation is an integral feature of Zen, with its love of philosophical riddles and paradox. *Karesansui* were designed not to be walked through but viewed and pondered from a fixed position, often the wooden veranda of the abbot's quarters. Many are enclosed by walls like a canvas, or framed through open sliding doors, providing a sense of oneness with nature. Tending the garden was an act of meditation for junior monks as much as pondering it was a meditative aid for Zen abbots. A lack of ostentation, a sense of tranquillity, and a desire to strip away illusion were all-important qualities that would give rise to the Japanese aesthetic of minimalism.

Finding Pleasure in a Strolling Garden
To be strolled in rather than studied, Kyoto's other main garden variety is the *shūyū* (strolling garden). *Shūyū* were often found on imperial or feudal estates, and were designed primarily for pleasure. Pavilions, teahouses and villas are typically set around a pond, with pursuits, such as fishing, boating, moon-viewing and poetry writing, taking place.

In the Edo period, these were known as *kaiyū* ('many-pleasure') gardens, and featured graceful arching bridges, moon-viewing platforms and stepped paths designed to gradually reveal the garden, one carefully orchestrated view at a time.

At Katsura Rikyū (p131), a Kyoto garden created by an imperial prince, famous Japanese landscapes are rendered in miniature, while stone lanterns on the pond's 'beaches' represent lighthouses.

Guests would travel between various themed teahouses by boat, in what amounted to a condensed, idealised world not unlike the modern theme park. Also playing with a sense of scale is the technique of *shakkei* (borrowed scenery) used in both *shūyū* and *karesansui* gardens, whereby elements, such as trees and hills, that fall outside the boundaries of the garden are skillfully incorporated into its design.

All in Harmony & Balance
For all the pruned perfection of Kyoto's gardens, the intention is that they should appear natural, or rather represent nature in an ideal state, and by extension, humanity's communion with it. The artful use of asymmetrical compositions – the irregular shape of a pond, for example – along with carefully chosen materials like rocks, water and plants, are all ways a garden designer can evoke untamed nature, and by extension nurture a kind of enlightened symbiosis between humans and the world around them.

As for whether you'll feel this oneness with nature when exploring Kyoto's gardens, a lot hinges on your approach. Slow down your footsteps, resist reaching for that camera phone, clear your mind, and be prepared to look longer and deeper than you might be accustomed to. Take in all those little details – the subtly shifting sunlight, a falling leaf, the murmur of a breeze. Above all, choose the garden less visited, avoid busy periods if you can, and you'll be giving yourself the best chance to make that special connection.

LEVELLING UP
KYOTO & THE MAKING OF MARIO

Home of the geisha, Japan's ancient capital is also where you'll find one of the world's most forward-thinking entertainment companies. By Thomas O'Malley

IF YOU HANG out at the Monkey Park in Arashiyama you'll see that Kyoto is well stocked with macaques, but did you know it once had a giant gorilla? Going by the name Donkey Kong, the lovable lunk was the girlfriend-snatching antagonist of a 1981 arcade game, developed by a struggling Kyoto firm called Nintendo.

The job of designer for this early venture into arcade machines fell to an inexperienced employee named Shigeru Miyamoto. As it turned out, *Donkey Kong* was a smash hit, the biggest selling arcade game in Japan and North America for two years straight. Players controlled a character called Jumpman, and had

Super Mario display, Takashimaya (p59)
BUDDHIKA WEERASINGHE/BLOOMBERG VIA GETTY IMAGES ©

to dodge Donkey Kong's barrels while climbing up through a construction site to rescue his beloved. With his red hat and moustache, Jumpman would later go by another name, known to the world as Mario.

But long before that, the story started with playing cards. Founded in Kyoto in 1889, Nintendo Koppai had a profitable line in brightly coloured Japanese playing cards called *hanafuda*. Over time, the cards came to be associated with gambling and the *yakuza,* Japan's largest organised crime syndicate, so in the 1950s Nintendo branched out. They had a crack at making instant rice, vacuum cleaners and photocopiers, and ventured into industries like taxis. None met with much success, until the company turned to the new technology of video games.

The success of *Donkey Kong* transformed Nintendo's fortunes, and its designer Shigeru Miyamoto would go on to develop iconic franchises like *Super Mario* and *The Legend of Zelda,* a game Miyamoto claimed was inspired by growing up in rural Kyoto prefecture. Both titles were released on 1983's Famicom, a home games console known outside Japan as the Nintendo Entertainment System. Selling 2.5 million units in its first year, the 'NES' has even been credited with saving the games industry, which at that time was suffering a grim recession due to a flood of poor-quality games. Nintendo implemented strict quality controls and developer standards, restoring consumer trust.

There are many more compelling twists in the Nintendo story, but until recently, travellers to Kyoto hoping to interface with the beloved brand have left disappointed. Mario, Donkey Kong and Zelda's Link were under lock and key in the company's corporate headquarters, a grey box that accepts no visitors. In 2023, however, 40 years after the release of the Famicom, the company teased the forthcoming launch of Nintendo Museum. Under construction at time of writing, the interactive museum will open a short train-ride south of Kyoto, at the site where the old Nintendo Uji Ogura Plant once manufactured playing cards.

The museum follows hot on the heels of Super Nintendo World, a 2021 add-on to Universal Studios Japan in neighbouring Osaka. The next best thing to being inside a Super Mario game, the immaculately themed zone has giant snapping piranha plants, a hi-tech Mario Kart ride and roving costumed characters. For a more grown-up Nintendo experience, the company's former Kyoto headquarters reopened as a boutique hotel in 2022. The art deco building, in operation between 1933 and 1959, is now Marufukuro, a luxurious, 18-room pad close to Kyoto Station. Retaining many of its original period details, the hotel has a library where guests can read up on the history of Nintendo and its founders.

If that sounds a bit cerebral and all you want is a Yoshi cuddly toy, you're in luck. Nintendo opened its first Kyoto shop in 2023, on the 7th floor of Takashimaya Department Store (p59). Packed with toys, video games, clothing and other Nintendo merch, it's even got a giant Mario head peering up from one of those iconic green pipes.

Clearly, then, Nintendo is at last embracing its Kyoto roots, and Kyoto is returning the love to its tech-forward progeny. If you think about it, what could be more quintessentially Kyoto than Nintendo? Meticulous in its artisanship, obsessed with perfection and unswerving in its principles but willing to adapt and move with the times - like Mario and Princess Peach, Nintendo and Kyoto belong together.

NINTENDO IS AT LAST EMBRACING ITS KYOTO ROOTS, AND KYOTO IS RETURNING THE LOVE TO ITS TECH-FORWARD PROGENY.

TRADITIONAL
ARTS & CRAFTS

The cultural heart of Japan, Kyoto is where the country's most celebrated traditional arts and crafts were birthed and refined.
By Tom Fay

JAPAN LIES AT the end of the Silk Road, so it is no surprise that it became a repository for all kinds of cultural influences from the vast Asian continent. The establishment of Kyoto (Heian-Kyō) as the nation's new capital in 794 CE heralded an era of cultural blossoming as fine arts developed in the city and the nation's best artisans and artists were employed by the imperial court, aristocracy and Buddhist clergy. Life for the privileged in the Heian court revolved around creativity; they spent their days composing *waka* (31-syllable Japanese poems), playing musical instruments and appreciating art, before the advent of the feudal era brought great cultural changes. New ideas and artistic styles flowed in from the continent, most notably in the form of Zen Buddhism, and the temples themselves became centres of creative artistry. Ikebana, the Japanese art of flower arranging, also has its roots in Buddhism and the tradition of leaving flowers for the spirits of the deceased.

The Edo era (1603–1868) saw increasing prosperity and the rise of a wealthy merchant class. While the noble elite continued their high-end pursuits, it was this new upper-middle class who became the largest patrons of the arts, notably in the form of kabuki theatre and *ukiyo-e* (woodblock prints). Economic prosperity also gave rise to practical art forms such as pottery, *washi* (handmade paper), fabric-making and lacquerware, and Kyoto remains the epicentre for these traditional trades and crafts.

Painting & Literature

Up until the Heian period, most painting and poetry in Japan had been in the classic Chinese style, but this all changed in the Heian courts of Kyoto. A new style of painting which came to be called *yamato-e* ('yamato' referring to the imperial clan) developed; it featured scenes of court life painted on long scrolls in vivid colours, often with an almost bird's-eye view of the goings-on inside courtly chambers. The most popular poetry of the time was *waka,* and courtiers went to great pains when writing it to convey subtle details of the natural world; it was also the language of love, and so the choice of *washi* and the quality of the calligraphy were all of great importance. Unfortunately, little art from the Heian period remains today; the largest collection is at the Kyoto National Museum (p95).

By medieval times, Zen Buddhism exerted a far greater influence on the arts. Minimalist and monochrome ink-wash paintings called sumi-e were often painted by monks, who also produced some of the great works of literature of the age. The Muromachi era (1336–1573) gave rise to *shoin-zukuri*-style architecture, and this saw paintings move from scrolls to *fusama* (sliding paper doors) and *byōbo* (folding screens). The Kanō school of painting took the simple conventions of *sumi-e* and added bolder lines and colour to make the artwork even more striking.

The short-lived peace of the Azuchi-Momoyama period (1574–1600) resulted in

Nō mask

from the lacquer tree and pigments such as iron oxide (for that deep vermilion pigment); multiple layers are added and it is polished to an incredible shine, which makes the wood extremely durable. The lacquerware decorative technique of *maki-e,* developed during the Heian period, involved sprinkling gold and silver powder onto liquid lacquer to form images.

The delicate art of *washi* was introduced to Japan from China as early as the 5th century, and is typically produced using mulberry trees. Kyoto has its own distinctive form of paper called *kyō-chiyogami,* which is traditionally used as wrapping for gifts. There are still several specialist washi stores in Kyoto.

Performing Arts

The oldest performing art that still exists in some form today is the dance-drama of *nō.* This theatrical art has been in existence since the 14th century, but draws on earlier traditions including Shintō, *gagaku* (music and dance of the imperial court) and more. The performance integrates masks, costumes, music and stage props in a stylised dance-based art form, and the drama usually tells a story from traditional literature where a supernatural entity is transformed into a human; *nō*'s iconic masks are used to represent females, ghosts or demons. The plays are interspersed with short, comic interludes called *kyōgen,* which feature everyday scenes and colloquial language.

Kabuki started in Kyoto around 1600, and later developed a stronghold in Edo (Tokyo). Featuring extravagantly costumed actors in dramas of acrobatic dance, the original all-female ensembles were eventually banned as some of them doubled as prostitutes, and the audiences, which came from a mix of social classes, were deemed to be too rowdy.

Kabuki eventually found more structure, males took over the acting, and following a dip in popularity in the mid-18th century, it has since garnered a dedicated following once more. Bunraku, which developed at around the same time as kabuki, is a form of puppet theatre that originated in Osaka.

a flurry of building and artistic patronage, and this was the age when the tea ceremony began to really take off. Between the 17th and 19th centuries, *ukiyo-e* flourished; these colourful paintings depicted a whole variety of scenes, encompassing everything from female beauty and sumo wrestlers, to historical events and landscapes – Hokusai's *The Great Wave off Kanagawa* is one of the most famous works of Japanese art.

Traditional Crafts

Kyoto has been home to highly skilled artisans since its founding, and while far fewer ply their trades today, the city is still the best place in Japan to seek out masters of their craft.

Kyoto was once famed for ceramics, and in the mid-1600s was home to more than ten kilns. Of these, only Kiyomizu-yaki remains today. Many of the pottery shops around Kiyomizu-dera sell its wares (among other Japanese ceramics).

Lacquerware is made using the sap

INDEX

Map Pages **000**

Map Pages **000**

'One of my earliest, and happiest, Kyoto memories was spending a balmy summer evening on the bank of the Kamo-gawa, drinking cans of *chūhai* with new friends, as giant kanji burned on a distant hillside – the city felt both instantly homely and intoxicatingly exotic all at once.'

TOM FAY

'A day trip out to Takao (p122) and its quiet temples can be an antidote to the downtown crowds. When I visited for this book, I was the only passenger on the bus for the last ten minutes of the trip.'

ROB GOSS

'Love sake? Try the tasting flight at Fushimi Sake Village (p51) – a whopping 18 glasses of sake, each with accompanying tasting notes! Just be sure to line your stomach first...'

THOMAS O'MALLEY

Mapping data sources:
© Lonely Planet
© OpenStreetMap http://openstreetmap.org/copyright

THIS BOOK

Destination Editor
James Smart

Production Editor
Claire Rourke

Assisting Editors
Nigel Chin, Pete Cruttenden, Michael Mackenzie

Book Designer
Catalina Aragón

Cartographer
Valentina Kremenchutskaya

Cover Researchers
Katherine Marsh (front)
Catalina Aragón (back)

Script Checker
Yuriko McLachlan

Thanks
Katie Connolly, Gwen Cotter, Melanie Dankel, Alison Killilea, Jenna Myers, Katerina Pavkova

MIX
Paper | Supporting responsible forestry
FSC
www.fsc.org   FSC™ C021741

Paper in this book is certified against the Forest Stewardship Council™ standards. FSC™ promotes environmentally responsible, socially beneficial and economically viable management of the world's forests.

Published by Lonely Planet Global Limited
CRN 554153
8th edition – Nov 2024
ISBN 978 1 78701 703 0
© Lonely Planet 2024 Photographs © as indicated 2024
10 9 8 7 6 5 4 3 2 1
Printed in Malaysia